Effective Science Communication (Third Edition)
A practical guide to surviving as a scientist

Online at: https://doi.org/10.1088/978-0-7503-6004-3

Effective Science Communication (Third Edition)

A practical guide to surviving as a scientist

Sam Illingworth
Department of Learning and Teaching Enhancement, Edinburgh Napier University, Edinburgh, UK

Grant Allen
Department of Earth and Environmental Sciences, The University of Manchester, Manchester, UK

IOP Publishing, Bristol, UK

© IOP Publishing Ltd 2024

All rights reserved. No part of this publication may be reproduced, stored in a retrieval system or transmitted in any form or by any means, electronic, mechanical, photocopying, recording or otherwise, without the prior permission of the publisher, or as expressly permitted by law or under terms agreed with the appropriate rights organization. Multiple copying is permitted in accordance with the terms of licences issued by the Copyright Licensing Agency, the Copyright Clearance Centre and other reproduction rights organizations.

Permission to make use of IOP Publishing content other than as set out above may be sought at permissions@ioppublishing.org.

Sam Illingworth and Grant Allen have asserted their right to be identified as the authors of this work in accordance with sections 77 and 78 of the Copyright, Designs and Patents Act 1988.

ISBN 978-0-7503-6004-3 (ebook)
ISBN 978-0-7503-6002-9 (print)
ISBN 978-0-7503-6005-0 (myPrint)
ISBN 978-0-7503-6003-6 (mobi)

DOI 10.1088/978-0-7503-6004-3

Version: 20240301

IOP ebooks

British Library Cataloguing-in-Publication Data: A catalogue record for this book is available from the British Library.

Published by IOP Publishing, wholly owned by The Institute of Physics, London

IOP Publishing, No.2 The Distillery, Glassfields, Avon Street, Bristol, BS2 0GR, UK

US Office: IOP Publishing, Inc., 190 North Independence Mall West, Suite 601, Philadelphia, PA 19106, USA

Sam: For Becky, Cora, and Grace —for enduring my endless efforts at effective communication. Your support is my secret superpower.

Grant: For Ian, Ken and Valerie —without whom I would not exist and for eternal guidance and course correction in all that I do.

Contents

Third Edition Preface	xii
Acknowledgements	xiii
Author biographies	xiv

1	**Introduction**	**1-1**
1.1	Introduction	1-1
1.2	How to use this book	1-3
1.3	Summary	1-4
1.4	Further study	1-4
1.5	Suggested reading	1-5
	References	1-5
2	**Publishing work in academic journals**	**2-1**
2.1	Introduction	2-1
2.2	Scoping your deliverables	2-2
2.3	Choosing a journal	2-5
2.4	Writing and manuscript preparation	2-8
2.5	The peer review process	2-10
2.6	Reviewing papers	2-13
2.7	Citations and metrics	2-14
2.8	Summary	2-17
2.9	Further study	2-17
2.10	Suggested reading	2-18
	References	2-18
3	**Applying for funding**	**3-1**
3.1	Introduction	3-1
3.2	What makes a good idea?	3-2
3.3	Finding funding	3-5
3.4	Anatomy of a research proposal	3-7
	3.4.1 Case for support	3-8
	3.4.2 Pathways to impact	3-11
3.5	Budgeting	3-12
3.6	The funding process	3-14

3.7	Summary	3-17
3.8	Further study	3-18
3.9	Suggested reading	3-18
	References	3-19

4 Presenting   4-1

4.1	Introduction	4-1
4.2	A three-way approach	4-2
	4.2.1 Developing your narrative	4-2
	4.2.2 Understanding your audience	4-4
	4.2.3 Managing yourself	4-6
4.3	Dealing with nerves	4-8
4.4	Rhetoric	4-9
4.5	PowerPoint	4-10
4.6	Timings	4-12
4.7	Answering questions	4-13
4.8	Poster design	4-14
4.9	Presenting digitally	4-18
4.10	Summary	4-19
4.11	Further study	4-19
4.12	Suggested reading	4-20
	References	4-20

5 Outreach and public engagement   5-1

5.1	Introduction	5-1
5.2	Objectives, audiences, and formats	5-3
5.3	Different publics	5-4
5.4	Working with children	5-6
	5.4.1 Children in a formal environment	5-8
	5.4.2 Children in an informal environment	5-10
5.5	Different formats	5-11
	5.5.1 Science talks	5-12
	5.5.2 Panel discussion	5-12
	5.5.3 Science busking	5-12
	5.5.4 Book clubs	5-13
	5.5.5 Workshops	5-14
	5.5.6 Citizens' juries	5-15

	5.5.7 Art exhibitions	5-15
5.6	Citizen science	5-16
5.7	Funding	5-18
5.8	Advertising	5-18
5.9	Evaluation	5-20
5.10	Initiative checklist	5-23
5.11	Examples of science communication initiatives	5-26
	5.11.1 Bright Club	5-26
	5.11.2 Think Like a Scientist	5-26
	5.11.3 Carbon City Zero	5-27
	5.11.4 Rhyme and Reason	5-27
5.12	Summary	5-28
5.13	Further study	5-28
5.14	Suggested reading	5-29
	References	5-29

6 Engaging with mass media — 6-1

6.1	Introduction	6-1
6.2	Why, when, and how to engage with mass media	6-2
6.3	Press releases	6-3
6.4	Constructing a narrative for mass media	6-5
6.5	Television and radio interviews	6-8
6.6	Summary	6-13
6.7	Further study	6-13
6.8	Suggested reading	6-14
	References	6-14

7 Establishing an online presence — 7-1

7.1	Introduction	7-1
7.2	Blogs	7-2
7.3	Podcasts	7-5
7.4	Social media	7-8
	7.4.1 X (the platform formerly known as Twitter)	7-8
	7.4.2 Facebook	7-10
	7.4.3 YouTube	7-11
	7.4.4 Instagram	7-12
	7.4.5 TikTok	7-12

	7.4.6 LinkedIn	7-13
	7.4.7 ResearchGate	7-14
	7.4.8 Others	7-15
7.5	The role of artificial intelligence in science communication	7-16
7.6	Digital collaborations	7-18
7.7	Summary	7-19
7.8	Further study	7-20
7.9	Suggested reading	7-20
	References	7-21

8 Science and policy — 8-1

8.1	Introduction	8-1
8.2	How science informs policy	8-2
8.3	What you can do to inform policy	8-4
8.4	Impact from research	8-6
8.5	Summary	8-7
8.6	Further study	8-8
8.7	Suggested reading	8-8
	References	8-9

9 Teaching science — 9-1

9.1	Introduction	9-1
9.2	Pedagogical approaches	9-2
9.3	Designing engaging and inclusive environments	9-5
9.4	Assessment and feedback	9-9
9.5	Turning frontier research into a module	9-13
9.6	Reflecting	9-16
9.7	Support and development	9-19
9.8	Summary	9-20
9.9	Further study	9-21
9.10	Suggested reading	9-21
	References	9-22

10 Other essential skills — 10-1

10.1	Introduction	10-1
10.2	Time management	10-3
10.3	Networking	10-5

10.4　Teamwork	10-8
10.5　Mentoring	10-8
10.6　Career planning	10-9
10.7　Integrity and malpractice	10-11
10.8　Promoting diversity	10-12
10.9　Recognising and managing stress	10-13
10.9.1　What is burnout and why does it matter?	10-14
10.9.2　How to recognise burnout	10-15
10.9.3　How to mitigate and recover from burnout	10-17
10.9.4　Practicing good mental health	10-18
10.10　Summary	10-19
10.11　Further study	10-19
10.12　Suggested reading	10-20
References	10-20

Third Edition Preface

Since the publication of the second edition of this book, science communication has continued to evolve, with the global landscape shifting dramatically in response to COVID-19 and the rapid development of artificial intelligence (AI) technologies such as ChatGPT. These changes have compelled us to revisit, revise, and add to the text, ensuring it remains a valuable resource for readers seeking to stay abreast of the latest developments in science communication.

In this third edition, we have introduced a brand-new chapter (chapter 9) dedicated to teaching science, providing guidance on how to effectively convey scientific concepts and foster critical thinking in various higher educational settings. We have also added new sections on recognising, avoiding, and mitigating burnout, given the importance of maintaining a healthy work–life balance for scientists.

The impact of COVID-19 has accelerated the adoption of digital tools, making it crucial for science communicators to be well-versed in these technologies. We have updated chapter 7 (Establishing an online presence) to reflect these rapid changes and consider the implications of AI advances on the practice of science communication and teaching.

Chapter 5 (Outreach and public engagement) now offers a more nuanced discussion on engaging with diverse audiences, especially those that have been historically underrepresented and underserved in science. We have included several new examples of successful outward-facing initiatives that demonstrate effective engagement with non-scientists.

Throughout the book, we have consistently emphasised the significance of ethical and rigorous scientific practices, inclusivity, and the celebration of diversity. In addition, the revised chapter 10 (Other essential skills) now includes an extensive section on identifying burnout and strategies for dealing with it. This chapter addresses a wide array of skills are particularly relevant to contemporary scientists as they navigate their ever-evolving priorities.

We are grateful to Paul Dickens for updating and creating new cartoons that continue to reflect the inclusivity we hope this book promotes. Our thanks also go to the IoP Publishing Team for continuing to standardise all images in the book, making them more visually appealing.

We hope you find this third edition engaging and informative, and we eagerly await your thoughts and valuable feedback.

Sam Illingworth and Grant Allen
December 2023

Acknowledgements

This book is the result of several years of hard work between the two of us, but there are many people who have contributed directly or indirectly through discussions and the experiences they have offered to us. We would like to thank everyone who has ever sat through one of our lectures, listened to one of our talks, or put up with one of our rants. Thank you to our scientific colleagues for the innovation, inspiration, and at times perspiration that was necessary for us to shape our ideas. Thank you also to our students and those we have met at the European Geosciences Union conferences for providing us with feedback and insight during the developmental phases of this book. We would also like to thank the team at **IOP Publishing** for their help in preparing this book for publication, in particular to Paul Dickens for the wonderful cartoons that appear throughout the book. We really think they help to illustrate some of points that we make and the issues that we raise. Special thanks must also be given to the reviewers, whose comments and constructive criticisms have helped to ensure that the book is consistent and effective in its message.

Author biographies

Sam Illingworth

Sam Illingworth is an Associate Professor at Edinburgh Napier University, where his work and research focus on using poetry and games as a way of developing dialogues between scientists and other publics. He is also an award-winning science communicator, poet, games designer, Principal Fellow of Advance HE (PFHEA), Chief Executive Editor of *Geoscience Communication*, and the founder of *Consilience*, the world's first peer-reviewed science and poetry journal. Find out more about Sam and his work via his website www.samillingworth.com.

Grant Allen

Grant Allen is a Professor of Atmospheric Physics at the University of Manchester. His research interests include pollution, greenhouse gas measurement methods, and remote sensing. After graduating with a PhD in satellite remote sensing at Leicester University in 2005, Grant was a postdoc at the University of Manchester, investigating tropical convection and pollution transport and chemistry. Grant received a Natural Environment Research Council Fellowship and became a lecturer in 2011, becoming a senior lecturer in 2013, reader in 2016, and professor in 2019. Grant has received over £10M in funding, with over 100 publications in high-impact journals. In 2012 he was awarded a Royal Society Westminster Pairing Fellowship to shadow a Member of Parliament to understand the science–policy interface. Grant has also featured in science documentaries on atmospheric phenomena and has been interviewed many times live on BBC and Sky News channels discussing topics from volcanic eruptions to flooding, and has provided commentary to hundreds of pieces of science journalism. He has served as an editor for several journals and sits as a core member on several UK and international research funding panels.

IOP Publishing

Effective Science Communication (Third Edition)
A practical guide to surviving as a scientist
Sam Illingworth and Grant Allen

Chapter 1

Introduction

I'm always interested in learning something new

—Katherine Johnson

1.1 Introduction

As scientists we are taught the skills and techniques which enable us to perform a range of extremely complex tasks, from detecting neutrinos to modelling future climate change scenarios. Despite this, very few of us are ever trained in how to effectively communicate our research or are asked to reflect on why doing so is important. We typically work in an environment where we are told that we must 'publish or perish', and training in communication often relies on a baptism of fire for the early-career scientist.

Such an approach means that some scientists still treat presenting their research at scientific conferences as being a necessary evil, while others view communicating with non-scientists as something akin to root canal surgery without an anaesthetic. The reality is that to be a successful (and impactful) scientist, we must be able to communicate effectively and confidently to a wide variety of audiences, using a range of different media. To do this well and with confidence, a relatively small amount of time invested in developing and reflecting upon communication skills can propel early-career scientists (and indeed those much further into their career) to new heights and take at least some of the sting out of those first forays into the public-facing role of science. Evidently, this is why you are here, and we hope to help you on that journey, drawing on the personal and professional experiences of the authors and the latest research in science communication.

For the purposes of this book, we have split science communication into two broad categories:

1. **Inward-facing**. That which involves communicating to other scientists through e.g. peer-reviewed publications, grant proposals, and conference presentations.
2. **Outward-facing**. That which involves working with non-scientists to both communicate our research more widely and to help diversify and broaden scientific discourse.

As scientists, the personal benefits of being able to effectively communicate our research inwardly (to a scientific audience) are relatively self-explanatory, with regards to both career progression and the impact of our work on our chosen discipline(s). However, at times, some may question what the purpose and/or benefit is of communicating our research outwardly, both to and with non-scientists. In 2017, University College London published a report into how engagement with science can be used to promote and develop social justice, stating that [[1], p 2]

> Scientific advances mean that people will need to be increasingly STEM-literate if they are to be active citizens who can have a say in society.

As practitioners of STEM (Science, Technology, Engineering, and Maths), the opportunity to create a more inclusive society through better science engagement and participation is a compelling reason why we, as scientists, have a responsibility to work with non-scientists in this way.

The purpose of this book is to provide guidance on how to be more effective at both inward-facing and outward-facing science communication. In addition to you becoming a more successful scientist, giving equal consideration to improving your communication in both directions will help to make you a more useful one as well.

1.2 How to use this book

Following the Introduction, this book is split into nine further chapters, each of which provides guidance concerning different aspects of inward-facing and outward-facing science communication. Each of these chapters presents an overview of the topic, drawn from both the literature and our own experiences and insights as successful scientists. In each of the chapters there are also several exercises to help you reflect on and put into practice what is discussed, as well as further study and additional reading, which have been carefully chosen and suggested to improve your knowledge and understanding.

Chapter 2 is dedicated to publishing work in academic journals. Writing your research in a format that is suitable for peer review is an essential skill for any scientist, and this chapter provides advice for how to do this. An overview of the peer review process and advice on how to review the work of other scientists is also included.

Chapter 3 introduces getting your research projects funded, guiding you through the typical application process for grant proposals and breaking down what makes for a good, and fundable, idea. Budgeting, pathways to impact, and the funding process itself are also discussed.

Chapter 4 is dedicated to improving your presentational skills, across a variety of media, for a mainly scientific audience. This chapter contains advice on how to structure your presentations, overcome nerves, and make use of rhetoric. It also provides advice on answering questions, designing scientific posters, and managing the associated timings and logistics.

Chapter 5 is focussed on outward-facing science communication and is centred around developing and delivering outreach and public engagement initiatives for a variety of different audiences. A consideration of the various formats that you may encounter is presented, alongside specific advice for working with children, and for funding, advertising, and evaluating your initiatives.

Chapter 6 presents information and advice for dealing with the mass media. This includes a consideration of how to construct appropriate narratives, how to write effective press reviews, and how to prepare for appearances on radio and television.

Chapter 7 will help you to establish an online presence and craft a unique and useful digital footprint. Blogs, podcasts, and other forms of social media are all introduced and discussed with reference to sharing scientific research, and advice for dealing with distractions and other potential difficulties is also discussed in-depth.

Chapter 8 introduces the topic of science and policy, outlining how the two interact, why policy is important, and providing information on what you can do to better inform policy through your own scientific research and expertise.

Chapter 9 introduces teaching science in higher education. It covers various pedagogical approaches, techniques, and strategies to effectively convey scientific concepts to a diverse range of students. Additionally, it offers insights into designing engaging and inclusive sessions, assessing student progress, and providing constructive feedback to support students' growth.

Finally, **chapter 10** catalogues a series of other essential skills, such as time management and networking, and outlines how and why you can develop each of these. We also provide advice and support on managing workplace stress, including tips on how to recognise the early phases of burnout and how to avoid it becoming a problem. This chapter also discusses in detail what it means to be an ethical scientist, and aids with planning your future career, either within, or away from academia.

Whether you are an undergraduate scientist embarking on your first steps into the existing world of scientific research, or a professor with dozens of years of experience, this book contains guidance and advice that will be (at least in part, if not completely) relevant to you. Being a scientist is an incredibly rewarding and enjoyable experience, but it can be a testing and difficult one as well. We hope that this book acts as a handbook for improving your ability to communicate effectively; and that in doing so it also serves as a practical guide to surviving, and thriving, as a scientist in the twenty-first century

---

Exercise: What do you want to improve?
Write down three personal aims for being a more effective scientist. These aims should be SMART, i.e. Specific, Measurable, Achievable, Relevant, and Time-Bound. For example, 'Write more publications' is not a SMART target, whereas 'Author or co-author two research articles by the end of this calendar year, in open-access journals' is. Try to include at least one outward-facing science communication aim in your list of three.

Now, turn to the table of contents and select the chapters that are most applicable to your three aims. After working your way through the appropriate sections, return to your aims and rewrite them to be more realistic. Alternatively, if you are one of those people who absolutely must read a book in page order, and from cover to cover, then refer to your aims as you reach the appropriate section, re-evaluating them as you work your way through the book. Keep you three aims in a location that is easily visible (e.g. on your desk or in the front of your lab book) and re-evaluate your progress in achieving these during regular intervals (e.g. once a month). Once you have achieved an aim cross it off your list, and once all three have been achieved do something nice to celebrate, then make another list and start again.

1.3 Summary

To be effective scientists, we need to master the skills of both communicating our research to the scientific community and engaging non-scientists with our work. By reading this book, working through the exercises, and following the recommendations for further study you will learn the skills that enable you to do this.

1.4 Further study

The further study sections at the end of each chapter in this book are an opportunity for you to reflect on what you have learned, and to develop some of these ideas through further reading and practice.

The further study in this chapter is designed to get you thinking more about outward-facing science communication, and the benefits that this can have for the wider society:

1. **Ask the news.** Visit the website for a news outlet of your choice and find the 'Science' section. Is what they are reporting based on peer-reviewed scientific research? Does it appear to be logical? Would somebody without your scientific training be able to follow the story and come to the same conclusions?
2. **Ask a non-scientist.** Find a family member or a friend who is a non-scientist and ask them about their opinions of science. Can they define 'science'? Can you define it? Do they think that scientists are good communicators? Do they trust scientists; and if not, why not? Do they think that science offers a positive contribution to society?
3. **Ask yourself.** Take a moment to reflect on what it was that made you want to become a scientist in the first instance. Did you have a particularly inspiring teacher at school? Were you encouraged by your family? Was it just something that you were good at and wanted to pursue further? Keep these reflections in mind as you work your way through the rest of the book and remind yourself of them when you next need some scientific encouragement.

1.5 Suggested reading

If you are keen on exploring science communication as an academic field and its practical applications, try the insightful *Science Communication: A Practical Guide for Scientists* [2]. For a more in-depth exploration into the history of science communication, cutting-edge research, and inclusive viewpoints on the subject within various cultural contexts, consider the comprehensive *Routledge Handbook of Public Communication of Science and Technology* [3]. Similarly, both *Creative Research Communication: Theory and Practice* [4] and *Science Communication Through Poetry* [5] provide a more creative approach to the discipline. There are also several journals that are dedicated to the development of this subject, including *Science Communication* from SAGE Publications [6], and the *Journal of Science Communication* from Sissa Medialab [7]. However, the format and nomenclature of these journals can at times be daunting to scientists who are new to science communication. *Geoscience Communication* from Copernicus Publications [8] provides a more accessible entry into the field, being written primarily by and for geoscientific researchers who are interested in applying their scientific training to their outward-facing science communication initiatives (see chapter 5).

References

[1] Godec S, King H and Archer L 2017 *The Science Capital Teaching Approach: Engaging Students with Science, Promoting Social Justice* (London: UCL Institute of Education)
[2] Bowater L and Yeoman K 2012 *Science Communication: A Practical Guide for Scientists* (New York: Wiley)

[3] Bucchi M and Trench B 2021 *Routledge Handbook of Public Communication of Science and Technology* (Abingdon: Routledge) 3rd edn
[4] Wilkinson C and Weitkamp E 2016 *Creative Research Communication: Theory and Practice* (Manchester: Manchester University Press)
[5] Illingworth S 2022 *Science Communication Through Poetry* (Berlin: Springer Nature)
[6] *Science Communication* https://journals.sagepub.com/home/scx (Accessed: 1 December 2023)
[7] *Journal of Science Communication* https://jcom.sissa.it (Accessed: 1 December 2023)
[8] *Geoscience Communication* https://geoscience-communication.net (Accessed: 1 December 2023)

IOP Publishing

Effective Science Communication (Third Edition)
A practical guide to surviving as a scientist
Sam Illingworth and Grant Allen

Chapter 2

Publishing work in academic journals

If I have seen further, it is by standing on the shoulders of giants.
—Isaac Newton

2.1 Introduction

This chapter offers advice on how to publish a peer-reviewed scientific paper, laying out a framework from conception to publication. Based on our personal experience as editors, reviewers, and authors, this chapter will provide practical advice and guide you through the process of publication in a typical modern scientific journal. We shall track a paper's journey—from deciding on when you have something to offer to science, to identifying an appropriate journal in which to publish; and then how to navigate the peer review process and ensure your published paper reaches its target audience. The advice in this chapter is especially relevant to those embarking on preparing their first scientific paper, but it may also offer helpful insights to maximise a paper's academic impact and reach for those with some existing experience.

Writing and publishing peer-reviewed journal articles remains the principal way that scientists communicate their research widely among other researchers. It also provides a way for science to be archived in perpetuity. Unlike other scientific communication methods, which may have a greater value in reaching wider audiences, peer-reviewed journal publications in reputable journals represent a time-honoured gold standard in academic rigour and provide a permanent record of contributions to humanity's body of scientific knowledge. This is because the checks and balances of the peer review and editorial process serve as an important quality control on the accuracy and rigour of the work presented to a journal, serving to keep science honest in the face of constructive criticism and independent oversight. On final publication, science can be reassured that independent experts have carefully and reasonably vetted an individual's or team's work, and that a published article has addressed any reasonable concerns.

Peer review (like any human endeavour) is not perfect (as we shall discuss later), but it does represent the best system we know of in science to ensure accountability and scrutiny. Primarily, peer review is intended as a constructive process, and should be approached in this manner by both reviewer and author; though that may not lessen the sense of anxiety some may feel when they receive reviews relating to their latest submission.

Bringing a paper to publication can be a daunting but also very enjoyable and rewarding experience. It is our duty as scientists to publish our work and bring it to the attention of others who may learn from it. The quote at the head of this chapter encapsulates the engine of scientific progress—all our current knowledge and teaching emanates from those that have previously published their findings for us to learn from. We build on each other's work and move our own forward incrementally. The record that is our academic literature ensures that our work is forever open to scrutiny such that it may be refined, disputed, or reinforced with time, in the light of future understanding and effort. In the modern scientific world, the number of journals (and the number of scientists) has been growing exponentially. This has many strengths but also some weaknesses, as we shall discuss later. However, the process and the result remain the same—to record knowledge and take it further. Let us now explore how you can make the most of this process in your work.

2.2 Scoping your deliverables

The word 'deliverables' is well-used in academia these days, implicitly commercialising science by its virtue as a term borrowed from the world of business. However, it serves its descriptive purpose. A journal article or paper is an academic output that contains a deliverable, or deliverables. These deliverables are the key conclusions of the paper that represent new pieces of information not previously known to science. They could represent enormous leaps forward in fundamental knowledge, or they could represent incremental advances or facts about the Universe (or anything in it).

The relative importance and the scientific field of those advances may dictate the journal to which you choose to submit (see section 2.3) but the fundamental fact remains that any paper must contain some new contribution to knowledge, no matter how large or small. This simple requirement is one of the first aspects that an editor or reviewer will look for and be asked to comment on concerning any submitted paper. Therefore, the first step in drafting a paper is to recognise when you have something new and useful to say. All that follows from that point (i.e. preparing a paper for submission) concerns framing the deliverables to provide clear evidence and explanation so that others can be confident in your conclusions.

A key tenet of the scientific process is that others should be able to reach the same result following the same methods using the same dataset. This is the principle of repeatability, and it goes to the heart and the origins of the scientific method. While the interpreted conclusions made in any paper may be tainted by subjective opinion, the data and results should be absolute according to a transparent and rigorous method. As datasets and methods become increasingly complex, because of the sheer volumes of data from modern instrumentation, and the analytical power of computers and algorithms, the principles of repeatability and transparency are getting increasingly harder to ensure, but no less relevant and important.

This modern problem has been recognised recently by many journals [1], several of which are leading a campaign on best methodological practice, and the open access and archiving of data (and metadata). After a string of high-profile academic malpractice cases [2], better processes to challenge and report poor practice (and outright malpractice) are also being introduced. Time spent becoming familiar with best practice and reflecting on how to embed the principle of repeatability in your work, will pay enormous dividends, both to yourself and to science, as those that follow your work will be able to have more confidence and respect for the outputs you make.

From experience of supervising students and early career researchers, and as former students ourselves, it is not always easy to recognise when a critical threshold has been reached in the context of having something 'useful' to publish. For some it may be easier than others; for example, if the deliverables were planned as part of routine analytical work that was carried out. But in many instances, science moves forward by stumbling on some unexpected new advance because of working on something else. At this point you should take a step back, explore what you have already found, and decide on three things before deciding on whether to write a paper:

1. Is what you have found thus far a scientific deliverable that others should hear about?
2. If so, does the work done to date represent enough information, data, or explanation to provide a coherent and substantial narrative from which to inform others of that advance?
3. If so, could that work be written up as a paper now, or could further work provide additional deliverables within the scope of the intended article?

Some of the words in the above list are necessarily subjective or vague. This is because every discipline and every piece of work is different. However, choosing the right point in the course of your work at which to publish is a skill that you learn to develop with practice. The difference between a mediocre paper and a truly groundbreaking one could be as simple as gauging when there is a neat package of work to create a clear and full story, as opposed to publishing as soon as there is something new but relatively incremental to say. However, delaying publication while waiting for new results is a risk that involves making educated decisions about the future direction and timescales of the work you might be engaged in. If in doubt, the less risky option may be to publish as soon as possible.

Prior to journal publication, an alternative may be to consider publishing a pre-print of your article [3]. Pre-prints are an excellent way to get scientific information out to a wide audience quickly, especially for work that may relate to something of high immediate public or scientific interest. Pre-prints also offer an opportunity to get alternative feedback from peers outside of a formalised journal peer review process. Some choose to do this because of the typically long timescales involved between submission and publication for many journals. However, because pre-prints are not always peer-reviewed, they are often considered as 'grey literature', meaning that it is not always seen as best practice to cite such work in more formal publications.

Implicit in point three above is knowing where to draw the line under a body of work and when to present it to others. Of equal importance to knowing when you have something to say, is to know when not to say too much. This is not about holding anything back, but it is about knowing how to properly scope an article. It is often just as hard for new researchers to know when to stop (and publish) as it is to know when there is something useful to say. There is always a temptation to keep going. There is always more to learn. It is therefore an important career skill to recognise when to compartmentalise your work and bring it to fruition in the form of a scientific article. This is not to say that you should abandon a thread of research once you have a good deliverable on a given subject, but a paper should be self-contained and address deliverables in the context of the proposed title. It may not make sense to produce a paper for every new deliverable where there are variations on a theme for example, but you should know when to stop before a paper runs the risk of becoming unwieldy and inaccessible to the intended audience.

Something to avoid is falling into the trap of believing that simply publishing more papers is always better for your career. In a world where the length of a scientist's publication record is a cursory symbol of academic success, it is tempting to add quantity to that list at the expense of quality. Both quality and quantity matter, and quality often matters far more. A long string of papers that have just made it past the threshold of publication acceptability, in a low impact journal (see section 2.3) with only meagre deliverables, may be meaningless if no one chooses to read the papers or cite them in their own work. Increasingly, academic reach and success is rated in terms of the number of citations a paper may receive (see section 2.7). Alternatively, a high-quality paper with useful deliverables on a well-scoped theme may attract a higher readership and hence more citations. Such an output is far better for your publication record and self-esteem, and more importantly, far more useful to science.

Exercise: Scope out your deliverables

This exercise is designed to guide you through the process of evaluating your current research, helping you discern which components are ripe for publication now, and which ones might be suitable for future papers. By methodically organising and prioritising your research, you will be better positioned to share your findings with the wider academic community in a meaningful way.

1) **Step 1: review and list**. Review your current research project, listing components that offer novel insights into scientific understanding.
2) **Step 2: categorise into themes**. Group related components to form distinct themes, labelling each with a descriptive title.
3) **Step 3: determine publication strategy**. For each theme, decide whether it warrants its own dedicated paper or if it fits as a section within a comprehensive paper.

> 4) **Step 4: evaluate research tasks**. Reflect on each theme, identifying any outstanding tasks or research steps required for completion.
> 5) **Step 5: prioritise for publication**. Assess themes based on readiness, prioritising those near completion or with substantial ready findings.
>
> By diligently following the steps outlined, you will have systematically organised your research components, laying the groundwork for future publications. You should now possess a clearer, prioritised view of your research's potential publication pathways, ensuring that your findings make the most significant impact possible within the scientific community. Remember, every piece of research has its place and significance; it is all about presenting it in the most fitting and coherent manner.

2.3 Choosing a journal

Once you have decided you have something useful to say, the next task is to decide on which scientific journal will best speak for you and your research. A journal is the medium through which we permanently record and communicate our research in its most complete form. Choosing a journal is analogous to deciding whether to present work at a large but general, or small but specialist, conference—each has relative strengths and weaknesses depending on the scope of the work.

The scientific journal landscape is vast and growing. Virtually all scientists (and many non-scientists) will have heard of, and read, publications such as *Nature* or *Science*. However, only a small number of specialist researchers may regularly read the *Journal of Waste Management*, for example. The relative reach and specialism of different journals reflects the scope and wider import of the articles that each publishes. For example, *Nature*'s readership may well not be too interested in the finer details of anaerobic digestion of organic waste in landfills, whereas the *Journal of Waste Management*'s readership may be surprised to read an article about new predictions of global climate catastrophe due to greenhouse gas emissions from landfill. Therefore, a key aspect when choosing a journal is to think about the scope of your conclusions and which group of people will be best served by hearing them. The journal you choose should then be analogous to selecting the loudest microphone positioned in the most appropriate room of people.

One of the metrics of a journal's reach is its Impact Factor (IF). This is defined as the ratio of total citations for the journal in some period (usually two years) to the number of articles published in the same period. These are routinely published by academic journals (usually on the homepage of their website) and in league tables produced by various organisations that can be found easily in any internet search. The higher a journal's IF, the more impact that journal's articles can be assumed to have, as measured by others referring to work published there. This IF ratio reflects both the magnitude of the journal's readership and the quality (and scope) of the articles it chooses to publish.

Many of the highest IF journals such as *Nature* and *Science* publish only the highest quality of articles with broad and societally important themes that carry interest to a wide (and even non-scientific) audience. Such wide-ranging articles are naturally positioned to be more readily cited by others, whereas more technical articles in specialist journals may be less obviously cited. Put simply, while you should attempt to publish in high IF journals to maximise reach and impact, your choice of journal may be limited by the scope and import of your subject matter and its conclusions. In all cases, your choice should be about reaching the attention of an appropriate audience for your work.

Not all articles are suitable for the highest IF journals. A specialist technical article may be best suited to a specialist journal with a smaller readership and a lower IF. In other words, the choice of journal should reflect both the IF and its scope, and as such you should try to target a journal with a high IF for the specific field of interest.

A recent proliferation of academic journals has accompanied the growth of science as a global commodity, driven by the profits that many publishing companies may stand to make from publication fees from a growing population of scientists. The era of digital online publishing has also removed much of the cost barrier in starting up new publishing enterprises that typically accompanied the print media of the past. Some of these new journals have become highly successful and respected and their IF has grown dramatically. But beware. Recent research has shown that this system is ripe for abuse [4, 5]. Some of the most unscrupulous of these 'predatory' journals pay lip service to the quality of the peer review process (or bypass it altogether) taking publication fees for profit at the expense of academic quality and rigour.

Unfortunately, some career-hungry scientists, jaded by rejection or heavy revision as part of the peer review process in more prestigious journals, have elected to feed the growth of these predatory journals to add bulk to their publication record. A growing awareness of these predatory journals and regularly updated blacklists does mean that this problem is slowly being dealt with within the academic community. However, for the uninitiated (e.g. employers outside of academia), a publication record can still, unfortunately, be taken at face value. Here, the advice is simple—do not publish in such journals and always check that a journal that you are considering is not included on any blacklist [6]. The easy ride they may appear to offer is at the expense of the quality of your published work and represents a blemish on any academic record.

To find a genuine and appropriate journal for your article, a good place to start is to read recent issues of journals that others in your field have published in, to get a sense of both their scope and quality. When conducting any literature review you may perform prior to embarking on a research project, or when writing the introductory and discussion sections for your own paper, you should naturally become familiar with a range of appropriate journals relevant to the context of your work. When you have compiled such a list, visit the journals' websites to investigate their IF and read about their aims and scope. Your choice of journal should then be concerned with which of them will give you the greatest reach based on the journal's IF, scope, and audience.

A further consideration in the realm of academic publishing concerns the journal's adherence to an Open Access (OA) model. Open Access signifies a shift in the funding model where articles, once published, are freely accessible to anyone with Internet access [7]. Historically, scientific journals aimed to offer scientists an affordable platform to publish while also serving as knowledge hubs for both the scientific community and wider audiences. However, over time, many journals deviated from this mission, prompting the push for OA. This model ensures that research remains free for public readership, ensuring the true democratisation of knowledge, with costs potentially covered by the author or another funding body.

Two primary routes to OA have emerged: the 'Gold Route' and the 'Green Route' [8]. The Gold Route entails authors paying to make their research freely accessible to all, often through article processing charges (APCs). In contrast, the Green Route involves authors placing their article in a free-to-access central repository, though journals may impose an embargo period. While there are nuances and challenges to both routes, institutions and funding bodies often provide guidance on the preferred path. For instance, the United Kingdom Research and Innovation (UKRI) funding body endorses both routes, leaning towards immediate, cost-free public access with optimal reuse potential. Given the enhanced visibility and the global push towards open access, we wholeheartedly recommend considering OA journals for your publishing needs.

2.4 Writing and manuscript preparation

In this section, we discuss some tips for journal publication preparation. However, in this book we do not offer detailed advice on scientific writing style, suffice it to say that the best way to learn is to read widely around your subject, to learn from the best practice of others, and then to put pen to paper (or rather finger to keyboard) yourself and be prepared to iterate tirelessly.

Before moving on to discuss preparing manuscripts for publication, one piece of advice on style and writing we would offer is to thoroughly check your manuscript prior to submission for typographical and grammatical errors. You should also get your work proof-read by a technical writer or proofreader if you have this resource available to you. This is particularly important if you are not confident in writing in English (the international language of science used by most journals). A well-prepared and clear text will go far with any reviewer. Similarly, nothing gets reviewers worked up more than having to write out a long list of technical errors such as grammatical and typographical mistakes. If you put your reviewers in a bad frame of mind over this avoidable aspect, then they may be less objective about your technical presentation, siding with a presumption of sloppiness. Put simply, typographical and grammatical errors push the burden of correction onto reviewers and editors who simply should not have to take on such tasks as part of a voluntary role that relies on the good will of busy people. And most importantly, remember that papers can, and frequently do, get rejected if the writing style is so poor as to affect the ease of reading, and therefore the clarity, of submitted work.

Once you have decided on a journal to submit your paper to, it is useful to thoroughly read any author guidance material that is available. This is usually accessible from the journal's website under a tab such as 'Guidance to Authors' or similar. This guidance will typically contain rules and advice on how your submitted article should be formatted or prepared, and it may detail how items such as figures, tables, and references should be provided.

Most journals will accept a word-processed document with embedded figures and tables for any initial review phase. But you can save yourself a lot of time later if you have prepared all material in any required format in advance. This is especially true for any figures, photographs, or illustrations which usually have strict file formats; for example, encapsulated post-script for data plots and raster graphics for any illustrations. As many scientific analysis software packages can output graphics in a range or file formats, it could save you hours (if not days) of time to prepare all outputs in the journal-required format at an earlier stage, as journals typically require separate files for each figure during the final stages of copy-editing. Other guidance to look out for includes any word or page limits, as some journals that take letter-style articles usually stipulate strict restrictions. It is also worth considering the graphics and colour schemes that are used in your article, as these can really make a big difference to how well received your article is by both readers and reviewers [9].

Before submitting an article to a journal, make sure that any co-authors have read and commented on your draft, and ideally pass it to someone uninvolved with the work (perhaps someone else in your research group) to provide a fresh pair of eyes and comment on how accessible the narrative is to someone at the edge of your field.

One crucial aspect of submission that frequently gets overlooked is the preparation of an abstract, and in some cases supplementary content such as video and image abstracts or plain language summaries. While every journal has its specific requirements for these materials, they should be viewed as opportunities to accentuate the key deliverables of your paper and maximise their impact. Scientists often use abstracts to gauge if the main content of the paper warrants further reading, potentially influencing future citations. Given the growing trend, it is also beneficial to prepare video or image abstracts and plain language summaries now, as they can offer a more engaging snapshot of your research and cater to a broader audience. Instead of viewing these requirements as tedious formalities, embrace them as chances to concisely communicate your work's significance. Doing so can be instrumental in gaining the recognition your research deserves (see section 2.7).

Finally, consider the cover letter that accompanies your submitted manuscript. Most journals will insist that you provide one, but it is good practice to always prepare one even for those that do not. This cover letter should be addressed to the editorial board of the journal, and it is your opportunity to explicitly explain what your deliverables are in plain language, and why they are relevant to this journal and its readership. Cover letters can be an opportunity for you to demonstrate to the editors of the journal exactly why your article should be considered for publication, especially if your research is particularly novel or on the fringes of what might be considered as suitable for that journal's aims and scope. Oftentimes a good cover letter can prove the difference between a paper being submitted for peer review or being rejected by the editor before it reaches this stage.

Since the launch of ChatGPT in late 2022, generative artificial intelligence (GAI) has become a significant disrupter in the academic world. Its introduction into academic writing is emblematic of this shift [10]. While tools like ChatGPT have the potential to revolutionise and refine the writing process, you should stay abreast of the perspectives held by many journals on this rapidly evolving technology. Although the use of GAI for manuscript preparation is a relatively new issue, numerous journals have established stringent guidelines about its use. And while comprehensive protocols are still in development, we advocate for an approach that draws a clear line between using AI to enhance content (generally seen as acceptable) and relying on AI for autonomous content creation (often approached with scepticism). Be forthright about how and to what extent you may have incorporated GAI in your work. Upholding this clarity and transparency both maintains academic integrity and preserves the robust foundation upon which scientific knowledge is constructed.

2.5 The peer review process

In all reputable journals, after you have submitted an article, it will first undergo a preliminary check, known as a 'desk reject' evaluation. This quick assessment is primarily done to ensure that the submission adheres to the basic standards and scope of the journal. Often, the journal's senior editor or editorial team makes this decision. If the article passes this initial scrutiny, it will then be assigned to a handling associate editor (AE) for the journal. This AE will typically have a reasonable (but not necessarily always high) level of expertise in the field of research your article addresses. While it is sometimes possible to examine or request a list of AEs for your chosen journal and to suggest one based on their expertise in a covering letter accompanying your submission, the final assignment of an AE is primarily determined by the publishing staff or a senior editor. The AE oversees the peer review process of your article and makes the ultimate decision regarding its suitability for publication.

On first receiving an article to handle, the AE may make an initial judgement on whether the subject matter of the article fits the scope of the journal and whether the initial manuscript is suitable to send on to reviewers, taking into consideration the arguments that you have laid out in your cover letter. It is common with some journals to receive guidance from the AE prior to further peer review at this stage. Any comments from the AE at this point should be carefully examined and answered to allow your paper to progress further. The AE will then select and invite several expert reviewers to comment on your paper. This phase can sometimes take several weeks while reviewers accept or decline invitations to review, requiring the AE to find suitable alternatives.

The peer review for journals is almost universally a service that other researchers provide for free. This can sometimes make it difficult for journals to solicit suitable reviewers quickly. Again, it is possible for you to suggest sensible reviewers to the AE. However, you should avoid bias in your choice and only suggest expert reviewers that are not linked to your work or organisation, as an AE will take a dim view of any attempt to undermine or subvert the quality of the peer review process. The AE may then choose to invite one or more of your suggestions, but this is entirely at their discretion.

Once expert reviewers have been assigned (typically two or more), the reviewers may take several weeks to complete their review of the submitted paper. They will be asked to comment on the suitability of the subject matter for the journal, to report on the quality and importance of the work, and to discuss any technical points where they may be cause for question or concern. They may also be asked to comment on the quality of the figures and tables, and to list any technical errors such as typographical and grammatical mistakes. Finally, the reviewers will be asked to make a recommendation for publication, and sometimes they may be invited to submit a score against a set of criteria. This score or recommendation may not be made visible to you, and any reviewers' comments and recommendations are advisory to the AE and do not represent a decision on publication, which is usually the decision of the AE alone.

After all the solicited reviews have been received by the AE, they will contact you and provide the reviews along with their decision on publication. Rarely, an article may be accepted outright in its current form, with no further modification necessary. However, most often, reviews will be returned to you with some guidance from the AE on how to proceed in their opinion. This can range from outright rejection, where the article has been deemed to be out of scope with the journal or of insufficient quality to be improvable for publication, to a suggestion for revision based on the comments of the reviewers. Suggestions for revision typically take the form of either a major revision, where significant further technical and/or presentational work may be required, or a minor revision where further clarity or graphical improvements are needed.

THE PEER REVIEW

On receiving the AE's decision and guidance, you will then be given several weeks typically to prepare a response to the reviewers' comments, provided that your paper has not been rejected editorially. In your response, it is always courteous to thank the reviewers for their comments and to briefly summarise what you see as the salient points of their collective reviews, before continuing to address each review and each reviewer's comments in turn and in order. This logical sequence will make it easier for the AE to follow your response.

Most reviewers are busy people that have chosen to give up their time for free to help you as constructively as possible. They have been selected to review your work as recognised experts in the field of your own paper. For the most part, peer review is a highly valuable and helpful process. But your skill as an author is in recognising which reviewer comments are accurate and helpful and which may be in error. It is not uncommon for a new author to feel that everything a reviewer says is correct and that the author is in the wrong. Self-doubt and reflection, and a willingness to revisit ideas and conclusions in the light of peer review, are an important and valuable quality in the scientific process, but not at the expense of the truth. When reading and reacting to reviewer comments, you must face up to them honestly; addressing instances where they raise important points, but also robustly and politely defending your work where there may be misunderstanding.

Most importantly, be sure to constructively address and respond to all the comments made, whether that is to agree with the comment or suggestion, or to discuss or argue your case. In all cases, you should detail where and why you have made changes to your paper because of any of the reviewers' comments and describe how your changes have addressed the points raised. Your reviewers are objectively working to help you improve the presentation and accuracy of your work, so if you see that a reviewer has misunderstood something, try to think about why they have misunderstood it and attempt to clarify any parts of the narrative or material that could lead future readers to similar misconceptions.

Very rarely, you may receive what can only be described as an unconstructive review. This class of reviews may take a very negative tone and may make unsubstantiated comments with no link to the content of your paper. Our advice here would be to make the point (politely) that you have no case to address if you have not been given cause to. Your AE will almost certainly have already identified such a review as being worthless to the decision process and may have selected additional reviewers to provide more objective comments. This said, be sure to differentiate between negative but objective reviews that do make specific comments linked explicitly to your work, and reviews that are generally ignorant of its content. In other words, never mistake a review you just do not like, but is genuinely raising comments about the content of your work, with a review that makes no substantiated comment at all. The former requires a detailed response, while the latter requires very little. Thankfully, such reviews remain extremely rare. But if you are unlucky enough to receive one, the checks and balances of both the other reviewers and your AE, coupled with your right to respond, all serve to optimise the quality of the peer review process.

On submitting your revised paper (if required to do so by the AE), your paper may be sent back to the original reviewers for further comment, or it may now be deemed acceptable for publication without further review. The AE will usually make any decision for further review based on your responses to the reviewer comments, considering whether you have satisfactorily addressed them all in your response, and if any appropriate and necessary revisions to the paper have been made. In some circumstances, this iterative process can happen several times before the AE is satisfied that all aspects have been sufficiently addressed and that final publication can proceed.

Finally, and often several months after you submitted your original article, you may receive an email from the AE (or an editorial assistant) informing you that your paper has been accepted for final publication subject to copy-editing and final typesetting. This is a heart-warming moment for any researcher at any stage in their career and it is a cause for celebration. At this stage, you can be rest assured that you have contributed to knowledge and that your work will be recorded for future generations to build on. You too now stand on the shoulders of giants.

2.6 Reviewing papers

Very shortly into any published research career, you may find that you are invited to review papers yourself. Such an invitation is an honour and reflects your growing reputation in your field of research; it also represents an altruistic duty that all researchers rely upon each other to perform. Without the unpaid work that expert reviewers and editors do for journals, the peer review process would grind to a halt. And without that process, the quality of published work and the rigour of scientific endeavour would suffer immeasurably. As often very busy people, some scientific researchers fail to see the value to themselves in peer-reviewing the work of others, but without that contribution from each one of us, their own work would be devalued. As a rule of thumb, we try to accept invitations to review at least as many papers as we publish, although we accept that this might not always be possible. As an emerging researcher, taking part in this process is of great value, affording you the opportunity to learn something new at the same time as critically evaluating others' work, thereby helping you to develop your own writing style and technique for future submissions.

Accepting an invitation to review for the first time can be as daunting as publishing your own work; it is a great responsibility and as such requires time and effort. You are being asked to provide a judgement on work that another researcher or team of researchers has spent a significant amount of time preparing. Your job is to remain objective, constructive, and honest, and to only accept a review if you feel that you are both reasonably well qualified to comment on the subject matter of the paper in question and without any conflicts of interest (you should not accept a review if you have recently published with one of the authors, or if they are based at your institute). If there are areas of the work that you cannot comment on, be sure to make this clear to the AE and the author(s) in your review.

A useful way to learn about writing reviews is to read the reviews that others have published online. Many OA journals also have an open peer review process, where the reviews of papers and the responses from authors are published publicly during a discussion phase. The review and discussion boards of some more contentious publications make for some very interesting reading indeed and can be just as informative as the final article itself. This open discussion is an exciting new addition to the modern era of scientific publication but unfortunately it can also (very rarely) attract some of the more negative aspects of social media such as anonymous trolling (see chapter 7). Thankfully, even here the checks and balances of the peer review process prevail in virtually all instances.

Exercise: Preparing for peer review
Choose an unread paper that is pertinent to your ongoing research. Picking something that is new to you ensures that you approach the review process with an unbiased and fresh perspective. By selecting something relevant, you will be able to gauge its significance and relevance more accurately, just as a peer reviewer assigned to the paper would.

Start by providing a concise summary of the paper's primary conclusions, offering your insights on its overall importance and quality. Then, move on to more specific observations. Highlight any areas that appear unclear or potentially flawed, framing your concerns as questions to the author. This approach fosters constructive feedback, encouraging the author to reconsider certain aspects rather than merely pointing out flaws. Lastly, even though published articles should ideally be devoid of typographical or grammatical errors, make a note of any you come across. These details, although minor, can influence the paper's overall perception.

Re-examine your review, adopting the mindset of the paper's original author. This shift in perspective will enable you to gauge the objectivity and clarity of your feedback. Consider the implications of your comments: are they constructive and beneficial for the AE's decision-making regarding publication? Your critique should not only identify potential weaknesses but also offer suggestions for how these might be addressed.

2.7 Citations and metrics

In section 2.2, we discussed how the quality of published work is more important than the quantity of publications in your record. One of the more explicit measures of your work's quality and its importance to science is the number of citations your paper may receive. Your choice of journal and its IF are a major influence on its exposure and therefore the chance that others will read and cite your work. However, there are other ways to raise your work's profile in your field. These concern how you advertise your work to others, and there is much that you can do to bring it to the attention of relevant researchers beyond simply relying on random internet searches that others may perform when conducting a literature review of their own.

There are several strategies to ensure that your work garners the attention of those who do not regularly peruse the contents of traditional journals. First, the title of your paper plays a pivotal role. A well-chosen title not only captures the essence of your research but also serves as a beacon for readers, guiding them to your work.

It should be both informative and engaging, providing a snapshot of your paper's core findings or questions. Second, be meticulous when selecting the search index keywords that many journals request during submission. Typically, you can designate several keywords or phrases that encapsulate the essence of your paper, such as 'greenhouse gases', 'nanoparticles', or 'unmanned aerial vehicles'. Consider the terms you would employ when performing a literature review related to your paper's content. Test these keywords to see if they yield papers akin to yours. Lastly, as highlighted in section 2.4, crafting a compelling abstract is paramount. It should crisply convey your research's salient findings. Given that researchers often sift through numerous articles on a specific topic (or keyword), a well-structured abstract serves as a crucial filter, helping them discern if the paper merits a thorough read.

Other more active ways to advertise your research include presenting your recent work at conferences, including references to your papers in any abstracts that you submit to them. You might also consider listing your most recent papers in your email signature. It is also useful to directly email any researchers you know in your field who you think may find your paper interesting, as well as taking every opportunity to advertise your paper through all the social media channels that you engage with. Some of these channels, such as ResearchGate and LinkedIn offer the ability to list your publications and form networks with other colleagues and researchers who may be automatically informed when you publish new work; a further discussion of some of these sites is given in chapter 7. Lastly, any organisational or personal websites should be kept up to date with your evolving research interests and publications.

Keeping track of your papers' citations is useful, as it will help you to recognise how your field is developing and to identify which of the papers that you have written have been the most well received. There are several conventional metrics that can be used to help formalise this process; these metrics are also often used in academic or scientific-related career promotion criteria, and as such they can be a hotly debated topic [11]. The more common of these metrics include the 'h-index' and the 'i-10 index'.

The h-index is the most common of the two and is based on a set of a researcher's most cited papers and the number of citations that this same set may have received in other publications. The value of this index is calculated such that a h-index with an integer value of 'h' represents an author that has published h papers, each of which has been cited in other authors' papers at least h times (see figure 2.1). As such, this index then reflects both the number of publications and the number of citations per publication. For example, an author with 20 publications but with only five papers that have been cited at least five times, will have an h-index of five, while an author with 20 publications, each cited at least 20 times would have an h-index of 20. This index favours those with consistently well-cited papers, but not those with one standout paper and several less well-cited papers.

The h-index, while valuable in comparing the impact of researchers within specific disciplines, loses its relevance across varied fields due to the unique publishing and citation practices inherent to each. For individual researchers within common disciplines, however, it provides a comparative measure of impact and reach. To bolster one's h-index, publishing high-quality papers and ensuring they gain visibility among peers is crucial.

In 2011 Google Scholar introduced another metric: the i-10 index. It quantifies the number of an author's publications that have received at least 10 citations, i.e. an

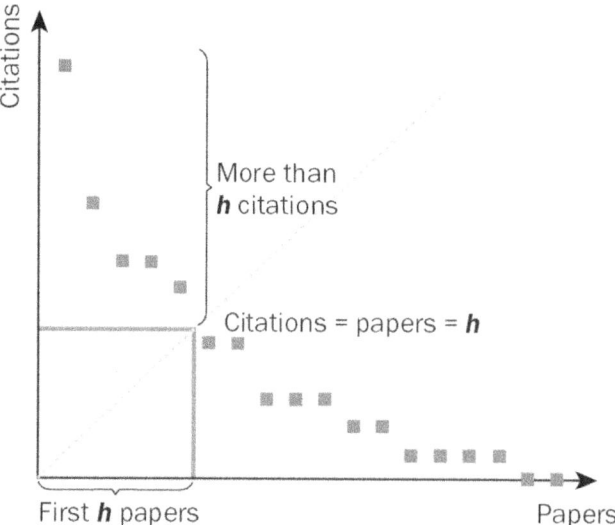

Figure 2.1. Calculation of the h-index using the number of papers attributed to a given author and the number of citations each has received. The h-index is then the maximum integer value where that number of papers has received at least the same number.

author with an i-10 index of 38 has 38 publications that have each been cited at least ten times. The i-10 index offers a more straightforward interpretation than the h-index, but it also accentuates the challenges of comparing impact across different disciplines.

There are many more exotic variations of these citation metrics, all of which are designed to remove a source of discrepancy, such as the discipline bias or age of the author, but not all metrics are readily recognised or understood by many [12]. A further point is that the value of these indices may vary wildly between different citation-indexing services, and that not all organisations recognise indices calculated from some services due to the perceived impurity, or chance of false positive data included in their calculation. It is your duty to honestly examine your citation indices to check that they have been calculated correctly, using the most up-to-date information. This may require you to routinely weed out (or add) any publications or citations that may have been wrongly attributed to you in any specific indexing service.

2.8 Summary

In this chapter, we introduced the critical importance of publishing within scientific journals, exploring their role as beacons of academic integrity and hubs for fostering rich scientific dialogue. We mapped out the journey of manuscript submission, providing a comprehensive understanding of the intricate peer review process and the checks and balances it introduces to ensure the quality of published work. We also touched upon the evolving landscape of Open Access and its transformative impact on disseminating research more broadly and democratically.

We have provided several strategies for researchers to amplify the visibility and influence of their findings, while also cautioning against the lurking shadows of predatory journals. The chapter also highlighted the emergent role of generative AI in the realm of academic writing, prompting readers to consider the implications and opportunities it presents. Throughout this chapter we have tried to champion the ethos of reciprocity in academia, emphasising that while publishing is a means to share discoveries, it is equally imperative for researchers to actively engage in peer review, upholding the foundational principles of collective scrutiny and collaboration that drive scientific progress forward.

2.9 Further study

The further study in this chapter is designed to help you think further about developing your paper writing and reviewing skills:

- **Read an article from outside your discipline.** Pick a scientific article from a reputable journal that lies outside your specific area of expertise. Read that article and see how it has been constructed in terms of its structure and layout. This will help you to defocus a little on the content of the paper, allowing you instead to reflect on its style and structure. Does the paper present its research findings in an innovative way, or is it overly verbose and

difficult to decipher? Are there any lessons that could be learnt for your own writing?
- **Follow an online discussion.** Pick a journal from within your field that has an online and open peer review system. Search through some of the articles until you find one that has a particularly long comments thread (ideally one that has inspired other members of the community, other than the compulsory reviewers, to comment), and see if you agree or disagree with some of the comments that have been made. Have all the comments been written in a constructive way, or are there instances of unprofessionalism or a lack of objectivity?
- **Compile some metrics.** Pick a couple of very well-known scientists in your respective field, both alive and dead, and compile a list of the various metrics that would be used to rate their publication records. How do they perform? See how they correlate to similar metrics of researchers from another discipline.

2.10 Suggested reading

While targeted specifically at the atmospheric scientist, *Eloquent Science* [13] is a book that contains a wealth of useful guidance on many aspects of scientific writing. The article 'The science of scientific writing' [14] also offers some helpful advice on how to improve the quality of your scientific writing. Similarly, if English is not your first language, then *English for Writing Research Papers* [15] is an essential guide for helping to avoid common mistakes and increase the readability of your work. If you are interested in developing your skills as a reviewer, then the article 'How to write a thorough peer review' [16] provides a straightforward methodology for constructing a considerate peer review and provides a useful worksheet for guidance. Finally, for readers wanting to find out more about the history of Open Access and what it is (and is not), the book *Open Access* [17] provides an excellent introduction.

References

[1] Tennant J P 2018 The state of the art in peer review *FEMS Microbiol. Lett.* **365** fny204
[2] Lockwood M 2020 Citation malpractice *Proc. R. Soc.* A**476** *20200746*
[3] Elmore S A 2018 Preprints: what role do these have in communicating scientific results? *Toxicol. Pathol.* **46** 364–5
[4] Mertkan S, Onurkan Aliusta G and Suphi N 2021 Knowledge production on predatory publishing: a systematic review *Learn. Publ.* **34** 407–13
[5] Mills D and Inouye K 2021 Problematizing 'predatory publishing': a systematic review of factors shaping publishing motives, decisions, and experiences *Learn. Publ.* **34** 89–104
[6] Strinzel M, Severin A, Milzow K and Egger M 2019 Blacklists and whitelists to tackle predatory publishing: a cross-sectional comparison and thematic analysis *MBio* **10** 10–1128
[7] Swan A and Brown S 2004 Authors and open access publishing *Learn. Publ.* **17** 219–24
[8] Harnad S *et al* 2004 The access/impact problem and the green and gold roads to open access *Ser. Rev.* **30** 310–4
[9] Zeller S and Rogers D 2020 Visualizing science: how color determines what we see *Eos* **101** 21 May

[10] Curtis N 2023 To ChatGPT or not to ChatGPT? The impact of artificial intelligence on academic publishing *Pediatr. Infect. Dis. J.* **42** 275
[11] Bihari A, Tripathi S and Deepak A 2023 A review on h-index and its alternative indices *J. Inf. Sci.* **49** 624–65
[12] Ioannidis J P, Klavans R and Boyack K W 2016 Multiple citation indicators and their composite across scientific disciplines *PLoS Biol.* **14** e1002501
[13] Schultz D 2013 *Eloquent Science: A Practical Guide to Becoming a Better Writer, Speaker, and Atmospheric Scientist* (Berlin: Springer)
[14] Gopen G D and Swan J A 1990 The science of scientific writing *Am. Sci.* **78** 550–8
[15] Wallwork A 2016 *English for Writing Research Papers* (London: Springer)
[16] Stiller-Reeve M 2018 How to write a thorough peer review *Nature* 21 May
[17] Suber P 2012 *Open Access* (Cambridge, MA: The MIT Press)

Effective Science Communication (Third Edition)
A practical guide to surviving as a scientist
Sam Illingworth and Grant Allen

Chapter 3

Applying for funding

I require 10,000 Marks.

—Otto Warburg

3.1 Introduction

Since the Renaissance period (and until surprisingly recently), academics were often self-funded—born of a wealthy family or made rich by some good fortune or industrial endeavour. Self-imprisoned in their archetypal laboratories, many of the famous names in medieval, and even nineteenth century science, used their personal resources to investigate whatsoever scientific direction they saw fit. Their unfettered free thinking and growing organisation gave us much of the fundamental understanding of the natural world and its governing physics that underpins all science and technology today.

However, the proliferation of science and technology during the Industrial Revolution, and the improvements in education that came from a more progressive society, soon meant that the deep thinkers and innovators of more recent modern history needed to seek external resource to fulfil their ambitions to learn and create. And with that need for resource came the necessity to justify and define the deliverables of projects to potential benefactors, from public agencies and charities to large corporations.

Increasingly, the 'impact agenda' features strongly in any request for funding—the ends must justify the means. Long gone are the days when a scientist could simply name the price of their research endeavours as in the case of the quote at the start of this chapter by Otto Warburg to the Emergency Association of German Science in 1921. Nowadays, most academic (and plenty of other professional) roles will at some point require you to make a case to a funder or funding body to invest resource in your projects and ideas, to allow you the time and resources you need to pursue them. In science, this case for support (or proposal) is typically a discussion of the current state of knowledge in a specific field, which aims to highlight a new frontier or challenge that you plan to address within a well-defined and achievable project design.

A potentially successful funding application needs just three things: a great idea, an effective project design, and excellent communication to those that might fund it. Like everything else in this book, a successful proposal often hinges on an ability to clearly communicate a narrative to a target audience. Your research idea may well be world-changing, but if you cannot convince others of that potential, you may never get the resources that you need to investigate it.

Referring to the 'triangle of effective communication' that will be discussed further in chapter 4, writing a proposal is about yourself (your idea), your audience (the funder), and your narrative (why your idea needs investment). The advice given in this book can help you to target and communicate effectively with your potential funding agency, or other investor, and give some useful insight into how to develop scientific ideas into workable projects. What this book cannot do is provide those exciting ideas—this spark of creative genius is still all very much down to you.

In this chapter, we aim to take some of the pain out of preparing a scientific proposal. From personal experience, even just the names of some of the elements of a proposal appear daunting to the uninitiated, and the process can appear very mysterious indeed. This chapter will look at the elements that comprise a modern scientific proposal and discuss how to formally develop your ideas into an achievable project, and then convince reviewers and funders of the need to invest in your work. We will begin by discussing the process of developing your ideas and your project narrative, and then offer insight into the machinations of scientific peer review and funding decisions. Much of what will be discussed is directly transferrable to any project proposal (e.g. a business case to a corporate sponsor and investors), but the focus and example here will be on scientific project proposals presented to public funding agencies.

3.2 What makes a good idea?

This is a highly subjective question, especially as someone working in a different field may not recognise the importance or feasibility of your idea or project. Thankfully, there are typically checks and balances in the review process that mitigate for this, but this is still something to be aware of when structuring the narrative in any proposal (see section 3.4).

Self-doubting researchers (especially those at the beginning of their careers) with truly great ideas can sometimes lack faith in their own creative ability and therefore struggle to express confidence in those ideas. Likewise, there are plenty of over-confident researchers who have mediocre ideas but believe in those ideas (and their ability) so much that they can present a very strong and convincing case for support. Therefore, the most important advice we can offer is to be honestly confident. If you are not confident about your ideas and your ability to deliver on them, then it will be impossible to convey that confidence in any research proposal and it will be doomed to fail. The opposite of this would be to present a hollow front for a poor idea, something that is usually obvious in the cold light of honest academic scrutiny, though of course mistakes do happen. In other words, confidence should flow naturally from a well-reasoned idea into which you have invested the necessary thought and time.

Your goal is therefore to think of an idea (or research question), to convince yourself that it is important, and then to invest time in the practical development of that idea into a feasible, costed project. After which you will be better equipped to convey that natural and bona fide confidence to those assessing the merits of your proposal.

Fundamentally, a good idea must represent an important new advance in some field of science, and ideally (and increasingly) provide direct and/or indirect benefit to society; for example, via public health, education, the economy, and/or the environment. Arriving at such an idea is typically a natural process after many years of research in a specific field such that you naturally find yourself at its cutting edge—for example after completing a PhD thesis. Identifying those ideas or scientific questions is the measure of a truly independent academic that can finally detach from the supervision of a senior academic (e.g. a PhD supervisor), and embark on their own path of investigation and discovery. True creativity often comes when we can push beyond our comfort zones; allow yourself the time and space to explore your ideas, discuss them with your trusted colleagues, and listen to their feedback. And then go ahead with writing your first funding proposal. It may well fail (most do, even for well-established scientists) but do not let that stop you from trying again and again (and again). Science is built on adventurous and resilient characters that push their own boundaries, and the boundaries of knowledge in the process.

Funding agencies often attempt to qualitatively (and sometimes quantitatively) assess the inherent risk in any project idea, and balance this with the impact and reward that might result in project success. A truly exciting and disruptive idea with high risk of failure but high potential for reward may well be prioritised over an incremental but relatively safe scientific advance.

Many of the projects we receive to assess as peer reviewers are often safe incremental projects with a sound project design. However, every so often a truly exciting project is submitted that really captures the imagination, but that may need a leap of faith to convince that it is a valuable use of resource. Our advice here is to be careful but not to be scared. As an experienced researcher with an excellent track record, reviewers and assessors may be more convinced of your ability to deliver on riskier projects, but this should not stop you from trying if you know you have an amazing idea. Just be mindful that any risky project must still have a good project design that minimises, identifies, and mitigates any risks, while also distilling the impacts and rewards that may come if the project is a success.

Let us examine two examples, one involving high-risk–high-reward, and the other with a moderate-risk-moderate-reward profile. While there are instances where proposals with low risk and high rewards can succeed, they are exceedingly rare.

One prime example of high-risk–high-reward is the discovery of the Higgs boson —a fundamental, force-carrying particle. This discovery, made in 2012, played a pivotal role in completing the Standard Model of particle physics and laid the groundwork for various breakthroughs in fundamental science and potential technological advancements. When the Large Hadron Collider (LHC) was built, it represented a collaborative effort between the European Organization for Nuclear Research (CERN), involving over 10 000 scientists, hundreds of universities, laboratories, and more than 100 countries. This monumental project, which spanned from 1998 to 2008, faced significant challenges. At the time, there was no hint of observational evidence for the Higgs boson. The financial commitment required for constructing the experimental infrastructure and recruiting skilled personnel was colossal, and success was far from assured. Additionally, the immediate pathways to practical technological advancements were not readily apparent. Nevertheless, the compelling nature of the case drew significant investment in the form of multi-billion euros and a continuous influx of enthusiastic researchers dedicated to the task.

The second example might be something like the development of a new model parameterisation for weather prediction requiring new field data to validate it—an incremental and achievable improvement on an already good weather forecast using new understanding gained from reliably obtained field data (though colleagues working in meteorology may well argue that such a new advance is far from incremental...).

Have the confidence to explore your ideas, take the time to research the field of interest, and develop a practical plan (see section 3.4) that turns these ideas into a proposed investigatory project. Consider and highlight the risks and rewards and mitigate, minimise, and maximise, respectively. Get advice from trusted colleagues, and if necessary, bring in the skills of those you need to help complete your project. And get thinking. Science needs you.

> **Exercise: Turn an idea into a project**
> Write down a list of three ideas you have that would represent novel advances in your field of interest. This could be the follow-on work you wanted to do when you finished your PhD thesis, some outstanding questions from a recent paper you wrote, or something completely different. Try to make one of these ideas something truly adventurous and risky (in terms of potential for successful investigation).
>
> Once you have this list, think about what you would need to do to investigate each of them. What equipment might you need? What data do you need? How will you obtain that data and equipment? What facilities do you need? How will you analyse the data or build your prototype? How long will each step take? What can you do yourself and do you need help from others (including people at different institutes) with specialist expertise?
>
> Put these activities into order in self-contained 'work packages' and work out the total project time and make a rough calculation of the cost. Think about what can be done in parallel, and which of these work packages depend on the outcomes of another.
>
> For each project, think about the risks at each step. What would it mean if you could not obtain part of the data? How could you minimise the chances of that risk becoming a reality, and what would you do if it became unavoidable? Think about the 'critical path' of your project and how you might still achieve project success if part of the project was not possible or yielded a null result.

3.3 Finding funding

When you have decided you have a good idea and a workable plan in principle, you need to identify a suitable funder or funding agency that fits your idea (and your budget). If your idea has industrial applications, you could approach specific companies for investment and ask about their research and development strategies and how to engage with them. For public funding agencies, look up your national science funding council(s) and read their webpages to learn what their scientific remit is, so that you can gauge whether your project is a good fit to their advertised strategy. Charities and other philanthropic schemes (e.g. the Gates Foundation) may also commission research relevant to their agenda.

In Europe, there is also an over-arching European Research Council that accepts proposals from across the European Union (as well as many non-EU countries such as Norway, Switzerland, and the UK) across many different scientific themes. Often, research councils will list contact information for you to informally discuss whether your idea is eligible within the council's remit, and you will usually be pointed in the right direction if not. Finally, a good chat with more experienced colleagues will normally save you a lot of time when working out where to apply for funding; as discussed in chapter 10, mentoring is a life-long asset in any professional career.

Research councils typically release calls for proposals, or announcements of opportunity, on set advertised dates (with specific deadlines). Other calls for proposals may be open and continuous with rolling deadlines. Spend some time looking at current and past calls for proposals and announcements of opportunity to learn more about what different funding agencies are interested in, and where you might fit in to their remit. Registering for email alerts for new calls from funding agencies is a good way to keep track of what opportunities are coming up, without having to remember to make return visits to webpages.

Sometimes, your idea may need to be adaptive to respond to a prescriptive call that the funder wants to commission. At other times, you may have an idea that is more suited to an open round that accepts ideas across the broader swathe of the funder's remit. Whatever the case, always make sure that you have identified the right place to submit your proposal to by reading the webpages associated with the funder and any call for proposals.

Perhaps the most important funding opportunity to any new academic, graduating PhD student, or early-career post-doctoral researcher, are early-career research fellowships. These are highly prestigious awards made to researchers with excellent ideas who show great promise for academic career development. While fellowship opportunities do also exist for researchers at various stages in their career, this chapter will focus on early-career fellowships only. Such fellowships are a truly career-advancing opportunity for any aspiring new academic; they are mostly designed to fully fund your salary and your project costs at a nominated host institute for the duration of the award, and as such mean that you may be free to pursue your project without conflicting demands of teaching and other academic duties (if this is what you desire and negotiate with your host institute).

Early-career fellowships are as much about an investment in the individual as they are about the investment in a project idea. Funding agencies and reviewers look for proposals from promising new academics with an already strong track record of research outputs, and who have an exciting idea that really capitalises on their existing skill as an independent researcher in their chosen field. Such fellowships may well be hosted at an institute where the candidate is not currently in residence, where the applicant may benefit from new skills and expertise working alongside a world-leading research group that complements their research idea. Equally, it may well be that the applicant has a good case to develop a fellowship at an institute with which they already have much experience. In either case, reviewers will look for evidence that the applicant has a strong record as an independent researcher, and that they know how to synergise with other teams and research groups to meet the objectives of an independently developed fellowship proposal.

Once you have identified a funding agency and a call for proposals that you intend to submit to, conduct some more in-depth research to check your eligibility, and to learn about what components may be required in your submission. There is usually guidance and a template that you can follow to make sure that you include all the relevant information the funder needs; for example: a CV, budget documentation, and a case for support (see section 3.4). You can typically find all this information in funding guidelines that can be downloaded or otherwise requested from the funding agency. If in any doubt, always contact the funding agency with any questions you have (it is part of their job to help you in this process), and there are also often online webinars (or in some instances face-to-face events) explaining the intricacies and processes of such schemes.

If you are hosted by an institute that is already eligible to apply for funding, then use the support that they can provide; find out who this is and let them know about your plans and learn what they can do to help you. For example, there may be a research finance office (or equivalent) at your institute that can help you with costing your project (see section 3.5). Again, speaking with your colleagues is a good way to learn more about what support is available. You should rarely be completely alone in developing a proposal, but you may have to spend some time in finding out where this support is and how best it can be accessed. Bear in mind that it can take many months to develop a good proposal and secure the collaborations you may need, so start early.

Exercise: Research your funding opportunities
For each of the ideas you explored in the previous exercise in this chapter, do some research in to which agencies, companies etc you might approach for funding, and find out how to submit a proposal to a call from that funder. Examine the remit of those funding bodies and whether that remit fits your idea. You could begin with an internet search for 'science funding agencies', or at the homepages of your national research council.

Sign up to the email alerts from any of these agencies that are of relevance and interest to your research, so that you can be kept up to date of any new announcements of opportunity. Also, take the opportunity to download any guidance that is available for preparing a proposal.

3.4 Anatomy of a research proposal

Unfortunately, there is no magic formula for what needs to be included in a research proposal. There are, however, some key aspects that are essential to all proposals, and others that may be interchangeable depending on the funder. Always check your funder's guidance to find out what information is mandatory, and if there are any templates that might need to be followed. Sometimes even formatting these documents with regards to specified page margins, font styles, and font size are mandatory and may result in outright rejection if the guidance is not followed exactly. This can be especially disappointing if you have spent several months of work developing your proposal, only to have it rejected without review due to one line in an attached CV being written in the wrong font.

Some typical components of a research proposal may include the following:
- **Case for support**. A justification of your science idea and work plan. More recently, this component may be called 'Vision and approach' by some funders.
- **Pathways to impact**. An outline of the benefits and legacy that will come from your work, and who this will affect.
- **Justification of resources**. An itemised budget linked to the work plan.
- **Data management plan**. A discussion of how you will safely and securely disseminate any data to others.
- **Curriculum vitae (CV)**. This should be written in an academic style.
- **Track record**. An outline of how your current experience and access to facilities fits the proposed project. More recently, this may be called 'Capability to deliver' by some funders.
- **Project management plan**. A guide that provides timelines and responsibilities, and which is linked to a detailed work plan with milestones and deliverables.
- **Risk management plan**. An identification plus minimisation and mitigation of project risks, linked to the work plan.

There may well be other components depending on the funder (e.g. summary documents that explain your idea to a non-scientific audience) and some of these elements may be merged into one document, but this will be clearly specified in the documentation associated with each specific funding call. Furthermore, while all these elements are important, the 'case for support' is (by definition) where reviewers will look to be impressed by your project, while the 'pathways to impact' is an essential aspect of justifying why your project will benefit the wider society. There now follows a more detailed look at these two components.

3.4.1 Case for support

This is the most important part of any research proposal. It is through the case for support that you need to convince reviewers that you have an important idea supported by a workable project that is worth investing in. This can be anything from a few pages of A4 to many volumes (e.g. for very large and complex projects with multiple work packages, such as a new satellite instrument). Often, it is a challenge to make your case in the space allowed, which is where your ability to communicate is essential. You must efficiently, succinctly, and transparently describe your science idea to the level and range of reviewer expertise.

Reviewers are usually selected by the funding agency (see section 3.6) and are typically leaders in the field in which your proposal lies. However, the subject matter of many proposals may be so cutting edge that not all reviewers will have a high level of expertise in the specific area. Therefore, you must prepare your narrative for an audience that spans from the general to the highly specialised scientist in your field.

For example, in the field of atmospheric science, a proposal about the aircraft-based measurement of greenhouse gases may be reviewed by both someone who is an expert in the mathematics of sampling theory or by someone who develops sensors to measure greenhouse gases on the ground. Each reviewer may understand some aspects of the proposal better than others, but it is your job to provide sufficient clarity such that any reviewer can both understand the general thrust of your proposal, yet also access the necessary technical detail they may be looking for in their area of expertise.

The best way to achieve this is to structure your case for support such that you 'funnel' the reader from the overall project idea and deliverables (e.g. an executive summary), through the general scientific context of the wider field surrounding your idea, before finally describe the cutting edge of that field which you plan to address and how you will do this. At each stage, it is useful to introduce and summarise each section in turn.

Like any good story, your case for support, and each section of it, should have a beginning (an introduction and leading summary or abstract), a middle (flowing from the general to the technical), and an end (legacy of the project). This rolling introduction and summary throughout each self-contained section really helps reviewers to digest your project ideas and works on the following principle of triplicate repetition and memory retention: tell your audience what they are about to read, give them the information, and then summarise it for them. Indeed, most textbooks (including this one) or research papers follow this exact principle.

Reviewers are typically very busy academics who are not paid for their review work—your job is to make the narrative of your case for support easy for them to understand, as quickly as possible. They want to know that you have a good idea right from the start. A busy reviewer will not have the patience to read over your proposal many times to try and understand it; you must capture them on the first sentence and retain their concentration until the last. By taking them on a journey from introduction to technical detail and back to concluding summary, this will make the digestion of the information much easier for the reviewers and will help them to commit it to memory. A pleasurable reading experience will put the reviewers in a better frame of mind to score your proposal more objectively; especially if you have facilitated their understanding of any technical detail by funnelling them through that detail gently and succinctly.

A generalised structure to a case for support might resemble the funnel in figure 3.1 following:

1. A short summary of the project and why it is important.
2. An introduction or literature review that discusses the scientific context and motivation to your field (e.g. previous work), culminating at the forefront that your project addresses.

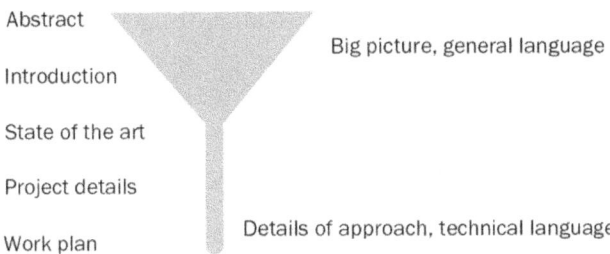

Figure 3.1. The proposal 'funnel'. This diagram outlines how your case for support can be used to create an engaging narrative journey for your reviewers.

3. A description of what your project will do, broken down into self-contained but cross-linked work packages.
4. A description of the deliverables and outputs of your project linked to those work packages.
5. A concluding summary on the legacy of the project and the future science that might be enabled by it.

Sometimes, project management, ethics statements, and risk strategies may also form part of the case for support—check the funding specifications of your chosen funding agency for detail.

First-time scientific proposal writers often possess experience in crafting peer-reviewed papers and encounter challenges in effectively balancing project design with scientific context, specifically the underlying literature review. It is crucial to encapsulate the current state of research in the field that forms the foundation of your project and pinpoint the void you intend to fill. However, this takes a backseat to the intricacies of the project you plan to undertake.

Given that most reviewers will already possess familiarity with the field, your introduction and literature review should serve as a concise summary that swiftly converges on the innovative aspect you intend to address, before following up with a more comprehensive description of your project. In other words, clearly tell your reviewer what is new and why is it important in as succinct a way as possible. If they can understand this from the start, the more technical detail that may follow will make far more sense.

Any contextual discussion is about demonstrating to the reader that you are well informed and at the forefront of your field; providing evidence for the importance of the work that you propose to do. It is not about regurgitating everything you know about your subject and exhaustively listing and discussing the merits of every paper ever published in the field. When you are limited on space, it is important to get into the project details as quickly as possible and not to bore or patronise your readers with what they may already know.

To demonstrate this in practice, we offer the following example of the aircraft-based measurement of greenhouse gases research project mentioned above, albeit in a very simplistic and abbreviated way so we can see the general flow and structure of a case for support:

1. **Summary.** Measuring greenhouse gases is important to understand climate change. Using aircraft sensors is a good way to measure them. This project will do that and provide new data to climate scientists.
2. **Context.** Lots of work has been done to measure greenhouse gases on the ground but more data is needed in places that only aircraft can get to. Complex computer models can be used to calculate emissions using this data.
3. **Work packages**. This project will: (a) install a new instrument on a plane; (b) provide data from the new instrument in a special field campaign; (c) interpret the data using complex computer models to derive new maps of greenhouse gases and their sources.
4. **Deliverables.** This project will provide: (a) new datasets for use by scientists; (b) new understanding of greenhouse gas sources in new places; (c) papers, conference presentations, etc
5. **Legacy.** New maps of greenhouse gas sources will allow future work to update climate predictions and target policies for emissions reduction.

If you can leave the reviewer with a clear and complete story about what you want to do, why it needs to be done, and how you will do it, then you will have succeeded in writing an effective case for support.

3.4.2 Pathways to impact

Pathways to impact are where you explain how the deliverables of your project will benefit others. It is about recognising how your work fits into the wider scientific community and society, and how to make sure that you are not the only human being to know about your exciting work. It is a more detailed description of the legacy of your work and should contain descriptions (pathways) of how each benefit potential will be realised in practice.

The first step here is to list the different communities impacted by your research—who benefits and why. These communities could be other academic beneficiaries who may wish to use your data for other projects. They could be members of specific publics who will benefit directly or indirectly because of some change brought about by your research (e.g. a new drug that will improve the lives of people living with a particular disease, or an improvement in air quality over a region due to new policy advice). They could be industrial partners who will use your research to develop new technology and generate economic benefit. Or they could be schoolchildren and other interested individuals who will learn about your work through targeted outreach and public engagement (see chapter 5).

The key here is to consider the wider beneficiaries of your research and then think of ways to maximise that potential through different pathways. For example, if your work has an economic benefit, how will you engage with companies who might want to use it? How will other academics learn about your new datasets? How will you inspire others? Do you need time and money to do this? Might journalists and media outlets be interested (see chapter 6)?

The primary driving force behind a project should indeed be its potential for genuine impact. There must be a societal need at its core, rather than merely pursuing knowledge for the sake of curiosity or interest. Your work should consistently revolve around the generation of fresh knowledge and its application for the betterment of society and the world at large. By keeping this fundamental principle in mind and dedicating time to contemplate how you can actualise it, the process of devising a roadmap for impact should seamlessly integrate into any proposal.

> **Exercise: Write your pathways to impact**
> For the ideas that you developed in the previous exercises in this chapter, list all the communities that you can think of for each project. These may be other research communities, specific companies, public bodies, policymakers, educators, or other publics. Write a line or two about which outcomes of your project are most relevant to each community, then think about how they might interface with your project or its outputs and how you might achieve this. For example, via publications, conferences, workshops, community events, policy guidance, one-to-one meetings, follow-on projects, etc. How will you engage with each community and at what point in the project? Finally, write about what might come from this engagement and the benefits to you and the other communities that are potentially impacted.

3.5 Budgeting

It can sometimes be difficult to know exactly what resources you will need to carry out a project. This is an area where you should seek help from finance administrators at your host institute, who can calculate specific costs for you once you have defined what you need (e.g. two years' salary for a research assistant at full economic costing).

The temptation to trim costs to present a more appealing proposal to potential funders is a common one. However, we recommend exercising caution in this regard. Our foremost advice is to allocate resources precisely in line with your calculated needs, providing a clear rationale for each resource requested, and not requesting a penny less or a penny more than necessary. Furthermore, ensure that your project's design aligns with the available budget. Avoid the inclination to propose an overly ambitious project that cannot be realistically funded within the available budget.

Reviewers and funders will scrutinise the justification for the requested resources and seek reassurances regarding the project's financial viability. For instance, if you have requested funding for a field-based project but overlooked expenses such as travel and accommodation, a reviewer may inquire about your plans to cover these costs. Similarly, if your budget includes stays at five-star hotels and three-course meals every evening, reviewers may question the rationale behind such expenditures.

Prioritising the comprehensive resourcing of your project to align with its design requirements is more crucial than omitting elements to create a facade of cost-effectiveness. In all instances, your total expenditure must not exceed the maximum budget established by your funding source. Your cost estimates should also remain grounded and reasonable. While it is customary to include some contingency, such as accounting for inflation over the project's duration, exaggerated cost estimates for items in your proposal may be perceived as excessive (is that laptop truly as expensive as you suggest?).

Furthermore, you may be obligated to obtain multiple quotations for costly new equipment, which might need to be included as part of your proposal. If your calculated costs surpass the allowed maximum, you may need to reevaluate the project's activities. It is far more advisable to undertake this revision during the planning phase than to discover that you are unable to execute the project after securing funding.

Typically, your institution's financial administration will assist you in, and often require approval for, expenses related to staff and other items. However, you are responsible for initially determining and then submitting the calculations for equipment, travel, or consumables costs. Additionally, all expenses should be clearly aligned to the project's requirements and presented in a detailed breakdown for scrutiny by funders in the resource justification documentation.

Lastly, it can prove to be a highly valuable exercise to strategize how you could capitalise on funding or in-kind contributions from other collaborators or grants you may have secured. For instance, a colleague at a different institution might offer you complimentary access to their specialised facilities, or someone else might agree to provide you with an exclusive dataset along with guidance on its use. These in-kind contributions significantly augment the proposal's worth, not only by providing added value but also by availing expert assistance and direction, thereby mitigating risks and augmenting the potential for impact and knowledge exchange.

To this end, carefully consider how you can enlist support from peers at other institutions and explore opportunities for collaborative efforts that align with shared interests and objectives. If such support materialises, ensure you obtain letters of endorsement from these collaborators, defining their intended contributions, and outlining their endorsement of both you and your project.

3.6 The funding process

One of the most exasperating aspects you may need to develop resilience for in your scientific career is the likelihood that most of your proposals may simply go unfunded. The reality within contemporary funding frameworks, whether in publicly funded science or the corporate sector, is that the financial resources are not limitless, and there exists a substantial pool of other outstanding scientists, all with remarkable ideas that frequently compete directly with your own. Your only recourse is to present your ideas and the rationale for support in the most compelling manner possible, celebrate when you succeed, and derive valuable insights from the feedback on your unsuccessful attempts.

Frequently, you might discover that reviewers and funders have endorsed your proposal as being of high priority for funding, only to encounter the limitation of finite funding resources, resulting in other proposals at a higher priority level receiving the available funding at that time.

Finding your potential funder and writing your proposal are the parts of the process over which you have complete control. Once you have submitted your proposal, the process of review and assessment begins. To give yourself the best chance possible after submission, ask senior colleagues to look over your proposal and provide an internal peer review. Do this well before any deadline and you will have time to build on their constructive comments. In any case, many institutes now require formal internal peer review prior to approval for submission to funding agencies.

The typical pathway to a successful (or unsuccessful) funding award may follow that outlined in the flow diagram shown in figure 3.2. You can find the exact pathway for your funder from their guidance information; for example, not all proposals require a face-to-face interview with a funding assessment panel, and not all funding calls allow you the opportunity to respond to reviews. Typically, your proposal will be first reviewed and scored by experts. Those reviews, sometimes together with your response to them, will then be passed to a specially convened funding panel consisting of several members, who will then judge the relative merits of each proposal based on the reviews and responses and make a recommendation on priority for funding (usually assigning a score against criteria you can examine). A rank order will be defined by this panel for any single call, and the funder will then award money to those proposals down the list until their funds are exhausted. We will now briefly look at each of these stages in turn.

On submission of your proposal, a funding agency will first check for the individual's eligibility and whether the science proposed is a fit to their remit.

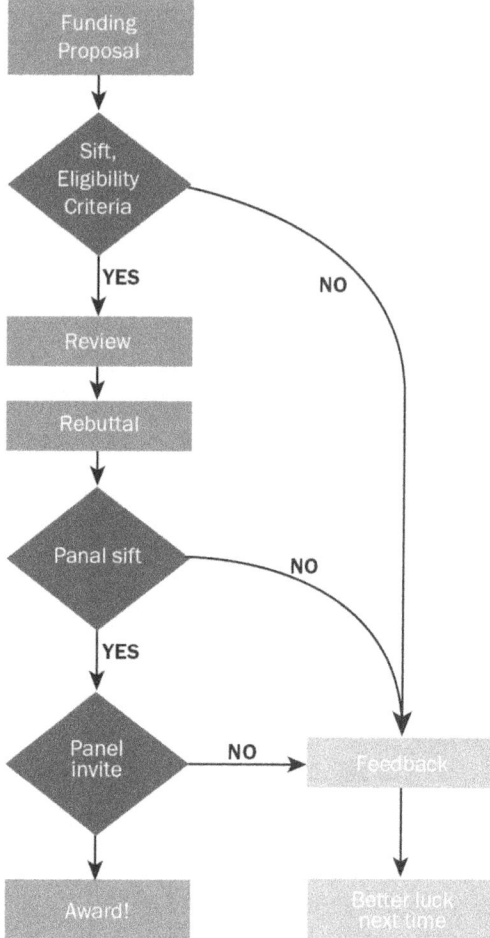

Figure 3.2. A flow diagram of the funding process, from proposal submission to award.

They will then check any formatting requirements and ensure that all components of the proposal are present. Some funding agencies can be quite unforgiving at this stage and may reject a proposal without scope to put things right, so make sure you have provided everything required exactly as it is asked.

Following this initial check, the funding body will proceed to select and extend invitations to potential reviewers to evaluate and assess your proposal based on predefined criteria. Typically, you can find information about the questions reviewers will be asked and the scoring criteria in the guidance offered by the funding organisation. It is always beneficial to review this information and ensure that your proposal provides clear and comprehensive details to assist the reviewer in their assessment.

Additionally, you might be required to provide contact details for potential specialist reviewers who have no affiliations with your project. While this does not guarantee that these individuals will be approached by the funder, it is considered best practice to provide names of professionals you are aware of who are well-suited to comprehend and provide input on your project concept. Subsequently, the funding body can assess the suitability of any reviewers you recommend and may choose to extend invitations to them.

The roster of reviewers engaged by a funding agency is typically meticulously curated, comprising prominent experts in the fields aligned with the agency's mandate. Nonetheless, certain proposals may find themselves under the scrutiny of academics or professionals possessing limited expertise in your specific domain. Reviewers are typically seasoned and impartial, and they will transparently communicate any constraints in their evaluation to the funding panel. They will be tasked with providing feedback on various aspects, including the scientific significance of your project, your proficiency as a project lead for its execution, and the efficacy of the project's design, evaluating both its strengths and weaknesses. Additionally, they may offer insights on potential risks and undertake a comprehensive assessment of the project's impact and the justification for allocated resources. In the case of fellowship applications, they may also be prompted to evaluate the applicant's track record and potential as an independent researcher.

Depending on the funder and the call, you may get the chance to respond to any reviews to help to clarify any misunderstandings. If this is the case, you may receive any number of reviews (usually an absolute minimum of two, and typically more). As discussed in chapter 2, you should not view your reviews as personal indictments—they are expected to be an objective discussion of your proposal—and your response to them should be equally objective. At times, you may feel like the review is an attack on your proposal. And in many ways, that is exactly what it is supposed to be. It is your job to defend your approach (if you believe the reviewer to be incorrect) and answer any questions raised. Address each comment in turn politely and be honest. If a reviewer has truly misunderstood some aspects of your work, the funding panel who make the final decision will read both the review and your response and reach a judgement. In many cases, the funding panel can completely disregard reviews it feels are not accurate or objective, so do not be too disheartened if you receive negative reviews. It is often better to have a detailed critical review than it is to have a very short, shining endorsement of your proposal that contains nothing that the funding panel can make a judgement on.

An awards panel is convened by the funder to prioritise and score proposals after peer review. The panel typically consists of leading academics drawn from the peer review pool whose expertise cover the range of topics in the submitted proposals, a chairperson (to manage the discussions and keep the panel on track), a secretary from the funding agency to advise on procedural issues, and a funding agency observer who may sit on several panels to monitor consistency in funding panel decisions across the various calls administered by the funding body.

Your proposal will normally be described to the entire panel verbally by a first introducer who has been asked to read your proposal, the reviews of your proposal, and your response to the reviews in advance of the panel meeting. A second introducer may then be asked to do the same in turn, following which the chairperson will then ask the introducer(s) to discuss the strengths and weaknesses of the proposal and invite others on the panel to comment. Ideally, all members of the panel will have read every proposal and are free to do so. However, in practice, each panel member may be asked to introduce many individual proposals and the total being assessed in any one panel may be very large indeed, meaning that panellists typically may only read and comment on those proposals most closely aligned with their expertise. The panel will then be asked to agree on a score that is recorded by the secretary.

Having sat on several such funding panels, we can confirm that it is an exhausting, but very objective and transparent, process. The panellists will do their best to assess the relative merits of each proposal, and the checks and balances of the panel process and peer review help to ensure neutral objectivity. However, the process works best for you when you can really make it as easy as possible for all concerned to fully understand and access your project. Try to put yourself in the position of a panellist when writing your proposal—make sure that every word and sentence is meaningful and useful, and that its structure allows a very busy person to absorb it easily. If you do not get this right, you risk your ideas being lost in the noise.

After the panel have scored your proposal and all others, a rank order of the scores will be compiled. Many proposals may have equal scores and those that do must be placed in priority order relative to those around them. At this point, the panel may briefly re-examine those proposals and rank them again such that a monotonic rank order is achieved.

Finally, the funder will allocate funding down the list and draw a line when the money is exhausted. If your proposal is above this line (and scored fundable in principle), then well done, your project has been funded. However, the vast majority will typically be below this line. It is not unusual for fewer than one in five proposals (and often a great deal fewer than this) to make the funding cut. Remember that you may have to write five good proposals before you have an odds-on chance of beating the average. Your job is to stack the odds in your favour by writing excellent proposals based on exceptional ideas.

If you find yourself facing disappointment, then explore the opportunity to request feedback from the panel. Their comments provide valuable insights into why your proposal was not successful. Take the time to reflect upon these comments, learn from them, and contemplate the possibility of resubmitting your proposal in the future, addressing the feedback provided by both the panel and reviewers. Remember, a significant amount of effort goes into developing your ideas, and recycling and refining them can be a wise approach.

Do not lose heart and try to avoid taking rejection personally. As scientists, our mission is to unearth, question, and advocate for the truth, and this aligns precisely with the principles of the peer review process. Embrace the opportunity to challenge yourself, your ideas, and the valid questions raised by others.

3.7 Summary

This chapter has provided guidance on the practical aspects of seeking funding and structuring scientific ideas into a cohesive proposal. It has also explored the intricacies of the peer review process within typical funding agencies, and in doing so we have dissected the various elements that constitute a funding application, offering insights into what makes a strong proposal.

However, beyond the technicalities, a truly outstanding proposal and project concept emerge from the confidence to nurture your creativity and engage in constructive introspection regarding your ideas. Embrace self-assurance, cultivate resilience in the face of challenges, maintain a methodical approach to your work, actively seek guidance from mentors and peers, and shed any fear of failure. The process of pursuing funding and advancing scientific innovation thrives on the blend of creative exploration and a steadfast commitment to learning and growth.

3.8 Further study

The further study in this chapter is related to your grant writing skills; it should make you think further about what is necessary for successful writing:

1. **Read some successful grants.** Ask the research and knowledge exchange office (or equivalent) at your institute to provide you with a selection of successful proposals. Alternatively go to a funding body's website and look for past examples of previously successful applicants. Reading a selection of successful applications will help you to understand what is required and will also help to develop your writing style.
2. **Make a list of upcoming deadlines.** Select several funding bodies that you are interested in working with and make a note of their upcoming calls and their respective deadlines. Are any of these achievable for you to apply for?
3. **Prepare a research proposal.** If you are ready, select your most promising idea and write a case for support, using the responses that you have provided to the other exercises in this chapter to help you. Note any deadlines for submission and plan your time for writing the proposal, allowing plenty of time for development and discussion with trusted colleagues.

3.9 Suggested reading

Scientific Writing and Communication: Papers, Proposals, and Presentations [1] covers both writing and oral presentation in significant depth. As one of only a few dedicated books that cover proposal writing, this resource is highly relevant to this chapter. *Writing Successful Science Proposals* [2] also provides very useful advice for how to get your ideas funded, while *Getting Funded: The Complete Guide to Writing Grant Proposals* [3] focusses entirely on proposal development from scoping an idea to the submission and review of a full proposal; it also deals with budgeting and human resourcing.

The article 'Ten simple rules for getting grants' [4] from the excellent '10 Simple Rules' series from *PLoS Computational Biology*, does exactly what the title suggests, providing a very helpful set of guidelines for writing successful funding applications. Finally, *Proposal Writing: Effective Grantsmanship* [5] covers proposal writing for submission to a wide range of potential funders including national funding agencies, corporate sponsors, and philanthropic foundations. It also provides some useful guidance on choosing an appropriate funding agency and deals with more logistical aspects such as budgeting.

References

[1] Hofmann A H 2014 *Scientific Writing and Communication: Papers, Proposals, and Presentations* (Oxford: Oxford University Press)
[2] Friedland A J, Folt C L and Mercer J L 2018 *Writing Successful Science Proposals* (New Haven, CT: Yale University Press)
[3] Hall M S and Howlett S 2003 *Getting Funded: The Complete Guide to Writing Grant Proposals* (Nottingham: Continuing Education Press)
[4] Bourne P E and Chalupa L M 2006 Ten simple rules for getting grants *PLoS Comput. Biol.* **2** e12
[5] Coley S M and Scheinberg C A 2008 *Proposal Writing: Effective Grantsmanship* (Thousandoaks, CA: Sage)

IOP Publishing

Effective Science Communication (Third Edition)
A practical guide to surviving as a scientist
Sam Illingworth and Grant Allen

Chapter 4

Presenting

Nothing in life is to be feared, it is only to be understood. Now is the time to understand more, so that we may fear less.
—Maria Skłodowska-Curie

4.1 Introduction

Eventually in your academic career you are going to be asked to give a scientific presentation. This may be at a face-to-face weekly research group meeting, or at an online international conference; each of which have their own unique set of challenges to address. Presenting to any audience, and in any context, can be a difficult and demanding exercise, and despite what some people might say, it requires practice. Colleagues that profess to making it up as they go along, or 'winging it', are either seasoned professionals who have delivered similar material many times before, or else they are deluded and are not as good at presenting as they may think.

There are various audiences that scientists need to communicate with, and we need to choose how to present our narrative accordingly. We must also consider how we present ourselves and our science in the process. Communicating to other audiences is addressed elsewhere in this book, in chapters 5 (non-scientists), 6 (the mass media), and 8 (policymakers). The focus of this chapter is about presenting your work to a scientific audience, centred around practical advice designed to help you become a better public speaker.

The best piece of advice that we can give is the most obvious: practice makes perfect. As the noted American author Mark Twain once said, 'It usually takes me more than three weeks to prepare a good impromptu speech.' Being an effective presenter is not a 'dark art', nor is it a gift that certain people are innately born with; rather it comes from taking the time to learn and develop the skills and approaches that are discussed in this chapter.

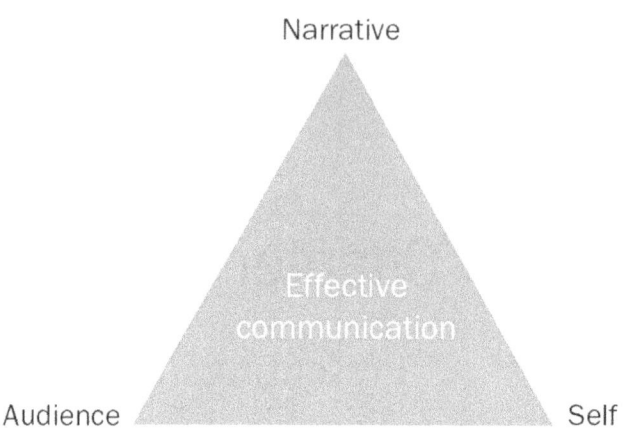

Figure 4.1. The triangle of effective communication. This triangle highlights the three key aspects that need to be considered to communicate: the 'Narrative' (what you are saying), the 'Audience' (who you are saying it to), and the 'Self' (how you are saying it).

4.2 A three-way approach

There are many theories on the best way to create and deliver a presentation, but the approach discussed here is based on the work of Edward Peck and Helen Dickinson [1], who outline three key properties that need to be considered for effective communication to take place: the narrative, the audience, and the self.

Figure 4.1 outlines this three-way approach in the form of a geometric shape: the triangle of effective communication; without all three of its components, the concept at the centre cannot exist. To communicate effectively, you need to consider the 'narrative', the 'audience', and the 'self', and if just one of these vertices is missing then the effectiveness of your message will be reduced. We will now discuss in turn how best to consider these three key properties.

4.2.1 Developing your narrative

The ultimate purpose of a scientific presentation is to communicate a message to your intended audience. This message might be that you have some interesting findings, or that you have an update on some recent challenges that you have been experiencing. To ensure that your audience have taken away from your presentation the message(s) that you intended, first you need to do a little planning. One way of doing this is outlined in the following exercise.

Exercise: Three take-home messages
Think about the next presentation that you are going to give. Now, imagine an idealised world in which your audience leaves the presentation knowing exactly what you wanted them to know. What would that be? Write down the three key, take-home messages for your presentation. For example, if you were giving a presentation entitled 'Effective Communication in Presentations', you might want your audience to leave knowing about the importance of the narrative, the audience, and the self.

> Once you have written down these three take-home messages, use them to create the structure for your presentation. We also recommend including these take-home points on the final slide of your presentation (see section 4.5), as doing so will serve to further highlight their importance to your audience.
>
> Determining the take-home messages and then using this to structure your narrative should not be restricted to presentations. This technique can also be used in any form of communication, from international teleconferences to one-to-one meetings with a supervisor or line manager. Next time you have something that you need to communicate, first take the time to work out what your key take-home messages are. This will help you to align your arguments and it will make it far more likely that you achieve what you set out to accomplish.

Once you have identified your take-home messages, it is time to start building the narrative that will allow for them to be communicated in a succinct and logical fashion. Giving a presentation is like telling a story, which means that the same basic concepts of narrative that are applicable to storytelling can also be applied when structuring a presentation.

In their most basic format, stories have a beginning, a middle, and an end. In this respect scientific presentations are no different. In a scientific presentation, this is often about setting the scene and telling your audience what you are about to tell them (the beginning), telling them something in detail (the middle), and then telling them what you just said (the end). As discussed in chapter 3, this principle of triplicate repetition and memory retention helps people to retain and understand information; especially complex technical information that is typical of many scientific presentations. Telling a story in this way, with running introductions and summaries, can go a long way to not losing your audience.

You should begin by introducing your audience to the narrative, i.e. by providing a summary of the background and context to the scientific field your work relates to. Without this introduction you run the risk of alienating your audience, but similarly if this introduction is overly long then you are in danger of losing their attention. The introduction is also necessary to justify why the story that you are about to tell is worth listening to. One way to link your introduction to the next part of the presentation is to pose a question (or hypothesis) that you plan to answer later; doing so prepares the audience mentally for what they will hear next.

The middle part of a story is where the crux of the plot takes place and develops. Having laid the scene with the introduction, the storyteller is now able to explore the more interesting elements of the narrative. In a scientific presentation, this is where the methods, results, and analysis would be found; having explained the context and justification in the introduction you now can take the audience with you on your journey of discovery. What did you find and how did you find it? What do you think that this might mean? Were there any unexpected or surprising results?

The end of a story is where the storyteller skilfully gathers all the different elements into a final passage which gives insightful context and objective interpretation to the preceding narrative. In a scientific presentation it is typically the conclusion that fills this requirement. Having laid out the experimental process and your reasons for doing so, did you succeed in answering your original hypothesis, how confident are you in your interpretation and conclusions, and what might those conclusions mean for any future research?

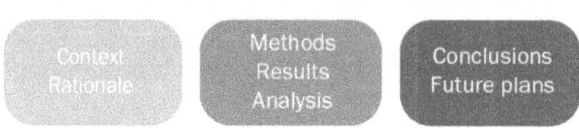

Figure 4.2. Telling your science story using a linear narrative for a scientific audience. Using this approach, your presentation should have a clearly defined beginning (context and rationale), middle (methods, results, and analysis), and end (conclusions and future plans).

Figure 4.2 provides a schematic representation of a scientific presentation, depicted as a continuous narrative. The nature of scientific research often implies that these narratives often pose a sequence of inquiries that call for additional exploration. The art of telling your story lies in sparking curiosity in your audience, making them crave more, whilst simultaneously eliciting helpful recommendations from them to further your work and collaborate. This linear storytelling technique, however, is contingent upon the nature of your audience. For instance, when addressing journalists, it could be more beneficial to commence with the key takeaways; a topic we will explore in greater depth in chapter 6.

4.2.2 Understanding your audience

The second vertex of the triangle of effective communication is your audience. Without an audience, you are delivering a speech to an unresponsive wall, and it is a disheartening truth that quite a few scientists prefer this method. Discussing your research is a fantastic chance to make a name for yourself and to underscore the significance of your work to those present. Yet, if your delivery implies a disregard for your audience's presence, then it is likely that the number of people captivated by your discourse will mirror that sentiment.

For a significant number of individuals, the thought of standing before peers and delivering a talk can be profoundly unnerving. We will tackle the issue of nerves in section 4.3, but it is beneficial to pause for a moment and contemplate how your audience is likely to perceive you. The scientific audiences you will be presenting to are understanding, thoughtful, and cheering you on to excel. Yes, there may be the odd exception, but remember that you are not warming up the crowd at a stand-up comedy gig. Your audience is not out for blood. They are there because they are genuinely interested in what you must share, and most of them will empathise, knowing that they have been in your shoes not too long ago.

Given the understanding, considerate, and patient nature of your audience, it would surely be unfair to dismiss them entirely out of hand and to speak as if they were simply not there. Your audience are an integral part of your presentation, and by working with them, rather than ignoring them, you stand a much better chance of not only communicating your take-home messages, but of also enjoying yourself in the process.

Exercise: Know your audience

Write down one sentence to explain your research to a five-year-old child. You should avoid using any scientific jargon, or indeed any words that would not be understood by this target audience. Once you have done this, read it aloud and see if it would be understood by a five-year-old, or even better find an actual five-year-old and see if they understand what you are talking about. If not try again.

Next, craft a sentence that encapsulates the heart of your research, this time for an educated adult who is not a scientist. Again, avoid any scientific jargon or words that could potentially confuse them. To assist you, consider using the 'Up-Goer Five text editor' [2]. This tool restricts you to the one thousand most common words in the English language, based on a comic from xkcd.com [3] that illustrates the Saturn V rocket using just these words. Test this sentence on a non-scientist adult. If they are puzzled, you will need to revise it.

Continue this exercise by penning two sentences: the first summarising your research for a scientist outside your field, and the second tailored for a scientist within your field. Run these sentences by their respective audiences and use the feedback to shape the key takeaways of a presentation (depending on your audience), as to proposed in the previous exercise.

Reflecting on your audience's level of scientific understanding, and the languages they speak, can assist you in striking a balance where you neither talk down to them nor confound them with complexity. With larger audiences, the task of meeting every person's individual needs can be quite the challenge. Nonetheless, gauging the range and extent of scientific expertise that your audience possesses can be a useful tool in keeping them captivated throughout your presentation.

Adjusting your presentation to cater to your audience's needs is not merely about using accessible language; it is also about shining a spotlight on the aspects of your research that will most engage them. For instance, if you are presenting to a gathering of environmental scientists, it is likely to be more captivating to say you are 'exploring the chemical composition of cave-dripping water to decode past climatic conditions', than to simply state that you 'employ instruments to investigate the chemistry of water that seeps within caves'. Equally important is gauging what facets of your research your specific audience might need more insight on, or which parts could be briefly touched upon. If, for example, you were discussing your study of global droughts on bird migration with experts in that field, they might need less of a preamble to the subject compared to hydrologists who might be novices when it comes to bird habitats or behaviours.

This consideration of your audience's experiences and attitudes might also be referred to as 'framing'. Framing theory suggests that how something is presented to the audience (i.e. the frame) influences how it is processed [4]. Framing involves explaining and describing the context of the problem to gain the most support from your audience, and so understanding their needs and experiences is key. A well-known example of the framing effect is a 2009 study which found that while only 67% of PhD students registered early for a particular conference when doing so was presented as a discount, 93% did so when the emphasis was instead on a penalty fee for late registration [5].

When tailoring your scientific presentation, be mindful of your audience, especially when it comes to jargon. Unleashing a flurry of unfamiliar terms is a sure-fire way to disconnect your audience from the topic at hand. Whenever you do introduce new terminology, make sure you spell out its meaning, ideally weaving it into a relevant context. Keep in mind, too, that jargon is not just the words your audience does not understand; it can also refer to words or phrases that carry different meanings across disciplines. Take, for instance, the term 'long timescales'. A meteorologist and a palaeontologist would interpret this in very different ways.

4.2.3 Managing yourself

The final vertex of the triangle of effective communication is you. Without you there is no presentation, and as such you should consider how to present yourself when addressing your audience with your narrative. Initially, the notion of self-management or self-presentation might appear quite nebulous. However, it can be conveniently distilled into a memorable acronym, as depicted in figure 4.3.

Stance

Assurance

Voice

Eye contact

Figure 4.3. The four components that are needed to successfully manage yourself when giving a presentation: stance, assurance, voice, and eye contact.

If you can master all four of these components, then you will have succeeded in managing yourself. Taking each one in turn:

Stance. The way you physically place yourself plays a pivotal role in reinforcing your perceived confidence as a presenter. This also encompasses any nervous habits or involuntary actions. For instance, do you tend to fidget with keys in your pocket while speaking, or do you pace around the room, eyes fixed to the floor? These actions can distract your audience, swiftly becoming the focus, much to the detriment of your narrative. Any movement you make should be conscious and intentional, maintaining an engaging focus on the audience.

If you are naturally expressive with hand gestures, don't hesitate to incorporate them into your speech. If you aren't, forcing these movements may feel unnatural, which could dent your confidence and detract from the quality of your presentation. Similarly, if you typically don't use gestures, avoid introducing them during your presentation to prevent them from becoming an unwelcome distraction for both you and your audience.

Being on your feet might not always be feasible or even ideal. For example, in an informal setting or a compact room, engaging your audience from a seated position might be more suitable. In all scenarios, endeavour to familiarise yourself with the room layout ahead of your presentation. This will bolster your confidence and ensure you can cater effectively to your audience's needs. Upon assessing the space, ask yourself: is there a prime position that offers most of the room a clear view of you? Is there a lectern available? Is the projection screen or monitor fixed or movable?

Assurance. Exhibiting confidence should not be mistaken for projecting arrogance. Your manner should underscore your authority on the subject, while simultaneously conveying approachability. Contrary to popular belief, its is ok for your personality shine through your presentation; indeed, many audiences appreciate this personal touch. However, in doing so, keep both your audience and your own comfort in mind. Avoid behaviours that feel forced or make you uneasy, as your audience will notice this discomfort.

Being a confident presenter does not necessitate being an extrovert; it is about feeling at ease in your own skin and creating a space where you feel comfortable speaking. For instance, while some presenters effectively incorporate humour into their presentations, others are better off avoiding it. Stay true to yourself, standing firm in your authenticity. So, brush off that persistent voice of self-doubt, and reassure yourself that you are indeed an expert in your field, that your insights are valuable, and that you can deliver them in a manner that is both engaging and comprehensible.

Voice. Your voice is the most dynamic and potent instrument you have as a presenter. Invest time in understanding its nuances. Reflect on how variations in pitch, rhythm, tone, and volume can shape your delivery. You also need to care for your voice. This includes doing warm-up exercises and avoiding alcohol, nicotine, and caffeine right before a presentation, as they can all strain your vocal cords. If your voice naturally has a softer volume, do not fret; that is precisely why microphones exist. Even if you have a robust, resonant voice and believe you do not need a microphone, you should still use one if it is available. The rationale behind this is twofold: first, the room's acoustics might hinder clear audibility from certain positions, and second, individuals might be using a hearing loop, which is directly linked to the microphone.

Eye contact. Aim to establish eye contact with each person in the room at least once throughout your talk. However, be cautious not to appear overly intense or to linger on any one person for an extended period, as it could create an uncomfortable environment. Instead, consider sweeping your gaze across the room, connecting with individuals sequentially. This tactic can keep your audience attentive and invested while demonstrating your interest in them. Eye contact can also serve as an effective strategy for managing nerves (see section 4.3).

4.3 Dealing with nerves

One of the most intimidating challenges that needs to be overcome when giving a presentation is nerves; specifically, how to deal with stage fright. Well-worn advice on this topic is that everybody suffers from nerves, and that you simply need to harness this nervous energy to give a presentation. While elements of this may be true, it is not particularly practical, nor is it helpful to the many would-be presenters who may be perfectly capable of rationalising their fears but are still unable to overcome them.

The most effective strategy for preparing for a presentation is practice. Familiarise yourself to the point where both content and delivery feel second nature. Nervousness often sprouts from fear of the unknown. Being thoroughly versed in your content and delivery style can significantly curb nervousness.

Strive to rehearse your talk until you can present it note-free. This approach not only alleviates nerves but also enhances your connection with the audience. Plus, without notes, you eliminate the risk of losing your spot. Equally, it is wise to avoid rote learning a script, as it can hamper your delivery and potentially escalate nervousness if you lose your thread or unintentionally deviate from your memorised text.

A proven method for mastering your presentation is to deliver it five to ten times, avoiding notes and scripts, focusing instead on key points and phrases that you can repeat consistently. This approach fosters the most organic delivery style and minimises stress linked to memory recall during the actual presentation. If you are employing slides, practice without them too. This allows you to visualise the transitions without excessive reliance on the screen.

If addressing a small group does not daunt you, but the prospect of speaking to a larger audience sends chills down your spine, consider rehearsing in front of an incrementally increasing audience size. Start with a small, comfortable group and gradually expand to a group of twenty to thirty people, say, during a weekly research group gathering. From there, you might find it challenging to practice before progressively larger crowds, but the confidence you have gradually built should equip you to address a larger audience. Another trick for handling larger audiences involves locating a friend or colleague in the crowd. Start by locking eyes with them and directing your talk to them, then slowly extend your gaze to the rest of the audience as your confidence grows, retreating to your friend if you feel your nerves creeping back.

4.4 Rhetoric

The Ancient Greek philosopher Aristotle defined rhetoric as 'the faculty of observing in any given case the available means of persuasion' [6]. In its infancy in Ancient Greece, rhetoric was often met with disdain, criticised for propagating the speaker's subjective truth rather than the objective truth inherent in the argument, as was the norm in dialectics. Nevertheless, Aristotle appreciated the need for rhetoric, recognising that individuals advocating for the pursuit of absolute truth could make use of the same tools as those promoting personal agendas. Today, rhetoric is sometimes dismissed as merely 'all show and no substance', or exclusively the domain of 'cunning politicians' and 'unscrupulous journalists'. However, this perspective does not have to hold. Familiarity with the three fundamental aspects of rhetoric can enhance your ability to craft and deliver outstanding presentations.

Ethos is an appeal to **ethics**, and it is a means of convincing an audience of the character or credibility of the speaker.

For example, when applying for a job your goal would be to persuade the interviewer that you are the perfect fit for the role. You might do this by citing past experiences and responsibilities as proof of your competence.

As scientists, we often overlook the fact that we are top-tier experts in our area, making us credible voices worth hearing when it comes to our work and research. As we have already touched on earlier in this chapter, stand tall in your expertise when conversing about your scientific research. Beginning your talk by introducing yourself as 'XXX from research institute YYY' serves as a handy reminder of your credibility to both you and your listeners. This approach can be particularly useful when addressing an audience that might be attending back-to-back presentations, such as at a conference or symposium.

Logos is an appeal to **logic** and is a way of convincing an audience by reason.

For example, when explaining to an audience the validity of your data, you might take them through a step-by-step account of your methods, in which you remove all doubt that what you have observed is spurious or unrepeatable.

As scientists, our research is built on a time-tested methodology. We formulate a hypothesis, put it to the test, and then either accept or reassess our hypothesis based on our findings. It is a logical progression, and if we conduct our work ethically (see chapter 10) and present our research in a similar vein, we have logos. Arguments stripped of logic lack a solid foundation, often tainting the reputation of rhetoric. As scientists, we are obligated to question any claims made by politicians, journalists, or even our peers, that lack solid arguments and independently corroborated results (where applicable). By doing this, we aid in shielding the more susceptible members of our community from false and potentially damaging assertions.

Pathos is an appeal to **passion** and is a way of convincing an audience of an argument by creating an emotional response.

For example, when having an argument with a loved one you might choose to recall a particularly hurtful example of when you had been let down by them in the past; pathos is an appeal to all emotions, not just positive ones.

In the realm of science, we tend to struggle most with this component of rhetoric. Often, we are told to present our scientific findings as nothing more than 'unemotional, concrete facts'. However, such a detached approach to our work could unintentionally create a gap between us and our audience. While we need to maintain absolute objectivity while conducting our experiments and testing our hypotheses, we can allow ourselves to express emotions when discussing the implications of our results. It is perfectly fine to experience feelings of anger, joy, elation, and even disappointment while discussing our work. For instance, scientists studying global warming and climate change are not immune to the negative effects of these phenomena.

While rhetoric primarily aids in crafting your narrative, it also finds utility in numerous other instances of audience interaction and self-presentation. For instance, in the UK, many public figures wear a poppy during TV interviews around Remembrance Sunday. This act communicates respectfulness (ethos) and triggers an emotional response (pathos) in viewers, depending on their personal associations with the symbol in this context.

4.5 PowerPoint

When enduring a particularly tedious or poorly organised scientific presentation, the term 'death by PowerPoint' may be uttered by the audience. However, it is unfair to blame the software itself, as it is the presenter's effectiveness that matters. Often, when it comes to the volume of material in visual aids, it is easy to overdo it. Some presenters tend to use slides to duplicate everything that they say, often as an aide memoir to themselves, but an audience cannot easily digest the contents of a text-heavy slide while simultaneously listening to the speaker's voice. Some of the best presentation slides typically have very little text, just enough to introduce a single graphic, while the substance is conveyed orally. PowerPoint and similar tools are highly versatile when used correctly; here are some tips to help you make the most of them:

1. **PowerPoint is not a substitute for you.** It is simply a software tool, and the success of your presentation relies on your delivery, not on PowerPoint itself.
2. **Less text is more effective.** Text-only slides are unengaging and distract the audience from your spoken words. Minimise the amount of text on each slide and instead support your narrative with appropriate graphs, diagrams, and images.
3. **Avoid PowerPoint karaoke.** If you must use text, refrain from reading it word-for-word from the screen. Your audience can read for themselves. However, there is one exception: you should verbally emphasise key points or take-home messages by reading them directly from the slide.
4. **Use take-home messages as the final slide.** After determining the key messages of your presentation (see section 4.2.1), present them as a concise list on the last slide. This provides the audience with a helpful summary they can easily reference. Avoid concluding with a slide asking for questions or thanking collaborators, as these can be addressed earlier.
5. **Double-check spelling and grammar.** Typographical errors in your slides undermine your credibility as a speaker. Take the time to ensure there are no mistakes, and if possible, have someone else proofread them for you.
6. **Pay attention to slide design.** Choose a suitable theme and colour scheme (see section 4.8 for further guidance). Select a font that is easily readable from a distance and maintain consistency by using the same font throughout your presentation. Aim for a uniform layout across your slides and consider including slide numbers to assist the audience in noting relevant points for discussion.
7. **Consider aspect ratio.** When designing your slides, think about the aspect ratio of the projector you will be using (typically 4:3 or 16:9). Adjust your presentation accordingly or create two versions if unsure. Neglecting this aspect can negatively impact the appearance and layout of your images.
8. **Be economical with animations.** Use them sparingly and with purpose, otherwise you risk distracting both your audience and yourself.
9. **Embed audio and video files.** This ensures smooth playback without the need for specific file locations or an internet connection.
10. **Verify everything works.** Always test your presentation beforehand, including any embedded videos or audio. Arrive early at the venue to set up and avoid unnecessary technical distractions. Additionally, check that your images are clear and that you have any necessary cables or adaptors to connect your laptop to the projector.

There are various alternative presentation software options available to you besides PowerPoint. It is recommended that you explore different software until you find the one that suits you best and provides you with confidence in your delivery. Here are five examples that you may find worth exploring:

1. **Prezi**. Unlike PowerPoint, Prezi allows you to create visually appealing presentations using frames of different shapes and sizes that can be zoomed in and out of. However, be cautious not to overuse the zoom function, as it can potentially cause discomfort to your audience.
2. **Google Slides**. A web-based presentation software that offers similar features to PowerPoint but allows for easy collaboration and cloud storage. It can be accessed from any device with an internet connection, making it convenient for remote presentations.
3. **Keynote**. A presentation software designed specifically for Apple devices, which offers seamless integration with other Apple applications. If you are using Apple devices, Keynote can be a powerful alternative to PowerPoint.
4. **Canva**. While primarily known for its graphic design capabilities, Canva also offers a presentation feature. With its intuitive drag-and-drop interface and extensive library of templates, images, and graphics, Canva allows you to create visually stunning presentations without prior design experience.
5. **Mentimeter.** An interactive presentation tool that allows you to engage your audience through live polls, quizzes, word clouds, and more. It enables real-time audience participation, making your presentations interactive and dynamic. With Mentimeter, you can gather valuable insights, receive instant feedback, and create an interactive dialogue with your audience.

Finally, you could consider using no slides at all, instead focussing on delivering your message to the audience in an engaging style. This may not be suitable for technical presentations requiring graphical data, but it can be a far more engaging method of delivery for less technical presentations. You might alternatively consider the use of a single image summarising your key, take-home messages.

Whatever piece of presentational software you decide upon, find one that you feel comfortable with, and which will help you to reinforce your narrative, rather than one which will cause the audience to become distracted.

4.6 Timings

When delivering a presentation within a limited period, you should adhere to the allocated timeslot. Overrunning is considered impolite, as it conveys the notion that your contribution is more valuable than others'. Moreover, it can disrupt the overall flow of a conference, particularly in cases of parallel sessions, where it can create frustration by causing delays in scheduled breaks. While the responsibility of keeping sessions on track typically falls on the chairperson, you should not rely on them to cut your presentation short. Instead, practice your presentation with strict timing in mind and avoid overstaying your welcome.

We recommend initially rehearsing with a visible stopwatch, which tools like PowerPoint provide. As you gain confidence and become familiar with the timings, gradually wean yourself off the stopwatch until you no longer rely on it. During the actual presentation, the chairperson will usually provide a two minute warning (or longer, depending on the duration of the presentation). If they do not, be sure to request one as it can help you stay focused. Many presentation venues also offer stopwatch features that you can refer to throughout your talk if needed. It is worth noting that adrenaline often leads to faster speech pace during presentations than during rehearsals. However, relying on a faster pace should be a consideration, not a strategy. It is unwise to prepare a 20 minute presentation for a 15 minute timeslot with the expectation that nerves will compensate for the time difference.

4.7 Answering questions

One of the most anxiety-inducing aspects of giving a presentation is the anticipation of having to answer questions about your topic. In most cases, this occurs during a formal questions and answers (Q&A) session following your talk, although there may be instances, such as in informal group meetings, where questions arise during the presentation itself. The following advice applies to both scenarios:

1. Whenever possible, take three questions at once. This technique, often used by politicians, allows you to address the easiest question first and gives you time to consider the more challenging ones.
2. If you do not feel confident answering a question in a formal setting, offer to discuss it 'off-line' with the questioner. This means engaging in a one-on-one conversation, such as over coffee at a conference, which provides more time for thoughtful consideration and fosters meaningful discussions.
3. If you get a difficult question but you still want to address it, try reframing or redirecting the question. This allows you to focus on a topic you are more comfortable with while still providing the questioner with a satisfactory response.
4. If you do not know the answer to a question, admit it. There is no shame in not having all the answers, and the questioner may offer valuable insights or perspectives you had not considered. Offer to continue the discussion off-line; it could be an opportunity for fruitful collaboration or a chance to clarify any misunderstandings.
5. Prepare additional material to address potential questions that may exceed your allotted timeslot. Whether this is extra slides, handouts, or well-rehearsed responses, having supplementary material ready will allow you to adequately address these queries.
6. Anticipate questions you expect to be asked. By practicing your presentation, you will become aware of areas that may require further explanation or topics that could generate controversy. If possible, rehearse in front of colleagues and solicit their questions. These are likely to resemble those you will encounter when delivering your presentation.

Asking questions after someone's presentation is a skill that requires practice and thoughtfulness. Here are some DOs and DO NOTs to consider before posing a question:

DO begin your question by offering a compliment or expressing appreciation for the content or delivery of the talk. It is a courteous gesture that sets a positive tone.

DO take notes during the presentation and use them to prepare a list of relevant questions to ask during the Q&A session. This is particularly important if you are the session chair, as you have a responsibility to ensure meaningful engagement.

DO consider speaking to the presenter privately after the talk, especially if you have complex or extensive questions that warrant further discussion.

DO try to thank the speaker after the Q&A session for their time and insights, regardless of whether you asked a question or not.

DO NOT ask a question solely to demonstrate your attentiveness or showcase your expertise in the field. The purpose of asking questions is to deepen understanding and facilitate meaningful dialogue.

DO NOT use a question as an opportunity to promote your own work. The focus should be on the speaker and their topic.

DO NOT ask a question that you cannot articulate concisely. Keeping your question clear and succinct respects the time of the presenter and the audience.

4.8 Poster design

Presenting a poster at scientific conferences should not be underestimated as it offers a valuable opportunity to discuss your research in detail, often in a more relaxed setting. To ensure your poster stands out and you make the most of your time, here are some guidelines:

DO structure your poster to tell a coherent story. Organise the layout to present a logical flow, from introducing the rationale and highlighting results to analysing findings and drawing conclusions.

DO NOT overload your poster with excessive text. Like oral presentations, your poster should primarily consist of visuals, such as images and diagrams, highlighting your work, accompanied by concise explanatory text. Use the opportunity during poster sessions to discuss intricate details in person and consider preparing handouts with additional information for interested readers.

DO stand by your poster for the designated time. Even if initial interest seems low, it may be due to your placement or concurrent sessions running late.

DO NOT use colour schemes that hinder readability. Use a colour wheel (see figure 4.4) to select complementary colours (opposite each other on the wheel). For instance, if your background is dark green, red text will be the most legible, and vice versa. Avoid excessive use of colour, as it can become distracting. Similarly, you should consider what your poster would look like to somebody who was colourblind.

DO pay attention to font selection. Avoid using fonts like Comic Sans that can be challenging to read. Use clear and legible fonts that enhance readability.

DO NOT approach people immediately upon their arrival at your poster. Allow them some time to read your poster and indicate your availability to answer any questions they may have.

DO consider including a QR code on your poster that directs readers to a webpage with additional information (e.g. your personal website or a recent publication). You can generate free QR codes quickly using online software.

DO NOT rely on printing your poster on multiple A4 sheets and taping them together. Prior to designing your poster, determine the dimensions of the poster board and consider the available orientation options (portrait or landscape). Create your poster accordingly to ensure a professional and visually appealing presentation.

DO take the opportunity to understand your audience. During a poster session, you have the advantage of interacting with viewers directly. Ask them about their expertise and background to tailor your explanations, accordingly, avoiding unnecessary explanations of basic concepts to experts in the field.

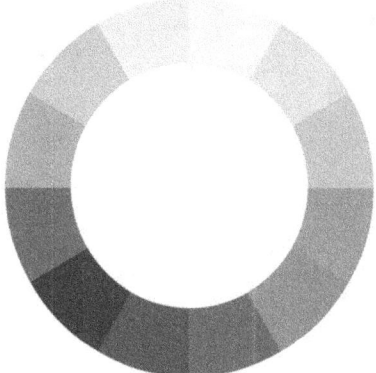

Figure 4.4. An example or a colour wheel. Complementary colours are those colours which are opposite one another on this wheel, and which can be used to provide the best contrast for reading coloured text on coloured backgrounds.

> **Exercise: You be the judge**
> Three posters are shown in figures 4.5–4.7. Which of these posters do you think most closely adheres to the rules for good poster design that are laid out above, and which of them needs the most attention? What would you improve about these posters and which do you think illustrate good practice in both design and storytelling?

Certain conferences incorporate a mix of oral and poster presentations, where you may have a moment, usually one or two minutes, to provide a verbal introduction to your poster. Rather than attempting to condense a full-length presentation into such a limited timeframe, view them as an opportunity to capture your audience's interest and leave them intrigued for more during the poster session that follows.

In addition, digital formats are increasingly being embraced for poster sessions. Some events offer interactive touch-sensitive screens for participants to present their work. Familiarise yourself with the relevant software packages for effectively conveying your central narrative in a logical and visually appealing manner. Embrace this opportunity to enhance your presentation through innovative digital solutions that engage your audience and facilitate a dynamic exchange of ideas.

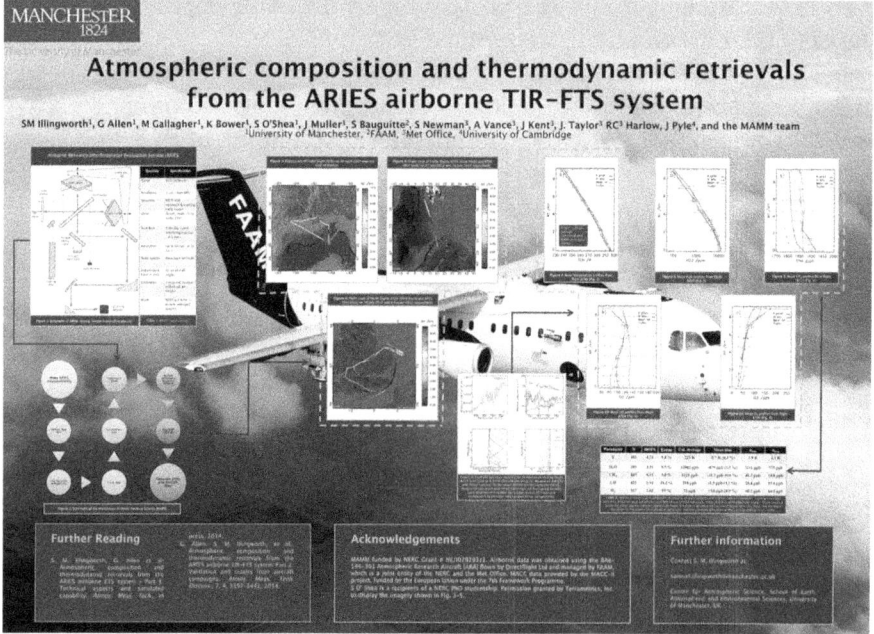

Figure 4.5. A poster displaying the results of a scientific instrument on a research aircraft (reproduced with the kind permission of The University of Manchester).

Figure 4.6. A poster outlining the development of a tabletop game about heat decarbonisation.

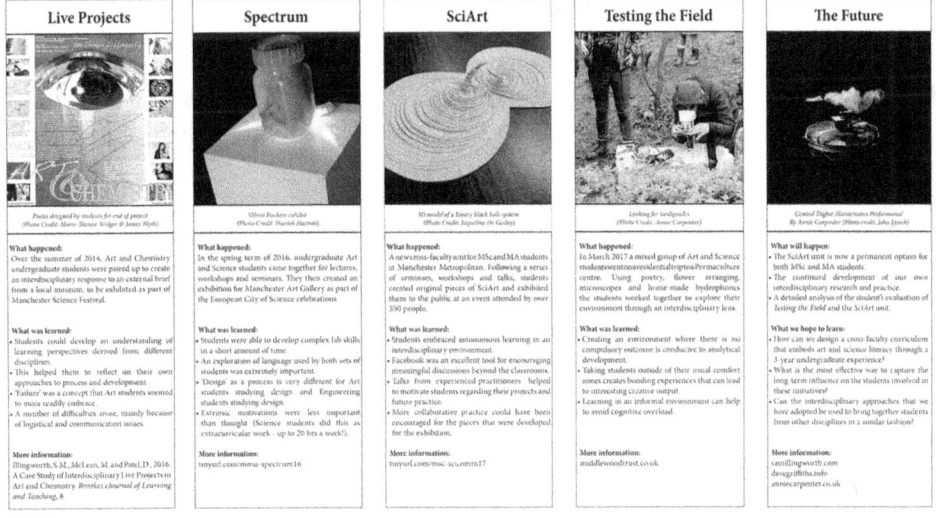

Figure 4.7. A poster based around the pedagogical development of an interdisciplinary science and art programme.

4.9 Presenting digitally

With the advent of COVID-19 and the subsequent global shift towards remote working and virtual conferencing, the need for effective digital presentation skills has never been more pertinent [7]. Many scientific conferences now offer hybrid attendance (with in-person and remote participation). This looks set to stay and offers many benefits, including widening participation for those without funding to pay the large expenses involved with attending a conference in another country, and the potential to reduce the significant carbon footprint of international travel. Drawbacks may include more restrictive networking and the toll of working on a different time zone. But overall, the hybrid approach offers flexibility and great opportunity.

Regardless of how you attend, scientific information needs to be communicated with the same clarity, coherence, and rigour, whether in-person or online. Although the principles remain the same, the delivery method must adapt to the constraints and possibilities of the digital platform. Here are some key issues for presenting scientific information digitally:

Do not forget your analogue training. Although digital platforms have their own unique set of challenges and opportunities, the fundamental principles of communication do not change. The triangle of effective communication (section 4.2.1), the SAVE acronym (section 4.2.3), and the rules of rhetoric (section 4.4) all apply, irrespective of whether you are presenting in-person or online. Therefore, do not disregard your analogue training; instead, adapt it to the digital platform. Keep your narrative coherent, your slides engaging, and your delivery confident and clear.

Understand the platform you are using. Each digital platform comes with its own set of features and constraints. Whether it is Zoom, MS Teams, or Webex, take time to explore and understand the platform's capabilities. Familiarise yourself with the platform's functionalities, like sharing screen, muting/unmuting, enabling/disabling video, launching polls, and managing breakout rooms. A hiccup with the platform during your presentation can disrupt the flow and engagement of your session.

Make the session interactive. Engagement is key to communication, especially in a digital setting where it is easy for participants to tune out. Use the interactive features of your platform to encourage audience participation. Incorporate polls, quizzes, or Q&A sessions to facilitate interaction. Breakout rooms can also be a useful tool to encourage smaller group discussions.

Create an environment in which all voices can be heard. The digital platform can sometimes make it challenging for everyone to have their say, especially in larger gatherings. However, features like 'raise hand', 'chat', and 'Q&A' can provide avenues for participants to voice their thoughts and queries. Encourage your audience to use these features and ensure that you allocate time to address these inputs.

Exercise: Digital presentation practice
To hone your digital presentation skills, set up a mock digital presentation with a few colleagues or friends. Choose a scientific topic of your choice, prepare a 15 minute

presentation, and use an online conferencing platform to deliver it. Experiment with different interactive elements, such as polls or quizzes, and make use of multimedia elements in your presentation.

After the presentation, gather feedback from your audience. Did they find the interactive elements engaging? Was the pace appropriate? Were you able to manage the digital platform? Reflect on the feedback and identify areas for improvement.

4.10 Summary

Throughout this chapter, we have presented the skills required to become a confident and engaging presenter. Effective communication hinges on understanding your audience, crafting a compelling narrative, and being mindful of your own presence. Harnessing the power of rhetoric enables you to convey your message in a way that resonates with your listeners. While PowerPoint and other presentation software are valuable tools, they are merely aids and cannot deliver a presentation on your behalf. Whether you are designing a poster or formulating questions for other presenters, there are key considerations to keep in mind. By actively participating in the exercises provided in this chapter, you will be well on your way to becoming an exceptional orator. And to reiterate once more, there is no substitute for practice when it comes to honing your skills in the art of public speaking.

4.11 Further study

The further study in this chapter is designed to enhance your presentation skills, encouraging you to refine a technique that suits you best:

1. **Engage in self-reflection.** Recall your last presentation and analyse how you addressed the narrative, the audience, and yourself. Reflect on whether you considered each aspect of the triangle of effective communication (figure 4.1). Identify strengths and areas for improvement in preparation for your next presentation.
2. **Record yourself.** Next time you have a presentation, record yourself practicing the delivery. Watch the recording and assess whether you embody the four elements of the SAVE acronym (figure 4.3). Evaluate if your message has a concise and logical narrative, and if it aligns with your target audience. Armed with these insights, practice your presentation a few more times and record yourself again. Compare the two recordings to see the progress you have made.
3. **Learn from skilled orators.** Observe proficient public speakers, either in person or on television, and dissect their messages into the three forms of rhetoric. Identify instances when they appeal to emotions (pathos), employ logical storytelling (logos), and establish their credibility as speakers (ethos). You will soon recognise that these adept orators make use of rhetoric to subtly influence their audience.

4.12 Suggested reading

There are many books and websites dedicated to helping you become a better public speaker, however some of the best are freely available via resources such as the Technology, Entertainment and Design (TED) talks. One of the most helpful of these is a TED talk from the audio expert Julian Treasure, entitled 'How to speak so that people want to listen' [8]. For those of you wanting further guidance on how to design aesthetically pleasing presentations and posters, *Designing Science Presentations: A Visual Guide to Figures, Papers, Slides, Posters, and More* [9] is highly recommended. There are also several short and useful journal articles on designing and delivering successful oral [10, 11] and poster [12] presentations. Finally, if you are interested in finding out more about rhetoric, Aristotle's *The Art of Rhetoric* [6] is the seminal text on the subject; in addition to expanding on the concepts discussed in this chapter, it also offers sound advice on how to survive in love, war, and everything else in-between.

References

[1] Peck E and Dickinson H 2009 *Performing Leadership* (London: Macmillan)
[2] Sanderson T 2023 The Up-Goer Five text editor https://splasho.com/upgoer5/ (Accessed: 1 December 2023)
[3] Munroe R 2023 xkcd: Up Goer Five https://xkcd.com/1133/ (Accessed: 1 December 2023)
[4] Nisbet M C and Mooney C 2007 Framing science *Science* **316** 56
[5] Gächter S *et al* 2009 Are experimental economists prone to framing effects? A natural field experiment *J. Econ. Behav. Organ.* **70** 443–6
[6] Aristotle 1991 *The Art of Rhetoric* (London: Penguin)
[7] Gibson H, Illingworth S and Buiter S 2021 The future of conferences: lessons from Europe's largest online geoscience conference *Geosci. Commun.* **4** 437–51
[8] Treasure J 2023 How to speak so that people want to listen *TED Talk* https://ted.com/talks/julian_treasure_how_to_speak_so_that_people_want_to_listen?language=en (Accessed: 1 December 2023)
[9] Carter M 2012 *Designing Science Presentations: A Visual Guide to Figures, Papers, Slides, Posters, and More* (New York: Academic)
[10] Collins J 2004 Education techniques for lifelong learning: giving a powerpoint presentation: the art of communicating effectively *Radiographics* **24** 1185–92
[11] Bourne P E 2007 Ten simple rules for making good oral presentations *PLoS Comput. Biol.* **3** e77
[12] Erren T C and Bourne P E 2007 Ten simple rules for a good poster presentation *PLoS Comput. Biol.* **3** e102

IOP Publishing

Effective Science Communication (Third Edition)
A practical guide to surviving as a scientist
Sam Illingworth and Grant Allen

Chapter 5

Outreach and public engagement

Science, I maintain, is an absolutely essential tool for any society with a hope of surviving well into the next century with its fundamental values intact—not just science as engaged in by its practitioners, but science understood and embraced by the entire human community. And if the scientists will not bring this about, who will?

—Carl Sagan

5.1 Introduction

So far in this book we have discussed how to develop inward-facing skills for communicating effectively within the scientific community. However, this is only a small section of society. Why then, as scientists, should we consider developing our outward-facing skills to communicate with people from outside of this community? How can we do this effectively? And what is in it for us?

As scientists, we communicate with non-scientists for three main reasons: because we must, because we want to, and because we should do. Most large research grants (see chapter 3) now require a consideration of pathways to impact, i.e. the development and delivery of initiatives that will increase the likelihood of potential economic, environmental, and societal impacts being realised. To develop and deliver these initiatives it is necessary for the scientists involved to fully understand the potential for these impacts and to recognise and search for them in all the work we do. Furthermore, it is the taxes paid by the wider society that fund much of our scientific research. and therefore, they have every right and expectation to be the ultimate beneficiaries of our successes and failures. *We communicate because we must.*

For many scientists, the main reason that we are in this profession is because we are passionate about our subject and have a thirst for knowledge, discovery, and truth. There are certainly far more financially rewarding and secure career paths available to those with the skills of a trained scientist (see chapter 10), but to most, science is a vocation. Given our appreciation of the subject, it follows that most of us also enjoy talking about our work and research, not only to other scientists but to friends, family members, and anyone with a passing interest in what we do. *We communicate because we want to.*

As discussed in chapter 4, as scientists we have a responsibility to question illogical and misleading arguments, falsities, and mistruths. In doing so we also have a responsibility to help train non-scientists to question the status quo objectively, and to give them the confidence and skills to interrogate failures of truth. It is easy to forget the educational and intellectual privilege that we enjoy as scientists, and that many other people are often not in a similar position. *We communicate because we should do.*

However, scientists are not just obligated to communicate their research and other scientific advances to the rest of society in a one-way flow of information. Science communication exists on a spectrum, with dissemination at one end, and participation at the other [1]. While participation and dialogue are often emphasised in science communication, there are cases where dissemination can be more effective. For example, science documentaries have demonstrated the potential to create a broader societal impact. Providing accurate and easily understandable information is also crucial in initiating dialogue, encouraging participation, and sparking inspiration.

We should view this spectrum as a tool for identifying the appropriate form of science communication based on the specific goals and audience needs. For example, if the goal is to develop connections with coastal communities and policymakers to address coastal erosion and climate change adaptation, engaging in dialogue becomes crucial to success. This could involve holding public forums, community workshops, and stakeholder meetings to facilitate discussions and gather local knowledge. Alternatively, if the objective is to engage various publics, such as farmers, landowners, and conservation organisations, in preserving biodiversity and restoring degraded ecosystems, a more participatory approach might be appropriate. This could include collaborative fieldwork, citizen science initiatives, and participatory mapping exercises to actively involve these publics in data collection and decision-making processes.

Aside from our responsibilities to engage with non-scientists, doing so also helps to develop us as scientists; for example, by improving our communication and organisational skills. Learning to communicate with different and varied audiences is also of direct benefit to how we communicate our research within both the broader scientific community (see chapter 4) and in university-level teaching (see chapter 9). Furthermore, the interpersonal and teamwork skills that we develop when engaging with non-scientists are also helpful in a variety of careers (see chapter 10).

Gaining experience in working with non-scientists is a recommended initial step before embarking on the development of your own initiatives, as it helps to enhance your skills and confidence in engaging with diverse audiences across various formats. Many research institutes offer free training and professional development opportunities, providing a wide range of initiatives to gain practical experience. Additionally, some funding bodies and learned societies provide training for researchers interested in creating science communication initiatives based on their research.

Certain scientists may perceive themselves as 'too busy' to engage with non-scientists or believe that the effort involved may yield little reward. Whilst developing effective science communication initiatives does require significant commitment, the benefits for all parties involved can be substantial. As scientists, we have a responsibility to foster a society where scientific understanding extends beyond mere factual knowledge, encompassing the ability to engage in meaningful discussions about the role and purpose of science. This chapter aims to provide guidance in pursuing these challenging yet rewarding and necessary objectives.

5.2 Objectives, audiences, and formats

Science communication has a rich history. In the UK, it can be traced back to the early nineteenth century when scientists like Michael Faraday and Humphry Davy dedicated significant time and resources to popularising science among non-scientists. Over time, science communication has evolved as an academic discipline, progressing through three main stages: scientific literacy, public understanding of science (PUS), and public engagement with science and technology (PEST) [2, 3]. This evolution reflects a shift in the approach to communication, moving away from a deficit model where scientists aim to fill gaps in public knowledge, towards fostering two-way dialogue and active participation between scientists and non-scientists.

As an academic discipline, science communication encompasses a wide range of topics [4, 5]. However, there is a need for better communication of research findings and best practices to scientists who are actively engaging with or planning to engage with non-scientists. Currently, much of the research in the field is conducted by scholars in science and technology studies (STS), which may result in a gap between their recommendations and the practices of scientists [6, 7].

Defining science communication is a complex task [8], given the diverse formats, target audiences, and objectives involved [9–11]. Terms such as widening participation, knowledge exchange, public engagement, and outreach are used interchangeably, reflecting institutional and national preferences, as well as individual interpretations within research practices [12]. This multifaceted nature highlights the dynamic and evolving landscape of science communication, with various perspectives shaping its implementation and impact.

Based on the current science communication literature, and the experiences of the authors, the following broad definitions are offered:

Outreach: a one-way discourse, in which scientists communicate their research to non-scientists.

Public engagement: a two-way dialogue or participation, in which scientists engage with non-scientists in a mutually beneficial manner.

Widening participation: any initiative that engages with social groups under-represented in higher education, to encourage them to attend university.

Knowledge exchange: any initiative that involves engagement with businesses, public, and third sector organisations (e.g. charities).

We acknowledge that there is still some overlap between these definitions. For example, a science talk at a local school given by a UK-based university researcher might be classed as being outreach, widening participation, and knowledge exchange. In this example, the researcher might classify the initiative as outreach, the university's widening participation team may catalogue it as widening participation, and the university's knowledge exchange offices could acknowledge it in reporting back to any funding bodies.

Widening participation and knowledge exchange as defined above are beyond the scope of this chapter, which will instead focus on outreach and public engagement, these being the most likely to be encountered by most scientists. For brevity, we will use the term 'science communication initiatives' to refer to both outreach and public engagement initiatives unless otherwise stated.

Exercise: Planning your initiative
When you are developing any science communication initiative you should begin by asking yourself these three questions:
  What is your objective? For example, do you want to raise awareness of the importance of diversity in scientific research? Are you interested in finding out the opinions of a local community group to inform your work on flood risk mitigation strategies?
  Who is your audience? How does this help you to achieve your objective, and how will you reach them? For example, if your objective is to raise awareness of air pollution amongst pensioners then how will you engage with this community?
  What format will you use? This needs to enable you to both achieve your objective and be appropriate for your target audience. For example, if you want to engage with local farmers to better understand the soil quality of arable farmland in the region, then a series of workshops might be more conducive than a one-off science talk.

Your objective is what will drive your science communication initiative, and as such it needs to be clear and achievable. You might also have a particularly aspirational long-term objective that can then be broken down into several short-term objectives. For example, your long-term objective might be for the health effects of air pollution to be more fully incorporated into your country's school curriculum. However, to achieve this, your short-term objectives might be to develop a card game that is used in 30 local schools to raise awareness of the subject, and the organisation of five panel debates with educationalists and policy-makers to discuss the potential for re-designing the curriculum. These objectives will depend on what you want to achieve, and so the remainder of this chapter will instead focus on providing support for the other two questions, i.e. how do you engage with suitable audiences, and what are the practicalities of the different formats that can be adopted.

5.3 Different publics

When thinking about which audience you want to engage with, the term 'general public' or 'lay audience' is misleading, as in reality there are many publics [10].

Simply targeting an audience that are not scientists is ineffectual, as 'not being a scientist' is not an identity, behaviour, or characteristic that people tend to identify and group themselves according to [13]. When designing these initiatives, you need to consider which publics you intend to target, and why. In some cases, the audience for your science communication initiative may already be determined as part of a larger project. It is important to assess whether this larger initiative provides a suitable platform for achieving your specific objectives. For instance, if your goal is to raise awareness of the climate crisis among local business leaders, organising a panel debate at a local primary school during working hours may not effectively target the desired audience.

When deciding which audience to engage with, you should think beyond those you have previously reached. There are two main reasons for this approach. First, sticking to familiar audiences can limit your perspective and confine you within an echo chamber, where existing beliefs are reinforced, and alternative viewpoints are overlooked. Second, there are numerous underserved and under-represented audiences in both science and science communication, and as responsible scientists, we have a duty to engage with these communities.

An echo chamber refers to an environment where individuals are exposed only to ideas and opinions that align with their own, leading to the reinforcement of existing views and a lack of consideration for alternative perspectives. As scientists, we should strive to break out of these echo chambers and move beyond engaging with the same audiences we have traditionally targeted. Instead, we should aim to establish more effective communication with diverse publics encompassing various demographics, socio-structural backgrounds, and value systems [14].

Engaging with underserved communities poses challenges, but it also provides significant opportunities for advancing scientific research and redefining the concept of meaningful impact [15]. The question then arises: how can we effectively engage with these audiences?

Start by establishing a connection with a community member who holds a position of responsibility within the group you wish to work with. For instance, if you are interested in collaborating with a local youth organisation, get in contact with one of the adult leaders. Building this relationship may require engaging in email exchanges, phone conversations, and in-person meetings over an extended period. Investing this time fosters trust, particularly when working with vulnerable individuals or communities.

Involve your community contact in the development of your initiative. They possess valuable insights into the specific needs and experiences of the target audience, allowing you to tailor your plans accordingly. Additionally, consider the location where the initiative will take place. While universities and research institutes may be convenient for scientists, they can be inaccessible and create physical and psychological barriers for many other publics.

Furthermore, when deciding which communities to engage with, reflect on the communities you already belong to. Are you involved in a local charity as a volunteer? Are you a member of a sports club or do you host regular board game nights? These existing communities present opportunities for developing initiatives, as you already have established relationships with members and are naturally attuned to their needs and experiences. This approach enables you to refine your objectives through a deeper understanding of the community dynamics.

When developing a science communication initiative involving scientists and non-scientists, you will often need to overcome perceived hierarchies of intellect [16]. These hierarchies arise when one party is seen as an expert while the other is not, which can hinder meaningful discussions. While scientists may possess expertise in their respective fields, non-scientists also bring their own valuable expertise and knowledge based on their personal and professional experiences. It is important to encourage and highlight this expertise to create an inclusive and conducive environment. For instance, if you are aiming to engage a rural community in discussions about genetically modified foods, create a platform where other publics such as famers and landowners are respected and invited to share their perspectives and expertise alongside scientific experts.

Once you have identified your audience and the means to reach them, consider how to frame your initiative. The concept of framing, as discussed in chapter 4 regarding science presentations, remains relevant. Understanding the needs and experiences of your audience is key to effectively framing your science communication initiative. When framing discussions on specific scientific topics, avoid promoting false expectations and maintain ethical conduct throughout the process, aligning with the principles of being an ethical scientist (see chapter 10).

5.4 Working with children

Since scientists often engage with children in science communication initiatives, it is valuable to offer more detailed guidance for this group. While these initiatives typically involve one-way communication (i.e. scientists sharing their research with children), there are other approaches as well.

Working with children can be immensely rewarding and enjoyable. However, it can also be demanding, challenging, and occasionally disheartening. It would be presumptuous to assume that simply being a scientist will automatically command the attention of children in a classroom or informal setting. Before embarking on a science communication initiative for children, it is advisable to seek relevant training and gain practical experience. The STEM Ambassadors [17], a national network of volunteers in the UK, offer opportunities for science communication in STEM subjects. They provide training, advice, and a range of pre-existing initiatives organised by schools and organisations. Participating in these initiatives can help you gain valuable experience in science communication. By acquiring appropriate training, practical experience, and engaging with established initiatives, you can effectively develop and deliver science communication initiatives for children, ensuring a positive and impactful experience for both you and your audience.

If you are engaging with children in the UK, you need to undergo a Disclosure and Barring Service (DBS) check to ensure your suitability for working with children. If you are working with children outside the UK, familiarise yourself with the specific regulations and requirements of the country or region in which you are operating. Each country may have its own screening and clearance processes such as the DBS check in the UK. Research and comply with the local laws and guidelines regarding working with children and ensure that you meet all the necessary legal and ethical obligations. There is typically a small fee associated with obtaining a DBS check. However, if you are delivering initiatives on behalf of your research institute, they usually cover the cost.

Even with an up-to-date DBS certificate (or equivalent), you should never be left alone in a room with a child or a group of children. Always having a teacher or guardian present in the room is necessary to prevent any potential allegations of misconduct. Their presence not only facilitates your interaction with the children but also helps create a controlled environment. Collaborating with a teacher can also enable careful co-design of the initiative (see section 5.4.1), ensuring its successful delivery.

The age of the children you are working with will determine the type of initiative you develop and deliver. It is incorrect to generalise, assuming that all teenagers are disinterested or lacking passion for science. However, some may hold negative attitudes due to limited engagement, ineffective teaching, or previous unsuccessful science communication attempts. Conversely, working with younger children can be an uplifting and exciting experience. They have yet to develop the scepticism and self-consciousness that can sometimes pose challenges when engaging with older children. Yet this enthusiasm can sometimes lead to behavioural issues and fatigue.

When working with children, it is crucial to follow the same advice discussed in chapter 4: avoid patronising your audience and instead seek to understand their needs and experiences. By carefully developing science communication initiatives, you can captivate and empower children, fostering a genuine passion for science during this formative and impressionable stage.

Exercise: What does a child know?
It is easy to forget that as a scientist you know (and are surrounded by colleagues who know) a lot of information about your research, its related discipline(s), and science more generally. What you consider to be common knowledge might be highly specialised information, especially to a child.

The next time that you can speak to a young child in an informal and supervised location, ask them what they know about science. Start off with questions that are quite general (What does a scientist do? What is physics?), and then begin to specialise (What is acceleration? What is gravity?). You will be surprised to find out what many children do (and do not) know, and you should use this to help structure your future science communication initiatives for this audience.

5.4.1 Children in a formal environment

When it comes to science communication initiatives involving children in a formal setting such as the classroom, they are often categorised as outreach efforts with the aim of engaging students, raising aspirations, and reshaping their perceptions of scientists. However, instead of focusing solely on the children's perceived lack of knowledge, it is important to adopt an approach that prioritises understanding the learners and the learning process.

To effectively engage schoolchildren, you need to have a comprehensive understanding of the school curriculum and consider the unique needs and abilities of each child in the classroom. This understanding requires time and cannot be rushed, but teachers can provide valuable information in this regard. Therefore, it is advisable to involve a teacher in the development process from the outset. Their familiarity with the curriculum and their insights into learning behaviours within the school environment will ensure that your initiatives effectively engage their students. Teachers can also offer constructive feedback on what will and will not work in their specific teaching contexts and assist with logistical aspects such as room set-up and student grouping.

Even if you have prior experience successfully delivering a science communication initiative in a formal environment, you should still engage with the teachers of the class before your session. Each group of students is unique, and what worked for one class might not work for another. By providing a basic summary of your plans to the teacher in advance, they can offer valuable feedback on what will and will not be engaging for their students.

Here are five further pieces of advice to consider when working with schoolchildren in a formal environment:

1. **The children are not your friends**. They are there to learn, and while they can have fun during the process, boundaries need to be established.
2. **Stick to time.** Schoolchildren will not thank you for eating into their breaks. For initiatives that take place in the afternoon, make sure that you finish with plenty of time to spare, as many of the children will have buses to catch or parents waiting to take them home.
3. **You know more science than they do**. A common fear of many scientists working in schools is that they will be 'caught out' on an area of science that they do not know. Ninety-nine times out of one hundred you will be able to answer any of the questions that you are asked. And for that one hundredth time, simply commend the questioner, and tell them that you will have to conduct some research before reporting back to them; alternatively, you could offer to work with the children to find out the question together. Admitting your lack of knowledge might also help to empower the teacher (who might not have a science background) when fielding difficult science questions from the children in the future.
4. **Expect the unexpected.** Be prepared to answer questions about your life as a scientist, and indeed your life in general. Young children will be fascinated about what it is like to be a scientist, which exotic locations you have visited in your fieldwork, and how often you get to use robots.
5. **Do not get disheartened.** On occasions things will not go as planned. This may be for several reasons: the children, the facilities, the alignment of the planets, etc. Do not dwell on any negative experiences, instead reflect on what went wrong and how it can be used to improve future initiatives (see section 5.9).

Exercise: Develop an outreach initiative for the classroom
Follow these steps and devise an initiative with schoolchildren in a formal learning environment:
1. What is your objective? Do you want to raise awareness of a particular subject, introduce the class to a famous scientist, or understand what they know about particle physics?
2. What format is most suitable for achieving your objective with this audience? Is it via a short presentation, a series of demonstrations, some hands-on experiments, or something more creative?
3. How does this tie into the school curriculum? Your initiative will be more effective if the topics that you are covering can be linked to the curriculum. This is especially true for more mature schoolchildren, where classroom time is often on a tight schedule.
4. Run your ideas past a teacher. They will be able to advise what will and will not work in their classroom and will also be able to help with linking your plans to the taught curriculum.

5. Beta-test your initiative. Aim to have at least a couple of practice sessions before taking the initiative into a school, as this will help you to iron out any issues beforehand. Undergraduate and postgraduate students are great for helping at this stage.
6. Trial your initiative. Contact the teacher that you spoke to in the development process and see if they are willing to let you try out your initiative with their class.
7. Reflect on the trial. What went wrong and what went right? Ask for feedback from the teacher and their class (see section 5.9), and from the people that were involved in the beta-testing process. How can you use this feedback to improve your initiative, and do you need any further support and/or resources to better implement it?

5.4.2 Children in an informal environment

Learning does not just take place in the classroom. There are many different environments outside of school where children can continue to learn about science in a more informal setting, including museums, science centres, and zoos. However, informal science education is not just defined by learning that takes place outside of the classroom, but rather as something that is self-motivated and guided by the learner's needs and interests [18].

Large science initiatives for children often take place in these informal settings, and include science festivals, science fairs, and public lectures. For example, the Royal Institution Christmas Lectures in the UK have been running since 1825 and are aimed at a teenage audience, taking place at the Royal Institution in London each year [19]. Informal science communication initiatives such as these have been shown to foster a strong commitment to science and science learning, and to have a significant impact on future career choices [20].

When running an initiative in an informal environment that is aimed primarily at schoolchildren, take account of the following:

1. A teacher might not accompany the children; instead, a guardian might be present, or they may be unattended. In any case, the children will behave differently outside of the school environment. They may feel less awkward, but similarly there may be behavioural issues that need to be kept in check without the presence of a teacher. In these informal environments it is just as imperative that you are never left alone with any children.
2. If your initiative is not part of a larger science festival or is alongside other initiatives that are not science-themed, then your participants may not be expecting to do any science. These 'science by stealth' opportunities [21] are an effective way of reaching new audiences, who might not otherwise seek out science-specific initiatives.
3. There might be a larger or a smaller influx of people than you were expecting. Plan for both eventualities, especially when arranging the number of scientists that will be involved. Where possible, have several activities that are flexible in the number of people they involve and the time they take to

run; doing so will mean that you can engage both small and large audiences accordingly.
4. Children have different learning styles and preferences. When designing your initiative, consider incorporating a variety of interactive activities and hands-on experiences to cater to different learning modalities. Some children may learn best through visual demonstrations, while others may prefer interactive experiments or group discussions. By offering diverse learning opportunities, you can accommodate various learning styles and engage a wider range of children in the process.
5. Encourage children's natural curiosity and sense of wonder by creating opportunities for exploration and discovery. Design activities that allow them to ask questions, make observations, and experiment with their own ideas. Encourage open-ended discussions and provide opportunities for children to share their thoughts and insights. By fostering a sense of curiosity and empowering children to explore scientific concepts on their own terms, you can ignite their interest in science and inspire lifelong learning.

5.5 Different formats

Just as there are a diverse range of publics, there are also a large variety of formats that can be used to achieve your objectives and engage your target audience. In this section several different formats, and the practicalities for running these, are discussed. While this is by no means an exhaustive list, the formats presented here have been chosen to demonstrate the wide variety that is available.

Some of the formats discussed below might be examples of outreach (one-way communication), some are public engagement (two-way communication), and some have the flexibility to be both. As noted in section 5.1, research in the field of science communication has tended to recommend public engagement formats as being more effective than outreach in engaging different publics [22]. This is largely because outreach is often associated with a deficit model of engagement, which has in turn been heavily criticised as being ineffectual, oversimplified, and derisory, in assuming that non-scientists are 'deficient', and scientists are 'sufficient' in knowledge [23].

However, while meaningful dialogue over science-related issues is needed for the development of science, and society more generally, providing reliable information in an accessible way is often a prerequisite for this to occur [24]. Furthermore, a gain in knowledge can have positive impacts on people's attitudes depending on their contexts and pre-knowledge [23]. If done correctly, outreach initiatives that are one-directional in format can still be extremely effective in achieving objectives and engaging audiences. We need only look at the impact that nature documentaries, such as those hosted by David Attenborough, have had to see evidence of this [25].

The following introduction to these selected formats should help you to think about how to develop your own science communication initiative, with both your objectives and your audience in mind. Section 5.11 provides some case studies of successful science communication initiatives that have made use of some of these formats.

5.5.1 Science talks

The most standard form of outreach is a science talk. This may consist of a lecture-style talk with an accompanying Q&A session, or a more informal discussion such as those hosted by Pint of Science [26]. Whatever the setting, the advice provided in chapter 4 still applies: consider your narrative, your audience, and yourself. Also, just because you are not speaking at an international scientific conference, do not assume that there are no experts in the room. Instead, try to find out who your audience will be, so that you can avoid either overestimating their knowledge or underestimating their intelligence. The advice that was given in chapter 4 with regards to preparation is also appropriate here: find out what AV equipment is available and try to arrange a practice session or sound check in advance if possible.

5.5.2 Panel discussion

When participating in a panel discussion, familiarise yourself with the format and your fellow panellists. Gain an understanding of how the discussion will be structured, whether it will be a round table, an open Q&A, or involve short presentations. Additionally, take the time to learn about the backgrounds, perspectives, and attitudes of your fellow panellists towards the topic at hand. This knowledge will enable you to engage in a meaningful and informed dialogue during the panel.

Promoting diversity among panellists is crucial. Strive to choose panellists who represent a diverse range of perspectives, including diversity in terms of gender, ethnicity, and career stage. By incorporating a variety of voices, you can enrich the discussion and provide a more comprehensive understanding of the topic to the audience, creating a space that welcomes and values diverse viewpoints.

When organising a panel discussion, carefully select a relevant topic that will resonate with the intended audience. Consider their interests, concerns, and the current relevance of the topic. Furthermore, invite panellists from various disciplines and backgrounds (i.e. not just scientists) to offer a broader range of viewpoints and insights. This diversity will contribute to a more engaging and well-rounded discussion.

If you plan to record the panel discussion, then obtain explicit permission from the panellists. Ensure that they are aware of the recording and its intended use, whether it will be streamed via social media or hosted on an institution's webpage. Address any concerns or preferences the panellists may have regarding the distribution and accessibility of the discussion.

Lastly, appoint an effective chairperson for the panel. The chairperson plays a vital role in facilitating a balanced discussion, keeping the conversation on track, and ensuring that all panellists have an opportunity to contribute. Look for someone who can manage time effectively and create an inclusive environment where diverse voices are heard and respected.

5.5.3 Science busking

Science busking [27] involves showcasing intriguing scientific phenomena in a captivating manner. For instance, you can create a cloud by using a bottle of water and a lit match or demonstrate surface properties by inserting a wooden kebab stick through a balloon without causing it to burst. When executed well, science busking can be an enchanting and innovative way to engage a potentially large audience.

Like other forms of street performance, science busking requires a skilful approach to engage the audience and inspire their curiosity. Connecting with people, irrespective of their scientific background, requires effective communication skills and the ability to simplify complex concepts. By presenting scientific ideas in a relatable and accessible manner, you can spark interest and foster a sense of wonder in those who encounter your demonstrations.

Furthermore, adaptability plays a crucial role in science busking. Being prepared to modify your approach based on the audience's reactions and interests allows for a more tailored and engaging experience. Adjusting your demonstrations to suit different age groups or incorporating relevant topics of local interest can further enhance the impact of your science busking performances.

5.5.4 Book clubs

Running a book club [28] provides an opportunity to explore science in an accessible and engaging way. When organising a book club, it is beneficial to choose a specific theme that is focused, such as 'time travel' rather than the broad category of 'science' itself. This allows for more in-depth discussions and creates a cohesive reading experience for participants.

To ensure a successful book club, it is recommended to schedule meetings once a month. This gives members ample time to read the selected book and prepare for the discussions. Opting for books that are easily accessible from local libraries helps to keep costs down and ensures that everyone has access to the reading material.

Planning and creating a book list in advance is a good practice. This allows members to have an overview of upcoming readings and ensures a diverse range of topics and perspectives. You should also try to give each member an opportunity to select a book and lead the discussion, fostering a sense of ownership and inclusivity within the group.

Consideration can also be given to setting up a digital book club, where members can connect and engage through social media platforms like X or Facebook. This format allows for broader participation, as members from different time zones can join in discussions at their convenience.

5.5.5 Workshops

The term 'workshop' encompasses a range of interactive sessions aimed at engaging an audience in meaningful discussions on specific topics of interest. These workshops can take various forms, from informal gatherings over tea and biscuits at a local community centre, where participants engage with scientists to explore their knowledge of the Solar System, to more structured initiatives involving scientists and other publics collaborating to brainstorm ideas for future clean energy solutions to be presented to local policymakers. Regardless of the format, all workshops should have a clear objective, tailored to a specific audience [29].

The key to conducting successful workshops is to create a safe and inclusive environment where participants feel comfortable expressing their thoughts and ideas. Everyone's voice should be heard and respected, fostering a collaborative and constructive atmosphere. To achieve this, facilitators can implement various strategies such as setting ground rules for communication, ensuring equal speaking opportunities, and actively encouraging diverse perspectives.

In addition to establishing a safe space, workshops should also be designed to be interactive and engaging. Incorporating hands-on activities, group discussions, and collaborative exercises can enhance participants' learning experience and promote active participation. Such activities should strike a balance between providing information and facilitating dialogue, allowing participants to contribute their own knowledge and insights.

When planning a workshop, careful consideration should be given to the specific needs and interests of the target audience. This includes adapting the content, language, and delivery methods to ensure accessibility and relevance. Understanding the participants' background, prior knowledge, and learning preferences can help tailor the workshop to maximise engagement and understanding.

By designing workshops with clear objectives, fostering a safe and inclusive environment, and tailoring them to the audience, we can create impactful and meaningful experiences that encourage dialogue, learning, and collaboration. Workshops offer a valuable platform for knowledge exchange and collective problem-solving, empowering participants to actively contribute to scientific discussions and potentially drive positive change in their communities.

5.5.6 Citizens' juries

A citizens' jury [30] is an extraordinary form of workshop that employs a specific method of deliberation. It brings together a small group of individuals, typically numbering between 10 and 20, to have in-depth discussions on a carefully framed question or issue over a period of two to seven days. The selection of jury members aims to represent the diversity of the target audience, and the primary purpose of the jury is to enable non-scientists to fully engage with a topic that is often contentious or of great societal importance.

Organising and conducting a citizens' jury is a significant undertaking that should not be underestimated, as it demands substantial resources in terms of time and finances. The success of a citizens' jury hinges on meticulous planning and execution. It begins with identifying the relevant topic or issue and formulating a well-defined question that stimulates thoughtful discussion. The selection process for jury members should prioritise diversity, ensuring representation from different backgrounds, perspectives, and experiences. This diversity enhances the richness of the deliberations and promotes a comprehensive exploration of the topic.

Providing clear guidelines, establishing mutual respect among participants, and fostering open and inclusive dialogue are all key components of a successful citizens' jury. Facilitators also play a vital role in guiding the discussions, ensuring that all voices are heard through constructive exchange, where participants can express their opinions freely and respectfully challenge one another's viewpoints.

The outcomes of a citizens' jury can be highly valuable, providing nuanced insights into public opinion and informing decision-making processes. The recommendations and conclusions generated by the jury should be disseminated widely, ensuring that they reach key stakeholders and policymakers. Doing so fosters transparency, accountability, and the potential for societal impact.

While citizens' juries demand substantial resources, their ability to empower participants and facilitate informed, democratic discussions on complex issues makes them a powerful tool for science communication. By enabling meaningful participation, citizens' juries contribute to a more inclusive and democratic approach to decision-making, where diverse voices and perspectives are considered and respected.

5.5.7 Art exhibitions

Art exhibitions provide a creative platform for science communication, merging the worlds of art and science to engage audiences in a unique and thought-provoking way [31]. Through visual displays, installations, and interactive exhibits, these initiatives offer an immersive experience that encourages dialogue about scientific concepts and discoveries.

In these exhibitions, scientific ideas are brought to life through artistic interpretation, capturing the imagination and emotions of visitors. Artistic media such as paintings, sculptures, multimedia installations, and digital media are used to convey scientific themes, making them accessible and relatable to a wide range of audiences. Art exhibitions provide opportunities for interdisciplinary collaborations between scientists, artists, and curators. Scientists can work closely with artists to communicate their research findings or concepts, bringing scientific expertise and authenticity to the artistic expression.

Art exhibitions also foster dialogue and reflection, as visitors have the chance to discuss the artwork and the scientific concepts it represents. Guided tours, artist talks, and panel discussions can further enrich the experience by providing context, explanations, and opportunities for interactive engagement. By merging art and science, these exhibitions invite a variety of publics to explore scientific concepts through a lens of creativity, curiosity, and aesthetic appreciation, creating lasting impressions and fostering a deeper understanding of the science that inspired them.

Whatever format you decide upon, you need to consider the ethical implications of your initiative. If you are planning to conduct any research or are carrying out an evaluation which involves collecting personal data from the participants (see section 5.9), then you should seek ethical clearance from your research institute. Even if you are not collecting any data from the participants, you should still think carefully about the repercussions of your proposed format. For example, if you are talking to a group of elderly people about the latest medical research on dementia, then be sensitive to the effect that this may have on some of the audience members. Similarly, if you are planning to discuss anything that others might perceive to be upsetting or offensive, then signpost this with appropriate content warnings and directions for further support if required. Developing your science communication initiative with members of your intended audience will help you to identify when and where such incidents may occur.

Planning and delivering science communication initiatives in the wake of the COVID-19 pandemic requires careful consideration and adaptation to the new landscape. The lessons learned from this global health crisis have further highlighted the need for flexibility and contingency planning, especially when prioritising the safety and well-being of both the audience and the science communicators themselves. For example, public transport strikes, severe weather warnings, or even the illness of a key participant may mean that in-person events may need to be modified or transitioned to virtual platforms at relatively short notice. Accounting for such events (however unlikely they may seem) is now seen as effective practice for most science communication initiatives.

Additionally, the COVID-19 pandemic has demonstrated the importance of adapting content to address current societal challenges and concerns. Science communication initiatives should reflect the relevance of scientific research in tackling pressing issues such as public health, climate change, and social inequalities. By addressing these topics, science communication initiatives can engage multiple publics in discussions that resonate with their daily lives and foster a sense of collective responsibility.

5.6 Citizen science

Citizen science is a public engagement format that brings together members of society (i.e. citizens) to actively participate in scientific research. It is a form of collaborative research where citizens play an active role in collecting, generating, and sometimes even analysing data. This involvement allows for a greater sense of ownership and connection to the scientific process.

Like citizens' juries, citizen science activities fall on the participatory end of the spectrum of science communication. They go beyond simply disseminating information and instead have the potential to empower individuals to become contributors to scientific knowledge. Such initiatives encourage people from all levels of society to get involved, regardless of their scientific background. Whether it is monitoring wildlife populations, documenting weather patterns, or classifying celestial objects, citizen science projects offer countless opportunities for people to contribute their observations and insights.

Citizen science initiatives often use digital platforms and mobile applications, making it easier than ever for individuals to get involved. Through these technologies, participants can easily access project information, submit data, and connect with other citizen scientists worldwide. The widespread availability of social media and online communities has further facilitated the sharing of experiences, knowledge, and collective findings.

By actively involving citizens in scientific research, citizen science not only fosters a deeper understanding of scientific concepts but also cultivates a sense of ownership and empowerment. Participants can witness first-hand how their contributions contribute to broader scientific endeavours and drive real-world impact. Citizen science projects provide a unique opportunity for individuals to connect with scientists, fellow enthusiasts, and experts in their respective fields.

One well-known citizen science project is Galaxy Zoo [32], an online initiative that invites participants to classify different types of galaxies based on their structures. By harnessing the power of human eyes, which are better at distinguishing these nuances than machines, Galaxy Zoo has received over 50 million classifications from more than 150,000 people. This project demonstrates the immense potential for collective knowledge and discoveries that can be made through the collaboration between scientists and citizen scientists.

Another notable project is Old Weather [33], which seeks to recover historical weather observations from US ships dating back to the mid-nineteenth century. By digitising old transcriptions recorded in ship logbooks, citizen scientists contribute to a better understanding of past environmental conditions, improving weather pattern modelling for the future.

In addition to contributing to existing data, citizen science programs actively involve the public in data sourcing. For example, the Community Collaborative Rain, Hail & Snow Network [34] is a community-based network of volunteers who measure and map precipitation using low-cost tools and an interactive website. With networks across the United States and Canada, this project involves thousands of volunteers and provides valuable daily precipitation observations.

While citizen science projects offer exciting opportunities for public engagement, there is a concern that participants' contributions may be seen as free labour, with scientists benefiting from their efforts without proper recognition. To address this, if you conduct your own citizen science initiative then you should ensure that citizens are appropriately acknowledged and involved throughout the entire process. An example of this approach was the UK Community Rain Network [35], where children across the UK monitored and analysed precipitation using homemade rain gauges, with all participating citizens acknowledged in the subsequent journal publication. By treating citizen scientists as valued colleagues and acknowledging their contributions, scientists can foster a more inclusive and collaborative approach, avoiding the risk of creating a second-class citizenry of scientists.

5.7 Funding

After determining how your science communication initiative will meet the needs of your objective and your audience, you need to consider how to finance it. Even the most basic of initiatives will have some consumable costs, while larger initiatives will also have to account for travel and venue hire, plus maybe even a contribution to the salary of those involved. Here are some potential revenue streams for you to consider:

1. **Science communication funding.** Many national funding bodies and international organisations such as the Simons Foundation now provide specific funding streams for science communication initiatives. When applying for one of these grants, follow the advice given in chapter 3; in addition, getting match funding from one of the other sources on this list will strengthen your application.
2. **Universities.** Almost all universities have a widening participation team, with many also having people dedicated to co-ordinating science communication initiatives. Find out who these people are and ask them for advice when developing your initiatives. Furthermore, they might have access to funds that you can make use of, especially if your plans align with the university's wider strategy.
3. **Existing research grants.** As discussed in section 5.1, most large research grants must now show how they are making a conscious effort to inform society of the research that they are doing, and the relevance that this has to the wider community. Funds will normally have been set aside to do this, and therefore represent a potential revenue stream for future initiatives.
4. **Learned societies.** Most academic or scientific societies offer some kind of support for science communication initiatives, both through formal grants, and via development funds for associated members and fellows.
5. **Corporate sponsorships and partnerships.** Many corporations have corporate social responsibility initiatives that support science communication projects. Research and get in touch with relevant companies for potential partnerships or sponsorships that align with their goals.
6. **Crowdfunding platforms.** Platforms like Kickstarter and Indiegogo allow you to highlight your science communication initiative and raise funds from a supportive community. Craft a compelling campaign highlighting the project's impact and engage with backers who are passionate about science and science communication.

5.8 Advertising

With your science communication initiative fully developed, tested, and funded, how can you ensure that you reach your intended audience? If you are planning an outreach initiative involving schools, you will need to make prior arrangements with the schools involved. As discussed in section 5.3, when working with traditionally underserved audiences, it is beneficial to collaborate with a community member who can provide guidance on locating, scheduling, and promoting your initiative effectively.

Engaging with specific audiences can also be done through mailing lists, such as PSCI-COMM (psci-com@jiscmail.ac.uk) and PCST (network@lists.pcst.network), which reach a wide range of individuals interested in science communication. Personalised emails to contacts who may be interested or can refer others to your initiative can also be an effective advertising strategy. However, sending generic emails to a large group is unlikely to yield significant results.

Getting in contact with local newspapers, magazines, and international publications with regional offices, like *Time Out* magazine, can be worthwhile. These publications often offer free listings alongside paid advertisements, both in print and online. Additionally, using posters and flyers in locations frequented by your target audience, such as elevators or toilet cubicles, can raise awareness about your initiative in a visually engaging way.

Social media platforms, as discussed in chapter 7, offer a powerful means to reach a large portion of your target audience within a short span of time. If your initiative is tailored for a specific group, such as amateur astronomers, or is aligned with local or global events like the International Day of Women and Girls in Science, you should share information about your initiative with the social media channels managed by relevant organisations. Additionally, it is advisable to notify learned societies, related organisations, and funders of such initiatives in advance.

The logistical aspects of ticketing have been simplified with online tools like Eventbrite. Experience suggests that a common attrition rate of around 30%–50% is expected for free events. It can be frustrating for individuals who are unable to attend a sold-out event, only to discover later that only half of the ticket holders showed up. To account for this, it is good practice to maintain a reserve list or consider implementing a small fee to encourage attendance. Surprisingly, even a few pounds, euros, or dollars can serve as a strong incentive for people to participate. There is also an argument that charging a modest fee for tickets can create perceived value, potentially increasing attendance rates.

"WE'RE GONNA NEED A BIGGER BOAT."

5.9 Evaluation

Neglecting the proper evaluation of a science communication initiative would hinder a comprehensive assessment of whether the objectives have been successfully achieved. At the very least, try to keep a record of the number of participants attending the initiatives, both for your own personal records and for the associated research institute or external funder. It is also good practice to provide a brief personal summary of each initiative, as reflecting on these experiences (see chapter 9) enables improvements to be made.

To thoroughly assess the extent to which the outcomes of a science communication initiative have been met, it is important to gather detailed feedback from both the audience and any colleagues involved in the delivery. When constructing a feedback survey, consideration should be given to the data required from participants. While many surveys include inquiries about demographic information, it is unnecessary to request such details if they will not be used in your evaluation. For instance, it may be more meaningful to ask participants about their enjoyment or to rate the accessibility of the initiative on a scale of 1–5 (with 1 being very poor and 5 being very good). Lastly, it is important to be considerate in the design and wording of the survey. For instance, if asking about gender association, providing an open space for individuals to specify rather than offering a binary option or multiple-choice selection of 'male/female/other' would be more inclusive and respectful.

Google Forms is a valuable and cost-free tool for managing feedback, as it enables the creation and distribution of surveys using a dedicated link that can be shared with participants via email. To address concerns about follow-up responses, participants can either be requested to fill out the survey on their electronic devices before leaving or provided with printed copies that can be later uploaded to Google Forms (other paid platforms such as SurveyMonkey are also available). This platform also offers basic analytical features to assess the responses, which can be exported to a spreadsheet for further analysis.

Whenever possible, it is beneficial to integrate feedback opportunities into the initiative itself, making the process innovative and enjoyable. For instance, during a science talk on the geographies of light and dark, a feedback form shown in figure 5.1 was distributed to participants. These forms were printed on both sides of A5 cards, with participants also provided with pencils and pens. This approach resulted in a fun and straightforward feedback method that was quick and enjoyable to analyse.

The feedback that we have discussed so far provides valuable insights into how people perceive and enjoy our science communication initiatives, allowing us to make improvements for future endeavours. However, to truly assess the success of these initiatives and determine if they have achieved their desired objectives, we need to adopt a more comprehensive approach. In figure 5.2, we see a visual representation of the scientific process, which involves formulating a hypothesis, designing experiments to test it, conducting those tests, and based on the outcomes, either accepting the original hypothesis or refining it and repeating the cycle. As scientists, we engage in this process regularly, yet when it comes to evaluating our science

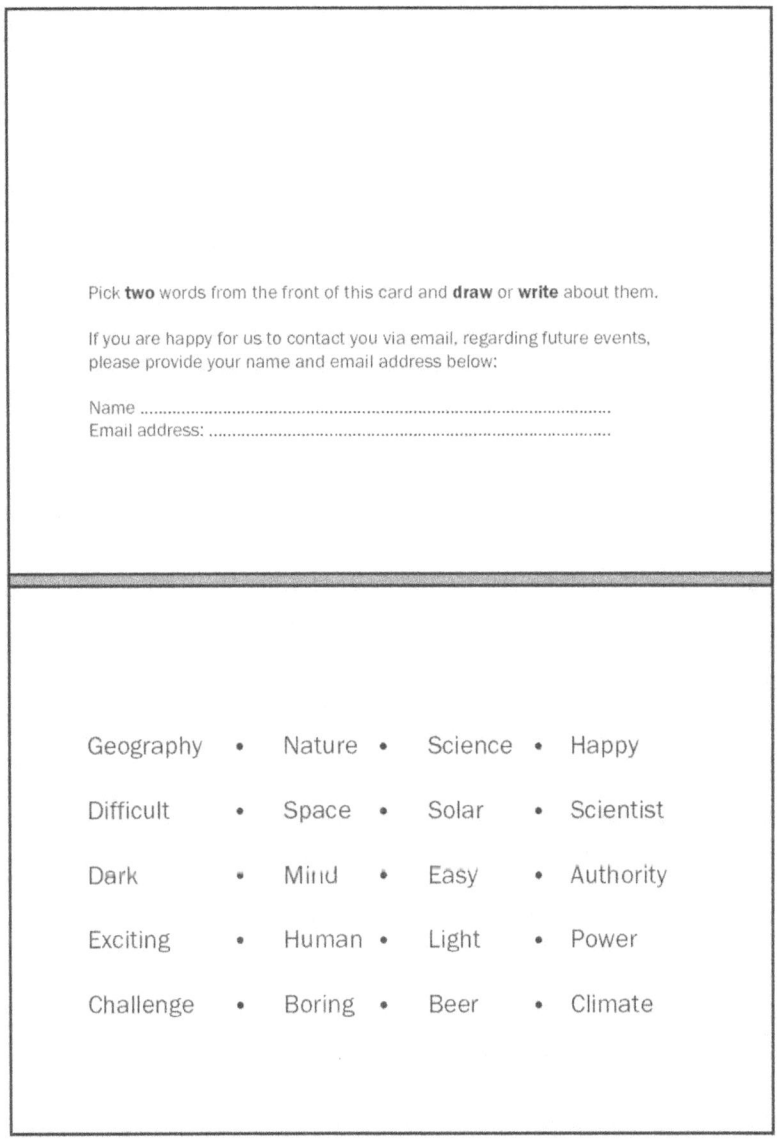

Figure 5.1. A sample feedback form for a science talk. Using feedback forms that are fun to fill out can help to enhance the audience's overall experience of your initiative.

communication initiatives, we often overlook our scientific training and fail to conduct thorough evaluations.

To address this, we should apply our scientific mindset to the evaluation process of our science communication initiatives. Just as we design experiments to test hypotheses, so too can we design evaluation methods to assess the impact and effectiveness of our science communication efforts. By systematically collecting data, such as pre- and post-initiative surveys, interviews, or observations, we can analyse

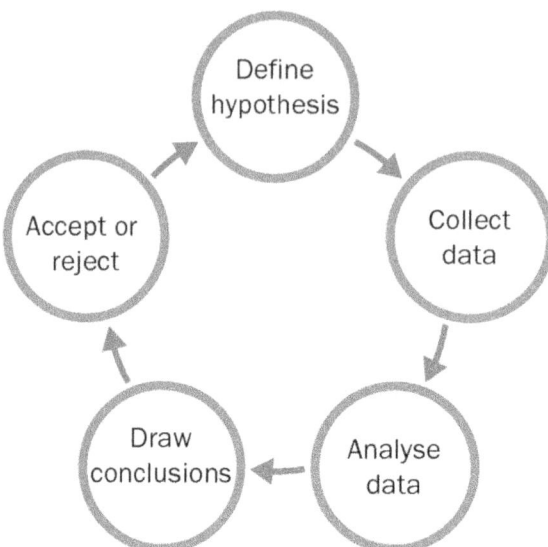

Figure 5.2. A circular diagram representing the scientific process. As scientists we follow this approach when we conduct our scientific research; we should adopt a similar approach when we evaluate our science communication initiatives.

and interpret the results to gain deeper insights into the outcomes and impacts of our initiatives.

As an example, suppose that you are developing an outreach initiative to raise awareness of ocean acidification for a group of schoolchildren between the ages of 10 and 12. In this instance, the hypothesis would be that 'this initiative raises the awareness of ocean acidification amongst schoolchildren between the ages of 10 and 12'. However, it is not possible to test this hypothesis without first assessing the level of awareness that these students had about ocean acidification prior to your intervention. In this instance, the evaluation process needs to begin before you even set foot in the classroom.

Assessing the audience's level of understanding or awareness does not have to be complicated. If our initiative aims to raise awareness of the climate crisis, we can gauge their initial familiarity by asking questions like: What is the climate crisis? What causes it? How does it affect humans and animals worldwide? After the initiative, we can ask the same questions again to compare their pre- and post-understanding. To evaluate any lasting effects, we can follow up with a short questionnaire six months later, as a form of longitudinal evaluation.

Unfortunately, some participants may perceive this approach as formal 'assessment', which can create negative attitudes toward our initiative. In such cases, a more informal focus group approach might be preferable. Participants can engage in open discussions about the topic before and after the initiative, and their comments and remarks can be recorded and analysed by you and your colleagues.

If the evaluation results will be used in reports or future publications, you must also obtain informed consent from all participants and seek ethical approval from your research institute, with participation information and consent forms that clearly outline how the information will be used and stored. Participants should also be informed of their right to have their responses redacted if they wish to do so later. You should also make clear that participating in the evaluation is not a requirement for participating in the initiative itself.

When working with schoolchildren and other potentially vulnerable audiences, you must take special care to ensure they understand the implications of their participation in any evaluation. If necessary, obtain explicit and informed consent from their guardian or responsible adult.

Adopting this rigorous approach to evaluating your science communication initiatives means that you might consider publishing the process and its outcomes, alongside what these findings mean for the wider scientific community, in a suitable journal such as one of those listed in chapter 1. Publishing original findings in peer-reviewed journals can help to justify the legitimacy of any science communication initiative to your institute, supervisor, or external funding body. Furthermore, such publications can help to develop your reputation, while also helping to advance knowledge and best practice in the field.

5.10 Initiative checklist

The table below will help you to deliver, develop, and evaluate your science communication initiatives.

	Your overall strategy
Objective	**What do you want to achieve?** Make sure that you have achievable and measurable objectives, focussing on both the short- and the long-term.
Audience	**Who do you want to target?** There are many different publics, so think carefully about your objective, and why you want to work with this audience.
Format	**How will this achieve your objective?** Pick a format that is suitable to both your objectives and your audience, and where possible discuss this in advance with a member of your intended audience.
	Development
Development	**Are you developing an initiative for schoolchildren?** If so, then work with a schoolteacher in the development process. Doing so will ensure that your initiative is suitable for the students and their school curriculum.
	Are you developing an initiative for a specific public? If so, then work with a member of this public in the development process, as this will help to ensure that your initiative is suitable and accessible for your proposed audience

(*Continued*)	
Funding	**How will you fund your initiative?** Look for internal and external funding schemes that you can apply for and remember to include transport and refreshment costs.
Advertising	**How will you advertise your initiative?** Use targeted email and social media advertising, and work with your intended audience to build a supportive and trusting relationship.
Staff	**Have you got enough facilitators?** Involve these people throughout the development process, checking that they have permission from their line managers or supervisors. Also, consider if these facilitators are 'volunteers', or if they require payment for their time and expertise.
	Have you provided suitable training? Anyone who is working with under-18s needs to be briefed on safe and appropriate ways of working with young people. The same goes for when working with any potentially vulnerable audiences.
	Is there appropriate identification for the facilitators? Wearing badges/t-shirts/fleeces etc can make it easier for participants to get help.
Insurance	**Do you have valid public liability insurance?** Your research institute should be able to help with this (see below).
Risk	**Do you have a risk assessment?** You should complete a risk assessment for each of your initiatives, and have it signed off by both your research institute and any external venue (see below).
Materials	**Do you need any materials?** Prepare any resources and take-away materials and include extra copies of everything just in case.
Venue	**Have you considered your AV requirements?** If you require computer/Wi-Fi access, then make sure that this will be available. Where possible bring your own equipment (e.g. portable speakers) that you know will work, and have a back-up plan in case of a power/IT failure.
	Have you confirmed the room with the venue? Contact a representative of the venue in advance to make sure that it is set up appropriately.
	Have you got adequate signposting? Make it easy for your audience to find the venue, and that once they are there they know where the toilets, parking, and other amenities are.
	Have you thought about accessibility? Try and pick a venue that can be accessed by everyone, and work with the venue to create a safe and inclusive space for all.

	Delivery
Participant Information	**If working with potentially vulnerable audiences, have you received consent from a parent/guardian and emergency contact information?** This should all be kept secure and destroyed after the initiative.
	Have you printed off photo and video consent forms? For larger initiatives, signpost that filming/ photography will be taking place and offer stickers to identify those people who do not want to be filmed and/or have their images used.
Health and Safety	**Are you aware of the fire procedure?** Check with the venue where the fire assembly point is, and if there is any planned fire drill. Make the participants aware of this information and ask the venue to temporarily turn off any smoke alarms if you plan to generate any smoke (e.g. through demonstrations).
	Do you know how you would access First Aid? You should have easy access to at least one person professionally trained in First Aid, with an up-to-date qualification. You might also consider asking an organisation such as St John's Ambulance (in the UK) to aid with larger audiences.
	Evaluation
Monitoring/ Evaluation	**Have you thought about feedback?** Record how many people have attended your initiative and produce a short personal summary for reflection. Also, create a feedback survey for all participants (including other facilitators) to fill in.
	Have you done a proper evaluation? Think about what hypothesis your initiative is trying to test and design an appropriate way of assessing this. If you are using data or information from any of the participants then make sure you have ethical clearance from your research institute, and that you have the informed consent from all participants.
	Have you advertised your success? Consider writing a blog post (see chapter 7) about your experiences and share any particularly engaging images via the social media accounts of your research institute and any host venue; first checking that you have permission to use any images in this way.

All science communication initiatives need a risk assessment. If you are using external venues, such as schools, they will require a copy of this information in advance. You can ask one of the health and safety officers at your research institute for the appropriate form or check if the venue has a standard format they prefer to use. When completing the risk assessment, consider the potential risks to all participants involved, including facilitators, audience members, and yourself. Take reasonable steps to mitigate these risks. For instance, if you are using wired microphones, ensure that any loose cables are securely fastened to the floor to minimise the risk of tripping. Once you have completed the risk assessment, it should be reviewed and approved by the relevant health and safety officer at both your research institute and any external venue you are using.

Certain venues may also require you to have public liability insurance, and you need to discuss this matter with the legal team at your research institute. Your initiative should be covered by your research institute's public liability insurance, even for external venues. However, it is essential to keep them fully informed about your activities. Failure to do so could leave you liable for any damages in the event of accidents or injuries occurring.

5.11 Examples of science communication initiatives

In this section we have highlighted some examples of successful science communication initiatives, each of which have a well-defined objective for a specific audience, with a format that has been chosen accordingly. They serve to highlight the wide range of science communication initiatives that can be developed and will hopefully serve as inspiration for your own.

5.11.1 Bright Club

Bright Club [36] is an innovative science communication initiative that blends comedy and academia to engage the public with science. Originating at University College London in 2009, it has since expanded to various locations in the UK, Ireland, and Australia. Each Bright Club event features researchers delivering short, humorous talks related to their areas of expertise and a themed topic for the night. A compere guides the evening, and live musicians often perform during the event, adding to the vibrant atmosphere. The initiative aims to break down barriers between academia and other publics by presenting scientific concepts in an accessible and entertaining manner.

Bright Club stands out as a successful science communication initiative that effectively combines entertainment and knowledge-sharing. By using comedy as a vehicle, it creates an engaging platform for researchers to connect with multiple publics, fostering dialogue and increasing scientific understanding in an enjoyable and accessible way.

5.11.2 Think Like a Scientist

The Think Like a Scientist project [37] aimed to address the issue of low self-agency and disengagement among students, particularly in STEM subjects. It specifically focused on the unique challenges faced by students in English prisons, where access to education is limited. The project introduced a STEM course designed to improve critical thinking and foster independent thought. Through a series of talks on science topics, such as climate change, plate tectonics, natural hazards, and space missions, the students were exposed to new information and encouraged to participate actively.

The aim was to enhance their self-agency and empower them to think critically. Teaching within the prison environment is complex due to various factors, including limited resources and the educational struggles faced by prisoners in traditional classroom settings. This project served as a pioneering initiative, addressing the educational needs of incarcerated individuals and providing them with a platform to develop their scientific thinking skills. By incorporating engaging science topics and promoting independent learning, the enhanced the students' educational experiences and contributed to their personal and professional development.

5.11.3 Carbon City Zero

Carbon City Zero [38] is a card game that was designed to facilitate dialogue and engagement around the topic of heat decarbonisation and transitioning to a zero-carbon economy. The initiative began by hosting workshops with various publics, including climate activists, policymakers, educators, journalists, schoolchildren, students, researchers, and industry representatives. Through these workshops, participants explored the challenges and opportunities associated with achieving a zero-carbon economy in the UK, co-creating and playtesting a card game in the process.

Carbon City Zero was developed to be played without facilitation, drawing on a growing body of research that has shown how analogue games can create a safe space for meaningful dialogue [39–41]. To date, the game has been downloaded and played by over 10 000 people from across the world, highlighting the value of community engagement and the importance of incorporating diverse perspectives to foster meaningful conversations and create impactful science communication tools.

5.11.4 Rhyme and Reason

Rhyme and Reason [16] was a public engagement initiative that consisted of a series of workshops run across the UK, in which people from traditionally underserved communities (refugees, asylum seekers, and people living with severe mental health needs) engaged in dialogue with environmental scientists by writing poetry together. These workshops were run in the community spaces of these different publics, and were developed to create a platform for participants to discuss their thoughts and fears about topics relating to environmental change (e.g. air pollution, global warming, soil degradation). This approach helped to break down the hierarchies of intellect that were discussed in section 5.3, by creating a shared space in which the non-scientists could freely discuss their opinions, and where the scientists could freely display their emotions.

By analysing the poems that were created during these sessions, researchers were able to demonstrate how this approach created a powerful way of generating what underserved audiences really know and think about environmental change, presenting a framework through which to understand differently, the lifeworld of these communities. Furthermore, bringing together scientists and other publics through poetry helped to platform the voices of the under-heard, giving those who could enact change an opportunity to listen.

> **Exercise: Developing your initiative**
> As these examples demonstrate, science communication initiatives encompass a wide range of formats, often influenced by the personal hobbies and interests of the scientists involved. So, take a moment to consider your own leisure activities outside of your scientific work. What do you enjoy doing in your free time? Reflect on how your hobbies and pastimes could be used as a platform to discuss either your scientific research or more general scientific topics. For instance, if you are a materials scientist that enjoys sports, then you could explore the connections between your discipline and sportswear. Or, if you are a geomorphologist who enjoys baking then you could teach people how to bake cakes inspired by natural landforms.

Leveraging your existing expertise and passion for your hobbies will also boost your confidence in delivering a successful and impactful initiative. Doing so also provides an opportunity to connect with a community that you are already a part of, strengthening the engagement and relevance of your communication efforts.

5.12 Summary

This chapter has provided an overview of how scientists can engage with other publics through science communication. It has introduced the terminology used in this field and highlighted the distinction between outreach, which involves one-way communication from scientists to non-scientists, and public engagement, which fosters a two-way dialogue between scientists and other publics. Several examples have been shared to illustrate these concepts.

The chapter has also offered guidance on developing effective science communication initiatives, emphasising the importance of defining clear objectives, understanding the target audience, and exploring appropriate formats for engagement. Funding, advertising, and evaluation strategies have also been discussed, along with the potential for contributing to the field through peer-reviewed publications.

Undertaking science communication initiatives can be demanding in terms of time and resources. However, the rewards can be significant, as it allows for the development of valuable skills applicable beyond academia, such as supervising, presenting, and networking. Recognising the various responsibilities scientists already have, it may be beneficial to collaborate with professional science communicators and social scientists. These experts can assist with logistical aspects, help establish long-term objectives, and provide valuable evaluation insights. Engaging them from the early stages of planning will maximise their contributions and alleviate the workload associated with science communication efforts.

5.13 Further study

The further study in this chapter is designed to help you think more about developing and delivering a science communication initiative:

1. **Evaluate an initiative.** Find an upcoming science communication initiative in your local area and attend as a participant. Can you identify the objectives of

the initiative? Is it aimed at a specific audience? Is the chosen format suitable and appropriate? Make a note of everything that you enjoyed and disliked about the experience and use this to help critique your own current and future initiatives.
2. **Become a citizen of (another) science.** Find a citizen science project that is of interest to you, but which does not necessarily align with your current area of research. For example, if you are an astronomer then consider taking part in a national wildlife survey. When you join this project consider how much agency and ownership you are granted by the process. Do you feel like you are genuinely collaborating in the development of new knowledge, or are you nothing more than an unpaid labourer? Use this experience to help shape any future citizen science project (or other initiative) that you are developing.
3. **Get support.** Track down the designated outreach, public engagement, or school's liaison officer at your place of work. Ask for their advice about your science communication initiatives and ascertain if there is any funding and/or training available to you. Making them aware of the work that you are doing will also make you more likely to be considered for future science communication opportunities.

5.14 Suggested reading

A concise and insightful review by D B Short [42] offers a comprehensive overview of the history of science communication in the UK, while 'Histories of science communication' [43] presents a more global overview. For a practical guide to developing and delivering science communication initiatives, *Science Communication: A Practical Guide for Scientists* [3] is an excellent resource. It features a range of useful case studies that are both informative and inspiring. Additionally, the article 'Delivering effective science communication: advice from a professional science communicator' [8] provides practical advice on defining objectives, considering the audience, and exploring innovative formats.

Furthermore, the references cited in this chapter serve as a valuable starting point for further exploration of the history and ongoing development of science communication as an academic discipline. They offer a wealth of information and insights for those interested in finding out more.

References

[1] Illingworth S 2023 A spectrum of geoscience communication: from dissemination to participation *Geosci. Commun.* **6** 131–9
[2] Bauer M W 2009 The evolution of public understanding of science—discourse and comparative evidence *Sci. Technol. Soc.* **14** 221–40
[3] Bowater L and Yeoman K 2012 *Science Communication: A Practical Guide for Scientists* (New York: Wiley)
[4] Grand A, Davies G, Holliman R and Adams A 2015 Mapping public engagement with research in a UK university *PLoS One* **10** e0121874
[5] Bucchi M and Trench B 2014 *Routledge Handbook of Public Communication of Science and Technology* (London: Routledge)

[6] Brownell S E, Price J and Steinman L 2013 Science communication to the general public: why we need to teach undergraduate and graduate students this skill as part of their formal scientific training *J. Underg. Neurosci. Educ.* **12** E6

[7] Besley J C, Dudo A and Storksdieck M 2015 Scientists' views about communication training *J. Res. Sci. Teach.* **52** 199–220

[8] Bubela T *et al* 2009 Science communication reconsidered *Nat. Biotechnol.* **27** 514

[9] Illingworth S 2017 Delivering effective science communication: advice from a professional science communicator *Semin. Cell Dev. Biol.* **70** 10–6

[10] Chilvers J and Kearnes M 2015 *Remaking Participation: Science, Environment and Emergent Publics* (London: Routledge)

[11] Prokop A and Illingworth S 2016 Aiming for long-term, objective-driven science communication in the UK *F1000Research* **5** 1540

[12] Illingworth S, Redfern J, Millington S and Gray S 2015 What's in a name? exploring the nomenclature of science communication in the UK *F1000Research* **4** 409

[13] McLoughlin N *et al* 2018 *Climate Communication in Practice: How Are We Engaging the UK Public on Climate Change?* (Oxford: Climate Outreach)

[14] Scheufele D A 2018 Beyond the choir? The need to understand multiple publics for science *Environ. Commun.* **12** 1123–6

[15] Illingworth S *et al* 2018 Representing the majority and not the minority: the importance of the individual in communicating climate change *Geosci. Commun.* **1** 9–24

[16] Illingworth S and Jack K 2018 Rhyme and reason—using poetry to talk to underserved audiences about environmental change *Clim. Risk Manag.* **19** 120–9

[17] Renaud G and Renaud K 2013 Computing science in the classroom: experiences of a STEM ambassador *Innov. Teach. Learn. Inform. Comput. Sci.* **12** 3–13

[18] Bell P *et al* 2009 *Learning Science in Informal Environments: People, Places, and Pursuits* (Washington, DC: National Academies Press)

[19] Gjersoe N L and Hood B 2013 Changing children's understanding of the brain: a longitudinal study of the Royal Institution Christmas Lectures as a measure of public engagement *PLoS One* **8** e80928

[20] Denson C, Austin C, Hailey C and Householder D 2015 Benefits of informal learning environments: a focused examination of STEM-based program environments *J. STEM Educ.* **16** 11–5

[21] Dance A 2016 Science and culture: avant-garde outreach, with science rigor *Proc. Natl Acad. Sci.* **113** 11982–3

[22] Bucchi M and Trench B 2008 *Handbook of Public Communication of Science and Technology* (London: Routledge)

[23] Sturgis P and Allum N 2004 Science in society: re-evaluating the deficit model of public attitudes *Public Underst. Sci.* **13** 55–74

[24] Dickson D 2005 The case for a 'deficit model' of science communication *SciDev Net* https://www.scidev.net/global/editorials/the-case-for-a-deficit-model-of-science-communic/ 24 May

[25] Farache F, Grigore G, McQueen D and Stancu A 2019 The role of the individual in promoting social change *Responsible People* (Berlin: Springer)

[26] Adhikari B, Hlaing P H, Robinson M T, Ruecker A, Tan N H, Jatupornpimol N, Chanviriyavuth R and Cheah P Y 2019 Evaluation of the Pint of Science festival in Thailand *PLoS One* **14** e0219983

[27] Villanueva Baselga S, Marimon Garrido O and González Burón H 2022 Drama-based activities for STEM education: encouraging scientific aspirations and debunking stereotypes in secondary school students in Spain and the UK *Res. Sci. Educ.* **52** 173–90
[28] Verran J 2013 The bad bugs book club: science, literacy, and engagement *J. Microbiol. Biol. Educ.* **14** 110–2
[29] Illingworth S 2022 *Science Communication through Poetry* (Berlin: Springer Nature)
[30] Street J, Duszynski K, Krawczyk S and Braunack-Mayer A 2014 The use of citizens' juries in health policy decision-making: a systematic review *Soc. Sci. Med.* **109** 1–9
[31] Rossi G *et al* 2020 Focus on glaciers: a geo-photo exposition of vanishing beauty *Geosci. Commun.* **3** 381–92
[32] Lintott C J *et al* 2008 Galaxy Zoo: morphologies derived from visual inspection of galaxies from the Sloan Digital Sky Survey *Mon. Not. R. Astron. Soc.* **389** 1179–89
[33] Eveleigh A, Jennett C, Lynn S and Cox A L 2013 'I want to be a Captain! I want to be a Captain!': gamification in the Old Weather Citizen Science Project *Proc. 1st Int. Conf. on Gameful Design, Research, and Applications* (New York: ACM)
[34] Reges H W *et al* 2016 COCORAHS: the evolution and accomplishments of a volunteer rain gauge network *Bull. Am. Meteorol. Soc.* **97** 1831–46
[35] Illingworth S, Muller C, Graves R and Chapman L 2014 UK citizen rainfall network: a pilot study *Weather* **69** 203–7
[36] Roche J, Fairfield J A, Gallagher Á and Bell L 2020 Bright Club: establishing a science comedy variety night in Ireland *Sci. Commun.* **42** 130–40
[37] Heron P J and Williams J A 2022 Building confidence in STEM students through breaking (unseen) barriers *Geosci. Commun.* **5** 355–61
[38] Illingworth S and Wake P 2021 Ten simple rules for designing analogue science games *PLoS Comput. Biol.* **17** e1009009
[39] Lean J, Illingworth S and Wake P 2018 Unhappy families: using tabletop games as a technology to understand play in education *Assoc. Learn. Technol.* **26** 13
[40] Illingworth S 2019 Developing science tabletop games: Catan and global warming *JCOM: J. Sci. Commun.* **18** 4
[41] Wake P and Illingworth S 2018 Games in the curriculum *Learn. Teach. Action* **13** 131–44
[42] Short D B 2013 The public understanding of science: 30 years of the Bodmer report *School Sci. Rev.* **95** 39–44
[43] Nielsen K H 2022 Histories of science communication *Histories* **2** 334–40

Chapter 6

Engaging with mass media

There are only two forces that can carry light to all the corners of the globe —only two—the sun in the heavens and the Associated Press down here.
—Mark Twain

6.1 Introduction

As scientists, we are driven to explore the unknown and analyse information honestly and rigorously. This curiosity to discover is, and should be, the essence of our professional identity. However, it is also incumbent on us as scientists to record and communicate any original knowledge that we discover, and to inspire curiosity in others. There is little point in being the sole person to know something and so it is our duty in equal measure to discover, disseminate, inform debate, and inspire new science.

The means by which we communicate our science to different publics are the various 'media'. Depending on the group or individual with whom we may wish to convey knowledge, different forms of media (or methods of communication) may be relevant. In academic circles, peer-reviewed journals (chapter 2) and scientific conference presentations (chapter 4) may be the most obvious media for this closed but specialised audience, but we also need to bring our science to the attention of other, non-scientific publics, and to use science to inspire and empower the wider society (chapter 5).

These latter forms of communication are often daunting to some scientists who typically (and stereotypically) feel much more comfortable communicating with their peer group. It is not unusual for researchers and academics to struggle to break down their often-technical scientific understanding for a wider audience. This potential mismatch between self, narrative, and audience can result in various misunderstandings, which can subtly yet significantly sway public and policy discussions in different directions. Despite these concerns, as scientists we should not avoid engaging with these media. Rather, we should recognise them as a potent tool through which our scientific work can genuinely create a difference and make a substantial impact. In doing so, we need to understand how we can use this power and agency effectively to uphold truth, raise awareness, and impart meaningful information.

In this chapter, we focus on what we might more conventionally think of as 'mass media', i.e. the mass communication methods of television, radio, and the printed press. The specific cases of engaging with social media and other digital forms will be discussed in chapter 7. Here, we shall discuss how to construct a useful and succinct narrative for the fast-paced environment of mass media, and how to remain focussed under the often stressful, and sometimes hostile, scenario of being interviewed by journalists and presenters. And finally, we shall discuss how to both maximise impact and bring science to the attention of those that might use it to make decisions.

6.2 Why, when, and how to engage with mass media

Mass media serve as pathways through which science can inform and enhance awareness about the findings and repercussions of research, exploring their potential impact on human society and the natural world. By disseminating information broadly, individuals from diverse fields can intersect your research with their specialised knowledge, taking it in various unexpected directions that may be unreachable through other routes. Mass media acts as a platform to inform vast audiences who might not typically access information from academic sources or from within the echo chamber of their social media algorithm.

Mass media is likewise a vehicle through which we can motivate the forthcoming generation of scientists and imbue within them the principles of scientific inquiry and the earnest quest for knowledge as fundamental elements of our civilisation and culture. By imparting this sentiment of academic liberty and knowledge to others, we embolden and empower them to question, to formulate informed perspectives, and to rationalise and comprehend the world around them. We can both recall childhoods replete with television appearances by the likes of David Attenborough, Neil deGrasse Tyson, Jane Goodall, and Carl Sagan. This brings us to the question of when and how we should seek to engage with mass media. For these four scientists, their wide and expert knowledge of whole swathes of science (as well as their innate passion, charisma and the skills of expert producers in the background) made them ideally placed to become the icons that they undoubtedly are. However, for most of us, especially at the start of our career, we must decide when we have a story worth telling, or a comment worth making, and how best to communicate it.

Engaging with mass media can be either a passive or an active process. You may wish to alert the media to something you have to say (e.g. through a press release) or you may be consulted for comment (e.g. by a request for comment through your organisation's press office). It will usually be up to you to determine when you have something worth saying, and if you have valid, accurate, and useful information to convey. However, a research institute's press officers can help to suggest when there is research done by a particular scientist that is of interest to the media.

Many scientists do not readily realise when their research may be of interest to mass media. We may assume that because we know something, that others do too. Contacting your institution's press office (or the press office of the publisher that you have submitted your work too), means that they can help you to find out whether your research is newsworthy; and if it is, how best to go about ensuring that it reaches the widest possible audience. The next step is to consider your narrative or message, to think about the audience you want to reach, and how best to say it in a succinct but accurate and informative way. In the rest of this chapter, we shall look at some of the ways you can engage with the media and how they may pick up your story.

6.3 Press releases

Press releases are an active way (from your point of view) of engaging with mass media. These are a useful tool when you know you have an important story that you feel a wider audience may want to hear.

A press release is a brief (usually not exceeding one A4 page) non-specialist summary of a fresh scientific conclusion, or a thrilling new project that holds appeal for the media. It commonly includes a succinct title (a sentence), an explanation of the science and its significance, and frequently features one or two quotes that might be used, along with contact details for journalists to reach you or your team for additional commentary. Crafting an effective press release typically demands training or skill, and it is advisable to seek assistance from professionals such as a press officer (should you have access to one). Nevertheless, with experience, most scientists can compose a sound press release with minimal aid. However, all press releases should be authorised and submitted through formal channels at most institutions, particularly where your affiliation may be used. This provides protection for you and may avert embarrassing or legal issues if grave errors are otherwise made.

Many of the science news stories you have seen on TV or heard on the radio will have first been picked up by a science journalist (who tends to specialise in scientific news) by reading a press release. Other press releases may be sent directly to specific news organisations' news desks. Those journalists will decide on whether they would like to pick up the story and then typically discuss it with their editor. They may then attempt to contact you to discuss the story further or they may take the information they need from your press release without further contact at all.

We have both submitted several press releases through our research institute's press offices that have resulted in hundreds of live or recorded TV news items, radio interviews, and newspaper articles over several years. We have also submitted releases that have not attracted any media interest, and there are often several factors that are simply beyond your control when it comes to whether a press release is successful. Often the success or take-up of your press release might depend on the coverage of big news stories in the press at the time, or on editorial policy, which is why it can also be important to consider the timing of releasing your story to the world.

An example may be useful here. In 2012, Grant was the Principal Investigator for a funded project to measure the air quality around London from a specialised research aircraft [1], which involved measuring how a cloud of pollution from London was moving over areas far away from the sources of pollution within the city limits. This measurement field campaign coincided with the 2012 London Summer Olympics, and there was a lot of attention to the problems of air quality in the news because of potential athletic performance impacts during the Beijing 2008 Summer Olympics.

As such, it was clear that Grant had something useful to add to the news debate at the time. He was also aware that being able to show people how we can make measurements of air quality from an aircraft would be a good and exciting way to highlight innovative research methods, helping people to understand how air quality impacts are felt much further away than the cities in which the pollution is originally emitted. As such, Grant issued a press release through his university's press office that described the project, which was picked up by the BBC Science Editor who then asked to join Grant and his colleagues on a research flight around London to film and interview the team while they recorded and discussed data in real-time as it was measured.

Before filming began, the editor and Grant discussed what each of them wanted to talk about and what questions would be asked. This allowed Grant to carefully plan his narrative and set constraints on what he would and would not be willing or able to talk about. Sadly, not all media interviews afford you the luxury of a detailed discussion on the contents of an interview in advance. Similarly, live interviews do not offer you the chance to re-record (see section 6.5) but setting your personal constraints in advance (if only in your own head) is always important for any interview, as we shall discuss in section 6.4.

> **Exercise: Draft a press release**
> Think about your research or a topic of research that interests you. Make a list of some of the recent key findings from that discipline or from results of your own research. From this list, rank or group those findings in order of which you think may be of most interest to a non-scientific audience.
>
> Next create a maximum ten word title that encapsulates your highest ranked finding or group of findings. Develop a 50 word summary or sub-title for this element. In a further 200 words, explain the context and background to this aspect and explain why it is an important story for a mass audience.
>
> To conclude, provide two quotes (each not exceeding 40 words) that succinctly express a key message about this research, and include contact details for further inquiries. If a press office is available within your organisation, forward this draft press release to them for review and suggestions. Ensure you inform them of your intention not to release it at this stage.

6.4 Constructing a narrative for mass media

Formalising and scoping a message for mass media depends on what form of media you are dealing with, and how much space (in the case of a written article) or time (in the case of an interview) you are given to present it. However, there are some common rules to all media content to keep in mind:

- **Keep it simple.** Talk in non-technical language wherever possible.
- **Keep it on point.** Define and discuss a narrow scope and do not stray too far from this narrative, ideally identifying one key point you know you need to make.
- **Be clear.** Do not make vague statements and do not use ambiguous language.
- **Be accurate.** Make sure you have researched what you are saying (or may be asked) and you know what you are talking about; otherwise, why are you doing it?

The paramount thing to bear in mind is ensuring that a journalist, reader, or viewer cannot extract and highlight any statement from your press release, article, comment, or interview that you are not comfortable making or did not intend. You may hear of individuals who have been aggrieved because they were misquoted or misunderstood in the press. In science, this is rarer than in a field like politics, where debate is often concerned with attitudes and viewpoints as they evolve. But contentious and emotional debates do surround science—take the climate crisis or vaccinations, for example.

Editorial policy may guide the context of how you might be quoted or questioned. However, much of the time any misunderstanding may be completely unintentional and due to an unbiased journalist simply not understanding what it is you are trying to tell them. Your job is therefore to minimise the risk of misunderstanding by carefully constructing any quote, article, or press release, and (where possible) taking the opportunity to first discuss your story with the press office, journalist, or producer informally so that you each have the chance to make sure there is a mutual understanding of the facts and the tone.

It is extremely rare that you will be led into a false sense of security and understanding only to be later thrown off balance through unexpected or off-topic lines of interviewing. This happened to Grant only once. He agreed to be interviewed live on a radio station about the impacts of volcanic ash on aircraft after a volcanic eruption in 2010. After a very quick telephone call with a polite producer telling him he would be interviewed about the science of volcanic ash in the atmosphere, he found himself personally accused (live) of being responsible for deciding to ground aircraft over Europe and inconveniencing the lives of thousands. Without any chance to reply, the phone was put down and he never heard from the producer again. In this specific case, the producer was may have just been looking for anyone that the radio presenter could have a one-way rant at. The station certainly wasn't interested in a meaningful interview. Pretty much all that Grant had a chance to say was 'hello'. And they certainly did not bother to find out if he was the right person to interview for what they wanted to talk about. Instead, they seem to have been looking for someone (anyone it would turn out) to blame to feed a public frenzy about travel inconvenience.

To mitigate the risk of something like this occurring to you, always conduct your own background check on the TV channel, show, presenter, or newspaper beforehand. Evaluate the likelihood of being allowed to present the honest message you want to communicate.

If you find yourself faced with an interviewer, panel member, or audience question where your viewpoint or science may be attacked, try to remain calm and objective, no matter how unsettled you may feel. It is helpful to bear in mind that mainstream mass media in many countries is concerned with open debate and public interest

Open debate is best served through a rational discussion of facts from the viewpoint of the researcher. The more politically biased elements of mass media and the rise of 'fake news' can, however, make such discourse very challenging. But our duty as scientists is to call this out where it occurs and passionately, yet honestly, defend objectivity and fact.

While heated debate and personal accusation can make for exciting reality television, scientific debate is rarely convincing or useful when it diverges too far from objective reasoning. In this scenario, you need to stay focused on discussing the facts as you understand them. Avoid being drawn into a wider discussion where you may not be qualified to speak; a calm and professional demeanour is always preferable while delivering any message. This is particularly true when being asked for an opinion on a politically charged subject. Scientists are trusted for their skill in objective reasoning; straying too far into opinion does not align with such values unless that opinion is properly weighted in the context of scientific consensus or is grounded in one's own research.

Most science journalists will take the time to ensure that they understand any story from your perspective and afford you an opportunity to comment or amend anything they write or present. Often, the more serious and professional media organisations may even go a step further and verify that what you have said is accurate by consulting other sources, and you may even be asked to reconfirm your story if inconsistencies of fact or opinion are discovered. Only rarely may you be asked to speak or comment without having an opportunity to discuss the detail of any interaction in advance, even when preparing for live interviews. If you're not comfortable or confident that what you have to say will be accurately presented, you should express this and withdraw from the process.

Now that you have decided you want to engage with mass media, how do you go about putting together a solid and accurate quote or story for everyone to see? There are several basic steps you should take to get ready beforehand, whether you are going live, recorded, or written. You need to break down the information you want to share into simple and self-contained parts and determine (at least for yourself) where your story starts and where it ends. This will help to prevent going too far off-topic and discussing things you are not professionally qualified to discuss. And if you ever mix personal guesses and scientific fact, make it clear which is which. Just like in the Q&A part of any scientific conference presentation (see chapter 4), do not try to answer a question definitively if you do not know the answer.

6.5 Television and radio interviews

Earlier in this chapter we looked at preparing a narrative for mass media in general terms. Here we will talk about what it is like in practice to give TV and radio interviews. We will approach this from the point of view of someone doing this for the first time and we certainly fall well short of discussing how to present a TV or radio show; something that requires specialist training and experience, and perhaps a broader career aspiration.

Of all mass media, subjecting oneself to a television camera or a live microphone can be the most unnerving. Even after over 100 such interviews, both live and pre-recorded, it is still natural to feel a little nervous. But it is equally important to keep calm and not panic. Different people will react differently—some of us are more confident than others—but with preparation, training, practice, and experience (and breathing), it can become easier and more rewarding. In this section, we will attempt to take some of the mystery out of the process of appearing on television and radio by citing personal experiences and offering some tips and advice. It is also worth noting that much of the advice presented in chapter 4 is also extremely useful for these situations.

As already discussed, preparation is the first step for any interview. This involves determining what you do and do not want to say and discussing the content of any interview or questioning with the journalist, producer, or presenter beforehand. In the case of live TV news or radio interviews, you will usually be contacted by a producer who will discuss and agree on any interview with you over the phone well in advance. This may be several hours prior to, or even the day before, any interview, where you will be invited to talk informally about the subject you will discuss on air. You will have a chance at this stage to ensure that both you and the producer know what you will and will not feel comfortable discussing. This is a two-way preparative exercise—the producer will be looking to gauge how well informed you are, and whether you will be able to articulate your message live on air, while you need to make sure you ask any questions to put your mind at ease. You may then be invited and given a time to arrive at a studio or told a time that a presenter and camera crew will come to you. This may then give you some additional time to prepare.

Live TV news interviews can assume one of three forms: a face-to-face interview with a presenter or anchor in a studio; a remote interview from a regional studio, where you will typically only hear (and not see) the presenter through an earpiece or headset; and face-to-face interviews with a presenter out in the field. The remote studio interview is the most unnerving for the uninitiated. You will typically meet with a producer or crew member in the Green Room of a studio, where you will have a final opportunity to discuss the interview before being ushered into a sound-proofed room. A technical crew member will then prepare you for camera and sound.

You will next briefly communicate over the microphone with a member of the Gallery, comprised of a team of directors and technicians. They will ensure you can hear the studio and inform you of when you will be live with the presenter. You can hear the live sound feed at this point, offering you a few moments to listen to the news as if you were at home. If well-prepared, overthinking the interview can be counter-productive and only add to your nerves at this stage. Remember to breathe deeply during any pauses in speaking and try to be conscious of any body language or nervous fidgeting. A good way to mitigate this is to practise in front of a webcam or camera at home, and to watch out for anything that may not look professional on camera (see chapter 4 for further advice regarding managing yourself). Actions such as scratching rarely come across well; but appropriate use of hand movements, head tilt and good eye contact with the camera can really help to emphasise your message. Body language such as this can be unnatural for some, but with careful thought and avoidance of more negative body language, it is possible to project confidence and clarity. Simple measures such as maintaining an upright and straight stance when sitting or standing can also help in this regard.

You may find your responses to the questions during the actual interview to be quite automatic, especially if you and the producer have scoped it out well in advance. Try to make sure that your key points have been made early. Answer any questions that you can, avoid those that you may not know the answer to, and make clear where opinion, rather than scientific evidence, may be introduced.

Face-to-face, live studio interviews are a little more comfortable as you can see the presenter and benefit from being able to interact with their body language in a way that you cannot in remote studios. From our own experiences, field interviews are more comfortable still, since the field presenter (if not acting as an anchor) typically has some time to talk to you ahead of the live interview and discuss any questions with you further, which you may find naturally helps to put you at ease.

Live radio interviews are not so very different from those for television. The process and setting are broadly the same—you may be face-to-face with a presenter in a remote studio (or speaking on the phone), or out with a roving reporter. We recommend approaching radio interviews in the same way as TV interviews, and when speaking to a presenter to behave exactly as you would in normal conversation, including using gesticulations or body language, which naturally help to project clear oral communication.

Some tried-and-tested tips on handling live interviews are to:

1. **Always be respectful.** Do not continue talking about a drawn-out subject when the presenter has asked you to stop.
2. **Do not interrupt.** Or be interrupted .... If you are interrupted, and the interview continues, remember to come back to your key messages if they have not been made already.
3. **Demonstrate passion (pathos).** Speak clearly, confidently, and with intonation.
4. **Be aware of yourself.** Be mindful of nervous body movements and actions like swaying, scratching your head, or playing with your clothes.
5. **Feel free to use gestures.** Use emphatic body language such as a head tilt and hand movements if these come naturally to you. But use these sparingly and with subtlety.

6. **Watch your posture.** Sit or stand as tall and upright as possible.
7. **Avoid filler.** Try to avoid using 'erm' or 'so' at the start of sentences. Instead, take a quiet moment to compose your answer if you need to. These 'filler' words are often used to help us formulate a response in stressful situations, but they do not present well.
8. **Be aware of your limitations.** Do not attempt to answer anything that you do not know about. Instead, answer by politely reminding the interviewer about what you are there to discuss. Or better still, explain how such a question could be answered with further science if appropriate.
9. **Behave appropriately.** Remember you may be on the record (and you should ask if unsure), be mindful about not saying anything you would not want to see reported or quoted and attributed to you.
10. **Practise in front of a camera yourself.** You will be surprised how any recording device can naturally force you to behave as though there was really an audience there.

As well as the interviewer–responder setting of a live interview, recorded interviews can also include features for science documentaries or other media outputs. These settings are broadly like live interviews, with the exception that you may have the chance to re-record any sections with which you are unhappy. In addition, the production team may have the opportunity to edit any material prior to release.

Curiously, we have both found that simply knowing that there is the luxury to re-record material means that you are more likely to make verbal mistakes in pre-recorded settings, while the pressure of live interviews seems to always ensure that you get it right first time. This has especially been the case when recording one-way monologues for documentaries and may be because the absence of someone asking specific questions means that you are often left to formulate your own thoughts, meaning that what you have to say becomes less of an automatic response and more of a voluntary choice. In such a setting it can help if you ask one of the presenters or other crew members to give you prompts. These could be written cues or verbal questions that remind you about what you have prepared in advance, thereby helping to break down any monologue into manageable sections. However, in all cases, it remains important to scope out and list the general content of what you need to say, especially if this concerns any important facts or figures that it may be important not to get wrong.

We need to clarify the distinction between offering an opinion and providing objective conclusions in any interview context. Imagine that you are being interviewed about air quality in a major city, and you are spotlighting measurements that you have recorded and published. Also, imagine that these data illustrate that air quality is often poor in the area where you recorded your measurements, and surpasses some regulatory threshold defined as a risk to health. Lastly, imagine that you are nearing the end of an interview and you have explained your measurements and have also (rightly) conveyed an objective viewpoint that there might be an impact on human health. This is a justified and appropriate objective viewpoint as it is based on your own published research, and in this instance, it is your own analysis that directly links your measurements to regulatory thresholds that define a risk to public health. But what if the interviewer asks you 'in the light of your research, would you live in this city?' This is entirely a type of question you might be asked, as it is a question very much related to the public interest that the media serves, and on a topic for which you are perceived to be an expert. Take a moment to think about what you would say before reading on? Would you answer the question directly? Would you answer the question honestly? Think carefully because your answer could be very powerful and influence the lives of many people. It may also anger some city authority should they disagree. If you said 'no', your answer may well be an honest opinion (especially if you do not live there). But ask yourself if you would honestly encourage others to move out of the city for their own health, as this is the true basis of the question you have been asked.

A more objective answer to the true basis of the question might be to refer to the science and suggest that your results relate to, for example, a fixed period and location, and that someone's choice of where to live may not be based solely on their exposure to air pollution, and that it is a matter of personal choice, made up of many different factors. You may also wish to say that the science on health risks is based on large population studies, that risk at a personal and individual level may well be different, and that further research is required to better understand the impacts on individuals. You could even go a little further and state that it is important that air quality should be improved through better policy. Such an approach steers your answer back toward the science you are discussing and away from a personal and emotional opinion, despite what the interviewer may want you to say.

These are incredibly difficult types of questions to prepare for in advance, but pondering potential questions and role-playing some scenarios with friends and colleagues can help train you to deal with them objectively. Very rarely, you might then be challenged on why you have not answered such a question directly. If that happens, you could politely reply by suggesting that it is not a decision you have to make or refer the interviewer to the response you have already given. If you do choose to give an honest (but personal and emotive) answer, always be clear that that is what you have done and be mindful of the authority and responsibility that your title as a scientist affords you.

A further salient example may help here. Climate science is a particularly politically charged subject area at the current time. We may hear of 'believers' and 'deniers' and some media outlets may be editorially aligned with one viewpoint or another, while yet others fall over themselves attempting to 'balance' a debate when the overwhelming proportion of practicing climate scientists subscribe to the objective view that climate change is real (and happening now) and a result of humanity's greenhouse gas emissions. A particular tactic used by some deniers who seek to undermine this scientific consensus has been to confront scientists with complex pseudo-science (read nonsense) during an interview. For example, by suggesting that we are currently in a natural glacial minimum and that climate change can be explained by orbital variations or sunspot activity. A climate scientist will know that the rapid changes observed this century do not correlate with the slow precessions of the equinoxes or with sunspot activity, and that climate models (with sound underpinning physics) show that (measured) increasing greenhouse gas concentrations do explain and predict observed temperature rise. Yet explaining all of this during an interview in detail and in full can take a significant amount of time. The denier will know that a throwaway question like 'isn't it all to do with sunspots?' will require you to give a lengthy and technical answer to fully satisfy the question.

The act of asking a short but catchy question and the act of giving a lengthy and technical reply can act to weaken the arguments of the climate scientist in the eyes of the audience. We have been faced with situations like this. If attempting to give a detailed technical answer in this scenario just is not possible given time constraints and the nature of the audience (who may not follow the technical details needed to explain it well), it can be better to reflect the question. For example, the climate scientist could reply with 'No—they do not correlate with measurements this century. Can you explain the physical evidence you have for such a claim?'. Such a reply can keep the debate objective and prevent others from putting you on the back-foot. To be clear, we would not advocate to avoid answering questions like the one above completely, but to think about the time you have available and if that time would be better spent asking the questioner to justify their position while reiterating your objective truth.

Exercise: Practise for a live interview
Pass your press release prepared the previous exercise in this chapter to a friend or colleague who is willing to help you by acting as a TV interviewer. Ask them to prepare a list of questions to ask you based on the press release but ask them not to share this with you in advance.

Set up a webcam or video camera with a microphone in a quiet room where you and your interviewer can attempt to recreate a live interview experience. Focus the camera on you from a frontal aspect but with your interviewer out of view. This is because we want to simulate the pressure and attention on you (and not your interviewer). Ask your friend or colleague to interview you about your chosen topic and record it. You could ask your mock interviewer to think of some particularly difficult questions, especially ones designed to elicit an emotive and/or personal response.

Watch the interview back, preferably with your friend or colleague, and reflect on how well your message(s) came across. Focus also on your style of delivery, confidence and clarity, and body language. Is there anything that you are unhappy with or which you could improve? Repeat this as many times as you can until you feel more confident and natural in front of a camera. To take this further, you could consider making this scenario a regular part of your professional life by recording a podcast or video about popular science in your field and uploading this to a video hosting site such as YouTube (see chapter 7 for more details).

6.6 Summary

In this chapter, we have explored several methods of interacting with mass media, offering valuable insights and guidance for researchers eager to communicate scientific messages effectively. From laying the groundwork for recorded media interviews to navigating live sessions, the chapter sheds light on various dimensions, ensuring that the researcher's perspective remains clear and understandable to their audience.

Even though facing the media can be a daunting task, the chapter highlights the significant impact of such engagement. It is not just about disseminating information; it is also about sparking inspiration and fostering a substantial societal change driven by scientific advancements.

6.7 Further study

The further study in this chapter is related to gaining experience with mass media, it should make you think further about how to best to get their attention and to promote yourself and your research in an effective way when you do:

- **Pitch an idea.** Go to the website of a popular science magazine or TV show and look for their submissions page. Using the press release that you have developed in this chapter, along with the guidance for submissions, pitch an idea based around your current or future research. One potential target for submission is *The Conversation*, a not-for-profit media outlet that uses content sourced from academics and researchers.
- **Listen to a science radio show.** Find a regular scientific radio show (e.g. 'The Life Scientific' with Professor Jim Al-Khalili on BBC Radio 4). Make a note of what you find interesting about the programme. Is there any aspect that you find unengaging? Could you imagine yourself being a contributor on that programme? If so, then how do you go about becoming one?
- **Watch other scientists.** Look online for a recent TV interview with a scientific researcher. Do they come across well? Are they able to communicate their research in a succinct and entertaining manner? Do they engage with the other people in the studio? Try and observe if there are any other examples of good practice that you could learn from, or any bad habits that you potentially see in yourself, and which should be avoided.
- **Register your expertise.** A practical approach to gain visibility is by registering your area of expertise with the press office at your own institute. Familiarise yourself with the press or media office at your institution and make your specialisation known to them. This proactive step ensures that your name is on the list for any relevant enquiries or opportunities, making it easier for the media to find you for expert commentary or insights within your field.

6.8 Suggested reading

Chapters 1 and 2 of *The Sciences' Media Connection—Public Communication and its Repercussions* [2] are especially relevant to this chapter and discuss the impact of science and science communication in society. *Introducing Science Communication: A Practical Guide* [3] also offers some helpful advice on dealing and engaging with the media. For a focussed analysis on news coverage and expertise, the article 'Are experts (news) worthy?' [4] looks at over 280 000 news stories on ten major issues. It finds that the news often highlights views that experts agree on rather than showing different perspectives. Similarly, 'Science audiences, misinformation, and fake news' [5] explores how and why citizens become (and sometimes remain) misinformed about science, while 'Understanding influences, misinformation, and fact-checking concerning climate-change journalism in Pakistan' [6] provides a case study for how we can tackle such misinformation.

References

[1] O'Shea S J *et al* 2014 Area fluxes of carbon dioxide, methane, and carbon monoxide derived from airborne measurements around Greater London: a case study during summer 2012 *J. Geophys. Res.: Atmos.* **119** 4940–52

[2] Rödder S, Franzen M and Weingart P 2011 *The Sciences' Media Connection–Public Communication and its Repercussions* (Berlin: Springer) vol 28

[3] Brake M L and Weitkamp E 2009 *Introducing Science Communication: A Practical Guide* (New York: Macmillan)

[4] Merkley E 2020 Are experts (news) worthy? Balance, conflict, and mass media coverage of expert consensus *Political Commun.* **37** 530–49

[5] Scheufele D A and Krause N M 2019 Science audiences, misinformation, and fake news *Proc. Natl Acad. Sci.* **116** 7662–9

[6] Ejaz W, Ittefaq M and Arif M 2022 Understanding influences, misinformation, and fact-checking concerning climate-change journalism in Pakistan *Journal. Pract.* **16** 404–24

IOP Publishing

Effective Science Communication (Third Edition)
A practical guide to surviving as a scientist
Sam Illingworth and Grant Allen

Chapter 7

Establishing an online presence

There was a time when people felt the internet was another world, but now people realise it's a tool that we use in this world.

—Tim Berners-Lee

7.1 Introduction

The twenty-first century has brought us many scientific breakthroughs and technological advancements, but one of the most transformative impacts has been the rapid evolution of the internet. From its humble beginnings as a limited collection of static webpages accessible to only a few, the internet has now become an omnipresent force that permeates every aspect of our lives.

While the internet has its fair share of distractions and critics, we cannot overlook the profound revolution it has brought to the field of science. Today, scientists have unprecedented opportunities to collaborate and share knowledge on a global scale. Through the internet, we can effortlessly exchange data, collaborate on documents, engage in video conferences with colleagues from around the world, and instantly access an immense wealth of peer-reviewed research.

The internet has empowered individuals in a personal capacity as well. We now can effortlessly share images, videos, and stories with friends, colleagues, and strangers, with just a click of a button or a gentle touch on our screens. The internet has opened new avenues for personal expression and connection, allowing us to share our experiences, passions, and ideas with a vast and diverse audience.

In the realm of digital communication, artificial intelligence (AI) tools have also emerged as invaluable resources for scientists. AI-powered algorithms can assist in analysing vast amounts of data, extracting meaningful insights, and automate repetitive tasks. Additionally, generative AI tools such as chatbots and virtual assistants have become increasingly prevalent in science communication. These intelligent tools can engage with an audience, answer questions, and provide personalised recommendations, enhancing the interactive experience and fostering deeper engagement with scientific content.

Considering the internet's remarkable capacity for sharing research, fostering collaborations, and leveraging AI tools, it has become increasingly important for scientists to establish and maintain a digital footprint. While this may initially appear daunting or burdensome, cultivating an engaging online presence enables us, as scientists, to expand our communication channels.

This chapter is dedicated to offering practical guidance on how to create a digital footprint tailored to your specific needs, experiences, and expectations. By leveraging AI-driven solutions alongside effective online strategies, scientists can unlock new realms of scientific discovery, enhance communication with different publics, and make significant contributions to their respective fields.

In this chapter, we have deliberately chosen not to provide references or direct links to the websites or tools mentioned. The reason for this omission is due to the dynamic nature of the internet, where websites and platforms can change or become outdated over time. Explore and discover these websites through your preferred search engine or web browser. We should also note that at the time of writing this third edition, generative AI had only recently been commercialised on a global scale, and we strongly expect that what is written here in 2023 will be already by somewhat dated by 2024.

7.2 Blogs

One of the easiest and most rewarding ways to start building your digital presence is by creating a blog. Blogs are online platforms where you can share your research findings, reflect on recent field campaigns, or raise awareness about important issues that demand attention. You may also choose to write reviews of recent publications or discuss the political landscape of science in a specific country. Blogs are not limited to text alone; you have the freedom to share pictures from your research or even display time-lapse videos of your experiments or fieldwork. With so many possibilities, you need to first define your message by considering what you want to say, why you want to say it, and who your intended audience is.

When determining the content of your blog, it is wise to explore existing science blogs to see what is already out there. Many active researchers maintain personal blogs where they share their work and experiences, while blog networks like Scientific American and IFL Science provide platforms for a diverse range of scientists to share their stories. As you read these blogs, you will quickly realise that the most successful ones, in terms of quality and readership, offer unique perspectives while maintaining a distinctive voice. Like writing for scientific journals, it is important to avoid simply rehashing existing content and instead strive to contribute something new. As discussed in chapter 4 and chapter 5, you also need to fully consider your target audience. Most science blogs cater to a non-scientific audience, as this maximises readership. However, if you aim to reach a more scientific audience, such as researchers in your field or scientists in general, make sure to justify why it is important to engage this specific audience. When writing for a non-scientific audience, consider any shared interests or characteristics your readers may have. For instance, if your blog focuses on environmental change research, consider targeting nature enthusiasts as well. Considering your target audience and the reasons for reaching them will help you tailor your blog content accordingly.

Here are some valuable pointers to help you craft a successful blog in your own style:

1. **Keep it concise.** Aim for blog posts between 400 and 600 words. While there may be occasions that call for more in-depth content, longer posts often attract a smaller readership.
2. **Seek input from non-scientists.** When writing your initial blog entries, enlist the help of friends or family members who lack a scientific background. Ask them to identify sections that may be unclear or in need of further explanation.
3. **Embrace originality and provoke thought.** Readers are often drawn to fresh perspectives or a unique spin on familiar topics. Feel free to express your opinions or emotions alongside scientific evidence if you are prepared to defend them when necessary, making sure to distinguish between scientific facts and personal viewpoints.
4. **Maintain a consistent posting schedule.** Begin by publishing one post every two weeks, gradually increasing the frequency to weekly or more regular updates as you gain confidence and refine your style. Consistency is key, as readers may lose interest if you only update your blog every six months.
5. **Engage with your readers.** Encourage interaction by responding to comments and engaging in meaningful conversations with your audience. Building a community around your blog fosters connection and encourages loyal readership. Blogging is not just about sharing your ideas, but also about creating a dialogue with your readers.

Once you have determined what you want to express, who your target audience is, and the format your blog will take, think about where you will host your blog. Numerous websites offer hosting services, either for free or at a fee. Take the time to explore various platforms and read blogs hosted on them to find one that aligns with the essence of your content. While WordPress, Blogger, and Tumblr are among the most popular blogging platforms, there are many others to choose from. These platforms provide detailed tutorials to guide you through the technical aspects of setting up your blog, and you can also find dedicated user groups within their communities to offer further support and assistance.

As noted above, engaging with other bloggers, both on your chosen platform and across different blogging sites, helps you in attracting followers and fostering a vibrant community. If readers interact with your blog or leave comments, try to respond promptly and in an engaging manner. While defending your opinions is important, as an ethical scientist, be willing to admit if you have made a mistake.

Engaging in public threads, especially on polarising topics such as the climate crisis, can sometimes lead to unwarranted personal attacks and severe abuse. For those who have experienced this toxicity, it is a harsh reminder of the darker side of online interactions. Therefore, it is crucial to approach these conversations with caution, armed with strategies to protect your mental wellbeing. Knowing when to step back, maintaining a professional demeanour, and seeking support from peers will help you in navigating this terrain. While this chapter does not deal with the toxicity encountered online, you need to aware of its existence and to prioritise your mental health (see chapter 10) when dealing with it.

You have probably heard of internet trolls—individuals who post defamatory and inflammatory comments while often concealing their true identities. If you encounter any trolls on your blog, which may be more likely if you are discussing a contentious topic, remember that as the blog owner, you have ultimate control. Simply delete the offensive comment without responding. If it violates the community guidelines of your blogging platform, you should also report the person to the platform's administrative staff. Depriving these bullies of the attention they seek is the best way to deal with them effectively. However, be careful not to cancel the honest (but polite) views of others, no matter how misinformed. Genuine and polite constructive disagreement should never be confused with abuse and can be engaged with in kind.

If the thought of maintaining a weekly blog post feels overwhelming, there is an alternative approach that you might find appealing. Consider joining a collective group of like-minded bloggers who share a similar vision and passion. By collaborating with colleagues or engaging with existing communities such as ScienceBlog and the PLOS Blogs Network, you can contribute to a collective platform where you share your own ideas and insights.

Another option to explore is writing a standalone piece and publishing it on a social journalism site. One of the most well-known platforms for this purpose is Medium, an online publishing platform that serves as a host for writers to highlight their stories. The advantage of using platforms like Medium is that you do not have to work as hard to build an audience from scratch, since you have the potential to reach readers across the entire site. However, your content still needs to stand out and catch the interest of readers, enticing them to click on your post and read more of your writing.

7.3 Podcasts

> **Exercise: Write a blog**
> Begin by planning out what you want to convey and how you want to express it. Will you share intriguing aspects of your research or captivate readers with tales of the mesmerising locations you explore during your fieldwork? Whichever path you choose, ensure that your theme remains broad enough to provide you with ample material to write about for months to come. It is good practice to plan and outline three to five engaging topics that align with your chosen theme.
>
> Once you have determined the 'how' and 'why' of your message, shift your focus to your target audience. Why do you want to engage with them and how do you know that they would want to engage with you (and your writing)? After you have identified your audience, explore a few different blogging platforms and identify the one that resonates most with your style and objectives. As you write your first post, try to incorporate the tips for successful blogging mentioned earlier in this section. Console yourself in the knowledge that your first few blog posts might not be particularly well written or well read, and that as with presenting (see chapter 4) both things will improve with time and practice.

A podcast is an audio blog that allows you to communicate with your audience through the power of sound. Recording a podcast does not require expensive equipment or extensive technical skills. All you need is a computer with free editing software, a decent microphone, and an online platform to host your recorded episodes.

Like writing a blog, the first step is to determine what you want to convey, why it is important to you, and who your target audience is. Once you have clarity on these aspects, consider the following steps:

1. **Choose your format.** Will you conduct one-on-one interviews, engage in round-table discussions, or create solo episodes? For sole episodes, you can

enhance your storytelling (and give listeners a break from your voice) by incorporating relevant sound effects or ambient noises. For instance, if you are discussing the atmospheric effects of a recent rainstorm, consider adding the soothing sound of rainfall in the background. Many different websites, such as Freesound, offer collections of Creative Commons-licensed sounds for you to use in this way.

2. **Plan and structure your episodes.** Before hitting the record button, outline the content of each episode. Consider the key points you want to cover, the flow of the conversation or narrative, and any supporting materials such as interviews, guest appearances, or sound clips. A well-structured episode ensures clarity for your listeners and helps you stay organised during the recording and editing process.

3. **Select recording and editing software.** Experiment with different toolkits until you find one that suits your preferences. Audacity®, a free, open-source software, comes highly recommended for professional-quality recording. It is user-friendly and compatible across various platforms.

4. **Find an ideal recording location.** If you are recording indoors, choose a quiet room devoid of distractions and external noise. Silence or mute any electronic devices that may disrupt the recording process. If you are recording outdoors, aim for an environment that complements your content, contributing to the overall ambiance and communication. Always capture a few seconds of background noise at the beginning and end of each recording, allowing for the removal of any unwanted sounds in the editing process.

5. **Invest in a quality microphone.** Consider purchasing a practical USB microphone that directly connects to your computer. These typically cost between £50 and £100, but the investment is worthwhile as such a device significantly enhances the professional quality of your podcast. If you frequently record in different locations or conduct interviews on the go, a digital voice recorder or a lapel microphone attached to your smartphone with a voice recording app are also recommended,

6. **Pay attention to transitions.** Just as a smooth transition between scenes in a theatrical play is crucial for audience reception, well-thought-out transitions between segments of your podcast can elevate its impact. Plan your segues and consider incorporating intro and outro music to create a more memorable listening experience.

7. **Choose a hosting platform.** Numerous free options are available for hosting your podcast, some of which offer premium features for additional data storage or marketing opportunities. Anchor, Podbean, and Buzzsprout are among the top choices to consider.

8. **Get listed in podcast directories.** Once you have selected a hosting platform, make sure that your podcast reaches a wider audience by submitting it to podcast directories. Apple Podcasts is perhaps the best known, but Google Podcasts, Spotify, and Stitcher all have significant user bases.

9. **Promote your podcast.** Spread the word about your podcast by informing your friends and colleagues, inviting them to subscribe and leave favourable reviews on their preferred podcast directories. Use your other social media platforms to keep your followers updated on new episodes and consider including a link to your podcast in your email signature.
10. **Promote and collaborate with other podcasters.** Networking and collaboration can expand your reach and introduce your podcast to new audiences. Engage with other podcasters in your niche by participating in cross-promotion initiatives, guest appearances, or collaborative episodes. Share each other's content on social media platforms, collaborate on joint marketing efforts, and leverage each other's audiences to mutually grow your listener base.

Many of the key strategies for maintaining a successful blog also apply to effectively managing a podcast. You should consistently release new episodes and try to actively engage with your listeners, rather than just sharing audio recordings without any further interaction.

To understand the potential of different podcast formats and find your own style, we recommend exploring the following five podcasts that demonstrate excellent content, production values, and a clear target audience. These diverse shows encompass various formats, ranging from panel discussions to intimate one-on-one interviews. You can easily find them in your preferred podcast directory, and listening to at least one episode from each will assist you in determining which approach aligns best with your own vision:

1. **The Infinite Monkey Cage.** Presented by physicist Brian Cox and comedian Robin Ince, this witty and entertaining podcast combines science and comedy. Each episode features a panel of experts and celebrities discussing scientific concepts, discoveries, and their implications in a light-hearted manner.
2. **Ologies.** Hosted by writer, actress, and science enthusiast Alie Ward, each episode of 'Ologies' focuses on a different field of study, exploring various '-ologies' such as anthropology, geology, and entomology. Alie interviews experts in their respective fields, uncovering their scientific insights and stories.
3. **Science Vs.** Hosted by journalist Wendy Zukerman, this podcast investigates popular topics and myths, applying scientific analysis and critical thinking to separate fact from fiction. It tackles subjects ranging from alternative medicine to the climate crisis, presenting evidence-based perspectives.
4. **The Poetry of Science.** This is a podcast hosted by Sam Illingworth, which uses poetry as a medium to present and convey new scientific research. It intertwines the beauty of language with the wonders of science, offering a distinct and artistic approach in bite-sized episodes of 5–10 min.
5. **Hidden Brain.** Hosted by journalist and writer Shankar Vedantam, 'Hidden Brain' explores the unconscious patterns that shape human behaviour. Through interviews, storytelling, and research findings, the podcast offers

insights into the workings of the mind and the influences that drive our decisions.

7.4 Social media

Social media platforms play a vital role in connecting people and facilitating communication in today's digital age. As a scientist, it is important to leverage these platforms to promote and advance your research. While there is a wide range of social media platforms available, including blogs and podcasts, you need to choose the ones that best align with your goals and preferences.

New social media platforms emerge frequently, and their popularity fluctuates constantly. It is impractical to provide an exhaustive list of all platforms, as the details become outdated quickly. Instead, we will highlight a few social media platforms that are currently considered effective for building a strong digital footprint as a scientist. Keep in mind that the technical aspects of these platforms may change, so it is advisable to explore and experiment with them first-hand.

When selecting social media platforms, prioritise those that align with your research goals and resonate with your preferred interface, accessibility, and ease of use. Try to manage your time effectively to avoid becoming overwhelmed by the multitude of platforms available.

As a scientists, you also have a responsibility to familiarise yourself with the social media policy of any organisation you are associated with or represent. Each institution may have specific guidelines regarding the use of social media platforms and maintaining an online presence. By understanding and adhering to these policies, you can ensure that your online activities align with the organisation's values and objectives. Pay attention to rules about confidentiality, privacy, appropriate language, and professional conduct. Remember to always adhere to ethical guidelines and privacy considerations when sharing scientific content on social media. Additionally, be mindful of copyright restrictions when using images or other media in your posts. Being aware of these policies not only safeguards your professional reputation but also demonstrates your commitment to responsible and ethical social media usage.

7.4.1 X (the platform formerly known as Twitter)

X (formerly known as Twitter before its recent rebranding) is a social media platform that allows you to connect with others and share your thoughts in 280 characters or fewer. While X does offer a paid premium version with additional features, the free version remains highly valuable for science communication even after the transition from Twitter, providing ample functionality to connect with a global audience, engage in conversations, and share scientific insights effectively. While some users have migrated to alternative platforms such as Mastodon, Bluesky, and Threads, X remains a valuable platform for science communication even after its rebranding

Here are some tips to make the most of X:

1. **Choose a memorable handle.** Pick a handle that is unique and easy to remember. Choose something like @samillingworth rather than @poems_science_games_sam. Also, include a clear profile picture, banner image, and a concise bio that accurately describes your interests and areas of expertise.
2. **Post regularly.** Aim to send out at least three to five posts per day to maintain and grow your followership. Be strategic about the timing of your posts, targeting morning and evening commutes, as well as lunch breaks when users are more likely to be active on X.
3. **Follow interesting people.** In addition to prominent researchers in your field, follow users who share intriguing insights about science in general. This broadens your network and exposes you to diverse perspectives.
4. **Advertise your research.** Share links to your latest publication or talk to expand its reach. Additionally, use X to promote other digital content, such as new blog posts or podcast episodes. The analytics function of X can also provide valuable insights into the impact of your posts.
5. **Use hashtags.** Hashtags (#) help categorise and organise ideas, making it easier for users to find your posts. Incorporate relevant hashtags, such as #scicomm for science communication-related posts, to increase visibility and engagement.
6. **Be concise.** With limited characters, focus on delivering concise messages. Embrace this challenge as an opportunity to refine and streamline your thoughts.
7. **Show personality.** Let your followers see your authentic self by sharing your interests, likes, and dislikes. If you are passionate about a cause, use X to promote it. Alternatively, if you prefer to keep personal opinions separate from scientific research, or if your institution discourages it, consider maintaining both a personal and professional account.
8. **Be polite.** Exercise good etiquette on X. Avoid posting anything you would not say in a crowded room or directly to someone's face. Remember, once your post is out there, it is public.
9. **Use alt text.** Alt text, short for alternative text, is a description you can add to an image to provide context for visually impaired or blind individuals who use screen readers. By including alt text, you make your content more accessible and inclusive, meaning that everyone can engage with your posts, regardless of their visual abilities.
10. **Post at conferences.** Amplify your visibility by using the official conference hashtag. Even if you cannot attend in person, following the hashtag allows you to stay updated on discussions and join online conversations.

7.4.2 Facebook

Facebook is a popular social networking service (owned and run by American technology giant Meta) that allows you to share information, photos, and videos with your friends and a wider audience. By creating a profile, you can showcase your interests, personality, and preferences to those you choose to share it with.

> **Exercise: Compose a post for X**
> Imagine an upcoming presentation you are giving. Condense the key points into a 280 character post. Focus on the core message you want to convey and express it in a clear, concise, and informative way. Consider using relevant hashtags to enhance its visibility and engagement. Challenge yourself to capture the essence of your presentation within the character limit while making it compelling and impactful.

Facebook's social aspect thrives on engaging with other users through reactions, comments, and personal messages. You can also create group chats and share files, making it a versatile communication platform. Additionally, Facebook offers the option to create pages for businesses or interests, serving as a central hub to share content, organise events, and invite followers.

Notable science-based Facebook Pages, such as 'News from Science', 'NASA', 'Physics Girl', and 'Physics World', have successfully built strong communities by posting engaging content that sparks interactions. While these examples may have broader scopes, they inspire the potential of Facebook Pages to connect with diverse audiences.

Facebook Groups provide an avenue for individuals to gather around common scientific interests and express opinions. From 'Basic Physics' to 'Quantum Mechanics', numerous science groups cater to specific topics. Some groups are open for anyone to join and participate, while others require membership approval. Discussions within Facebook Groups, especially on contentious scientific topics, may sometimes become heated and divisive. Many groups have established rules and entry questionnaires to discourage disruptive behaviour. However, with large memberships, complete moderation might be challenging, and instances of personal abuse can occur. In such cases, it is advised to follow the guidelines for dealing with online abuse, avoiding engagement with the abuser and reporting the incident to the Facebook Group administrator.

The issue of addressing abuse on social media platforms remains a topic of ongoing debate, reflecting the challenges of our society. As ethical scientists, we have a responsibility to speak out against such abuse and to respectfully consider diverse opinions. Actively seeking out and listening to differing perspectives is necessary to avoid echo chambers and promote constructive dialogue (see chapter 5), but not at the expense of our (or anyone else's) mental health or wellbeing.

7.4.3 YouTube

YouTube is a video-sharing website that allows users to upload, share, and interact with videos. It serves as a central platform for various channels, where content from individuals or organisations is organised. Subscribing to channels enables viewers to stay updated on the latest releases from their favourite YouTubers.

In addition to the abundance of cute cat videos and do-it-yourself tutorials, YouTube is home to many innovative science channels that exemplify effective science communication. Two highly acclaimed channels in this regard are vSauce and Veritasium. These channels boast millions of subscribers and offer engaging content covering a diverse range of scientific topics, from exploring concepts such as dark matter to analysing the discoveries of well-known scientists.

If you are considering creating your own YouTube channel, it is advisable to incorporate the advice discussed in sections 7.2 and 7.3 relating to blogs and podcasts, respectively. Additionally, collaborating with colleagues who possess filming and visual editing expertise (and equipment) can further enhance the quality of your videos. Many potentially captivating YouTube videos suffer from amateurish filming techniques, so leveraging the skills of experienced collaborators can make a significant difference. As you work on building your subscriber base, actively engage with other YouTube communities and consider guest appearances on the channels of successful YouTubers to bring your work to a wider audience.

Exercise: Get inspired by video
Visit YouTube and watch videos from channels such as vSauce and Veritasium (or choose another channel of interest). Read the comments section of popular videos and observe what resonates with the audience. If you have valuable insights to contribute, feel free to join the discussion.

7.4.4 Instagram

Instagram is a social media platform that allows users to share photos, videos, and stories with their followers. Because of its strong visual content, Instagram can be a valuable tool for science communication. Here are some tips for effectively using Instagram to engage with your audience and share your scientific work:

1. **Curate visually appealing content.** Instagram is all about captivating visuals. Take high-quality photos or create engaging graphics related to your research or scientific interests. Use compelling imagery to grab the attention of your audience.
2. **Craft informative captions.** Use the caption space to provide context and convey key information about the content you are sharing. Write in a concise and accessible manner, using language that is easily understood by a wide range of people. Consider including relevant hashtags to increase the discoverability of your posts.
3. **Show the human side.** Instagram is a platform where personal connections are valued. Share behind-the-scenes glimpses of your scientific work, such as lab experiments, fieldwork, or conferences. Highlighting the human aspect of science can help people relate to your work on a more personal level.
4. **Engage with the community.** Respond to comments on your posts, ask questions to initiate discussions, and interact with other science-related accounts by liking, commenting, and sharing their content. Building connections with fellow scientists and science enthusiasts can broaden your reach and foster meaningful collaborations.
5. **Use Instagram Stories.** Take advantage of Instagram's Stories feature to share real-time updates, short videos, or interactive polls. Stories provide an opportunity for more spontaneous and informal content that can give your audience a glimpse into your day-to-day scientific life.

7.4.5 TikTok

TikTok is a social media platform that allows users to create and share short videos. While it may be known for its entertaining and viral content, TikTok can also be a valuable tool for science communication. Here are some tips on effectively using TikTok to engage with your audience and share scientific knowledge:

Embrace the format. TikTok's format is unique, with videos typically lasting between 15 and 60 s. Use this short time limit to deliver quick and engaging scientific content that grabs attention. Consider creative ways to present scientific concepts, experiments, or interesting facts in a concise and entertaining manner.

Use storytelling techniques. TikTok thrives on storytelling. Craft your videos in a narrative format that captures viewers' curiosity and keeps them engaged. Tell a scientific story, explain a research breakthrough, or share an anecdote in an entertaining and relatable way.

Leverage trending challenges. TikTok is known for its viral challenges and trends. Participating in relevant science-related challenges or creating your own can help your content reach a wider audience. Put a scientific spin on popular challenges, adapting them to highlight scientific experiments or concepts.

Engage with the TikTok community. Interact with other users by commenting, duetting, or stitching their videos (the 'stitch' tool allows you to use clips of videos from other creators as part of your own video). Collaborate with fellow scientists or science enthusiasts on joint videos to amplify your reach. Respond to comments and questions and foster a sense of community around your scientific content.

Be authentic and relatable. TikTok values authenticity and relatability. Show your genuine enthusiasm for science and share personal experiences or insights. Use humour, storytelling, or visual effects to make complex concepts more accessible and enjoyable for viewers.

Exercise: Make a TikTok video
Create a TikTok video displaying a simple science experiment, such as a vinegar and baking soda volcano. Use visual effects and catchy music to make it captivating and memorable. In the caption, provide a brief explanation of the experiment and its relevance to broader scientific principles.

7.4.6 LinkedIn

LinkedIn is a professional networking service primarily used for business connections. It differs from Facebook by focusing on building and maintaining professional relationships. After creating a profile, which acts as a digital resume, you can join groups and connect with individuals on personal or professional grounds. In terms of effective science communication, LinkedIn is best used as an interactive discussion board and job market.

To leverage LinkedIn as a discussion board, join relevant groups related to your research field and scientific interests. Some groups require evidence of suitability, such as alumni affiliations or relevant expertise. Participating in these discussion boards helps you stay updated on current debates and collaborate with colleagues worldwide. Remember to respect others' opinions, contribute meaningful content, and avoid treating groups solely as advertising spaces for personal projects.

In addition to job searching, LinkedIn serves as a platform to highlight your professional profile and discover future opportunities. Keeping an updated profile, actively engaging in groups and discussions, and highlighting your employment history, qualifications, and achievements enhances your visibility to potential employers. Uploading key publications manually can be time-consuming, so select a few representative publications and provide links to other platforms like ORCID, Web of Science, or Google Scholar for easy access to your full portfolio.

LinkedIn allows you to list your skills, which can be endorsed by your connections, demonstrating your expertise to prospective employers and collaborators. Recommendations from previous employers and colleagues further strengthen your professional credibility.

We recommend creating a unique LinkedIn URL, which can be done for free. This URL can be placed at the top of a traditional CV, allowing potential employers to easily access more information about your achievements. Look at figure 7.1 for an example of a typical CV header, including LinkedIn and ORCID identifications (refer to section 7.6).

Sam Illingworth PhD

E: s.illingworth@napier.ac.uk • Edinburgh, UK
linkedin.com/in/samillingworth • orcid.org/0000-0003-2551-0675
www.samillingworth.com

Figure 7.1. Example of a CV header, showing LinkedIn and ORCID information.

Exercise: Update your LinkedIn profile
If you already have a LinkedIn profile, it is important to regularly update your information. Take some time to review and enhance your biography, ensuring it is concise and up to date. Choose a professional profile picture that reflects how you look in the current decade. Update your education, skills, and experience sections with thoughtful and relevant content. Request recommendations from current or previous collaborators to strengthen your profile, and highlight any recent accomplishments or achievements. Lastly, consider joining groups that align with your scientific interests to expand your professional network and stay informed.

7.4.7 ResearchGate

ResearchGate is a valuable platform tailored specifically for researchers, providing a range of features to enhance scientific collaboration and engagement within the research community. By creating a comprehensive profile, you can highlight your areas of research expertise, academic affiliations, and professional accomplishments, much like on LinkedIn. This detailed profile allows fellow researchers to understand your background and interests, fostering connections and potential collaborations.

One of the key advantages of ResearchGate is its publication-sharing capabilities. You can upload your research papers, conference proceedings, and other scholarly works, making them easily accessible to the research community. Alternatively, you can link your publications using Digital Object Identifiers (DOIs), providing a direct pathway to your work. This not only facilitates knowledge dissemination but also increases the visibility and impact of your research.

ResearchGate goes beyond being a repository for publications. It fosters active discussion and engagement among researchers through features such as the ability to ask questions directly to authors. This open dialogue allows for deeper insights into research methodologies, findings, and potential collaborations. Additionally, the platform enables you to follow other researchers whose work aligns with your interests, keeping you informed about their latest publications and activities.

Another valuable aspect of ResearchGate is its comprehensive analytics. Researchers can track the citation rates of their publications, monitor the number of views and downloads, and gain insights into the impact of their work within the research community. These metrics provide a valuable assessment of research visibility and allow you to further gauge the influence and reach of your scholarly contributions (see chapter 2).

ResearchGate also features a jobs board tailored to researchers, suggesting relevant job opportunities based on your expertise and publication portfolio. This makes it a useful resource for exploring career options and staying updated on the latest job openings within your field.

7.4.8 Others

The world of social media is constantly evolving, and while the platforms discussed earlier in this section are valuable for establishing a digital footprint as a scientist, there are many other platforms worth considering. In the realm of researcher-focused social networking, alternatives to ResearchGate include Mendeley and Academia.edu. These platforms also enable researchers to connect, collaborate, and share their scholarly work with peers. They offer additional avenues for highlighting expertise and engaging in discussions within specific research communities.

Reddit, known as the 'front page of the internet', hosts a multitude of discussion boards covering almost any topic imaginable. It serves as a vibrant platform for scientific conversations, where researchers can participate in various science-related subreddits to share insights, seek advice, and connect with like-minded individuals.

Clubhouse is an audio-based social networking platform where users can join virtual rooms and participate in live discussions. It provides a unique opportunity for scientists to host conversations, panels, and Q&A sessions on various scientific topics. Clubhouse also offers an interactive and inclusive space for knowledge sharing and networking within specific interest groups or scientific communities.

While originally designed for gaming communities, Discord has evolved into a versatile platform that can be used by scientists for communication, collaboration, and organising virtual events. Discord servers can be created to facilitate discussions, share resources, and foster collaboration among researchers with similar interests. It provides a casual and interactive environment where scientists can connect and exchange ideas in real-time.

The social media landscape is vast, and it is important to explore platforms that align with your goals and resonate with your target audience. By leveraging these platforms effectively, you can expand your scientific network, enhance visibility, and promote meaningful science communication to broad and diverse audiences.

7.5 The role of artificial intelligence in science communication

Artificial intelligence (AI) has emerged as a powerful tool in science communication very recently, offering potential for numerous applications that enhance efficiency, personalisation, and engagement. AI refers to computer systems capable of performing tasks that typically require human intelligence, such as understanding natural language, recognising patterns, making decisions, and learning from experience. This presents an opportunity for transformative change in science communication.

Machine learning, a subset of AI, enables analysis of large volumes of data to identify patterns, trends, and correlations, enhancing our understanding and communication of scientific information. For example, machine learning can analyse social media sentiment on climate change, allowing communicators to tailor their messages to address concerns or misconceptions. Likewise, natural language processing (NLP) allows computers to understand and generate human language (i.e. generative AI), making it possible to create chatbots, and other tools, that can explain scientific concepts or guide users through virtual experiments.

Generative AI can also automate routine tasks such as content scheduling for social media posts, freeing up time to focus on creativity and strategy. Similarly, AI-powered chatbots such as ChatGPT and BARD generate human-like text and explanations, enabling scientists to draft content and respond to queries efficiently. DALL-E, a generative AI image creator generates images from textual descriptions, potentially providing accessible representations of complex scientific ideas.

To use generative AI tools efficiently, you need to learn how to develop effective prompts, remembering to always check and scrutinise AI-generated content. A prompt is a specific input provided to an artificial intelligence system to initiate a desired response or action. It can be a phrase, question, or partial sentence that guides the AI model's generation of text (or imagery), enabling it to produce coherent and relevant output based on the given prompt. When crafting prompts for AI in science communication, consider the following tips:

Be clear and specific. Provide a clear context and specific instructions for the AI model to understand the desired output. Specify the type of information or response you are looking for, whether it is a scientific explanation, a summary, or a creative piece.

Example prompt: Provide a concise scientific explanation of the concept of natural selection and its role in evolutionary processes.

Set boundaries. Clearly define any limitations or constraints for the AI model. This can help guide the response and ensure it aligns with ethical considerations or specific communication goals.

Example prompt: Generate a creative story about space exploration, but ensure it adheres to ethical guidelines and avoids promoting harmful stereotypes.

Tailor the prompt to the AI model's capabilities. Different AI models have varying strengths and limitations. Familiarise yourself with the specific capabilities of the AI model you are using and tailor your prompts accordingly to optimise the quality and relevance of the responses.

Example prompt: Using the GPT-3 language model, summarise the key findings of this research paper on climate change in a few sentences.

Consider the target audience. Adapt your prompts to cater to the specific needs and understanding of your intended audience. Adjust the language, complexity, and tone to make the AI-generated content more accessible and engaging.

Example Prompt: Generate a simple and engaging explanation of the concept of gravity suitable for a group of 12-year-olds.

Test and iterate. Experiment with different prompts and evaluate the quality and relevance of the AI-generated responses. Refine and iterate your prompts based on the feedback received, ensuring that they consistently produce meaningful and accurate content.

Validate and fact-check. Even though AI can generate seemingly impressive content, it is important to validate and fact-check all the information provided. Ensure that the generated responses align with scientific accuracy and verify the content before sharing it with your audience.

As the use of AI continues to develop, we need to carefully consider the ethical concerns when using AI in science communication. One of the primary ethical challenges is the potential for AI algorithms to perpetuate and amplify mistruths. If AI models are trained on biased or inaccurate data, they may inadvertently reinforce existing misconceptions or promote false information. This can have detrimental effects on public understanding of scientific concepts and undermine the credibility of scientific communication. To mitigate this risk, you should always double-check the information generated by AI models before sharing it with your audience. Cross-reference the content with established scientific knowledge and if needed consult experts in the field to validate its accuracy. As such, generative AI should be seen as a productivity tool and not a final source of objective truth.

Ethical considerations also extend to the responsible use of AI in shaping public opinion and behaviour. AI algorithms can be designed to personalise content and recommendations based on user preferences, which can lead to filter bubbles and echo chambers, reinforcing existing beliefs and limiting exposure to diverse perspectives. This can hinder critical thinking and impede the dissemination of accurate scientific information. To address this, science communicators should strive for transparency and balance in content delivery, ensuring that AI-driven recommendations promote diverse viewpoints and provide a comprehensive understanding of scientific topics. Additionally, promoting digital literacy and critical thinking skills among diverse audiences can help them to navigate the information landscape and discern reliable sources from misinformation.

AI should be seen as a valuable tool that aids and enhances productivity, rather than something to be trusted blindly. Whilst AI has the potential to automate tasks, generate content, and provide insights, we must approach its outputs with critical thinking and human oversight. AI algorithms are only as reliable as the data they are trained on and the instructions they are given. They may be prone to biases, inaccuracies, or unexpected errors. By maintaining a thoughtful and responsible approach to AI, we can harness its potential to improve productivity, enhance decision-making, and advance science communication, whilst still prioritising human oversight and expertise.

> **Exercise: Visual enhancement with AI**
> Experiment with DALL-E to generate visually appealing representations of a specific scientific concept or phenomena. Describe a complex scientific idea and use DALL-E to create an image that visually communicates the concept for your target audience. Share these visuals with a member of your target audience and reflect on the opportunities and challenges that they might present.

7.6 Digital collaborations

In addition to its role as a vital resource for advertising skills, finding information, and managing research portfolios, the internet facilitates collaboration with just a few clicks or taps. While emails have replaced traditional letters and faxes as our preferred communication tool, there are numerous innovative and effective ways to collaborate with scientists worldwide.

Video conferencing is an efficient method for conducting group meetings, eliminating the need for unnecessary travel and saving time, money, and the environment. Various video conferencing facilities, both free and paid, are available, and it is advisable to experiment with different platforms to find the most suitable one for your needs. Zoom, Webex, and Google Meet all offer free video conferencing with additional features such as screen sharing and recording. When organising or participating in a video conference, test connections in advance, making sure that all participants have the necessary accounts and software. For larger groups, making use of instant messaging within conferencing suites can facilitate smoother communication when multiple people want to speak.

Document sharing platforms such as Google Docs, SharePoint, and Dropbox facilitate collaboration on documents or presentations by allowing real-time sharing and co-editing. These platforms enable the creation of folders for different research projects, making it easy to share them with collaborators and allowing them to contribute from any location with internet access. Additionally, Slack, a cloud-based collaboration software, offers features like direct messaging, notifications, alerts, document sharing, and group chat. Integrations with services such as Google Docs and Dropbox make it an effective tool for organising research projects. Many users prefer Slack over email due to its superior navigation and conversation tracking capabilities.

SlideShare is a platform that facilitates sharing and discovering slide presentations, infographics, and documents. Scientists can use SlideShare to display their research findings, conference presentations, and visual materials in a user-friendly format, reaching a wider audience and disseminating scientific knowledge in an engaging manner.

GitHub, primarily used by programmers, is a web-based platform for version control and collaborative development of software projects. However, many scientists increasingly use GitHub for sharing and collaborating on data analysis code, computational models, and scientific software. Its version control features, and change tracking promote transparency, reproducibility, and collaboration in scientific research.

Lastly, ORCID is a persistent and unique digital identifier that distinguishes individuals from other researchers and can be associated with their publications. ORCID is especially valuable for researchers who have used various name combinations across their publications. This personal identification number can also be applied to research grants, ensuring proper credit for one's work. Including a link to an ORCID profile serves as a reference for publications in a traditional CV, overcoming space limitations (see figure 7.1).

7.7 Summary

In this chapter, we have discussed the importance of creating a manageable, informative, and visually appealing digital footprint. We have provided practical advice on establishing successful blogs, podcasts, and social media profiles, while also addressing the evolving landscape of science communication, including the role of artificial intelligence.

With a plethora of digital tools and platforms available, you need to avoid overwhelming yourself. Instead, focus on a select few mediums that align with your skills and objectives. By leveraging innovative content and fostering meaningful communities within these chosen platforms, you can create a powerful and enjoyable digital portfolio.

Furthermore, we must consider the ethical implications of our online presence. Understand the guidelines provided by your employer regarding social media usage and think about the consequences of your posts. Ask yourself whether you would be willing to defend your statements in a professional setting. When discussing preliminary results, be mindful of protecting future publications for yourself and your colleagues.

Finally, we discussed how AI offers opportunities to automate tasks, enhance personalisation, and engage audiences in new ways. In doing so, we need to use AI tools responsibly, ensuring privacy, transparency, and adherence to ethical standards.

By following these guidelines and maintaining a balanced approach to your digital presence, you can effectively highlight your expertise, connect with your audience, and contribute to the advancement of both science and science communication. Continuously evaluate the impact of your digital footprint and adapt your strategies accordingly to stay at the forefront of this ever-evolving field.

7.8 Further study

The further study in this chapter is designed to help you think about developing your online presence and digital footprint:

1. **Record a podcast.** If you think that audio is the media for you, then follow the advice given in section 7.3 and set up your own podcast. Take the time to plan out in advance what you will be talking about (be warned though, as fully scripted podcasts can sound a little unnatural), how you will market the podcast, and how you intend to develop a community around it.
2. **Create/update your ResearchGate profile.** Fill in all your details and upload your publications. Then connect with some colleagues and co-authors and endorse them for any skills that you think they possess. Read some of the general questions that have been posted about topics in your field of expertise and see if you can provide any answers or contribute to any ongoing debates.
3. **Build a website.** If your digital footprint is starting to feel stretched, then it might be an idea to start thinking about building a personal website. Doing so will enable you to either host or advertise all your digital output from one easily manageable location. There are many examples of free and paid-for website builders; make use of the free-trial periods that most of these builders offer to find the one that works best for you and your audience.
4. **Host an online seminar (webinar).** Use a platform like Zoom or Google Meet to host webinar on a scientific topic of interest. Plan the content and structure of your webinar in advance, ensuring it caters to your target audience, and engage participants with interactive elements such as polls or Q&A sessions (see section 4.9 for advice on how to do this).
5. **Explore AI-generated content.** Craft a prompt such as 'Explain the process of photosynthesis in simple terms' and generate AI-generated content using your chosen chatbot. Evaluate the generated response for its clarity, accuracy, and engagement. Verify the information provided by cross-referencing it with trusted scientific sources. Finally, reflect on the strengths and limitations of the AI-generated response and refine the prompt for better results.

7.9 Suggested reading

The journal article 'An introduction to social media for scientists' [1] lays down the groundwork for understanding the role of social media in science communication. It unravels the complexities of crafting a scientific presence across various platforms, offering insights into reaching and engaging a diverse audience effectively. Equally, 'Twenty-five years of social media: a review of social media applications and definitions from 1994 to 2019' [2] is a valuable read for scientists interested in using social media as it provides a comprehensive review of social media applications and definitions across this time. By providing guidelines for studying social media and finding practical applications, this paper offers clarity and guidance for scientists looking to use social media in their research, communication, and engagement efforts.

If you are leaning towards setting up a science blog, *Science Blogging: The Essential Guide* [3] walks you through the process of communicating scientific research and discoveries online, from the craft of writing engaging content to how to make sure people can access your blog. Likewise, 'Science podcasts: analysis of global production and output from 2004 to 2018' [4] is a valuable read for individuals interested in creating a podcast as it offers insights into the landscape of science podcasts and their production and dissemination.

On a broader scale, 'Fostering public trust in science: the role of social media' [5] examines the relationship between social media news use and trust in science, demonstrating how to use social media for good. Similarly, 'The Notorious GPT: science communication in the age of artificial intelligence' [6] is a valuable read for scientists interested in using AI for science communication, specifically focusing on the emergence of generative AI and its implications. The paper highlights the potential of AI in providing translational and multimodal science communication at scale but also addresses concerns related to accuracy, as well as job market implications. Finally, 'Artificial hallucinations in ChatGPT: implications in scientific writing' [7] provides an excellent reminder of the limitations that AI tools still possess, and hence the need to use them as aides that need fact-checking rather than content-generators to uncritically adhere to.

References

[1] Bik H M and Goldstein M C 2013 An introduction to social media for scientists *PLoS Biol.* **11** e1001535

[2] Aichner T, Grünfelder M, Maurer O and Jegeni D 2021 Twenty-five years of social media: a review of social media applications and definitions from 1994 to 2019 *Cyberpsychol., Behav., Soc. Netw.* **24** 215–22

[3] Wilcox C, Brookshire B and Goldman J G (ed) 2016 *Science Blogging: The Essential Guide* (New Haven, CT: Yale University Press)

[4] MacKenzie L E 2019 Science podcasts: analysis of global production and output from 2004 to 2018 *R. Soc. Open Sci.* **6** 180932

[5] Huber B, Barnidge M, Gil de Zúñiga H and Liu J 2019 Fostering public trust in science: the role of social media *Public Underst. Sci.* **28** 759–77

[6] Schäfer M S 2023 The Notorious GPT: science communication in the age of artificial intelligence *J. Sci. Commun.* **22** Y02

[7] Alkaissi H and McFarlane S 2023 Artificial hallucinations in ChatGPT: implications in scientific writing *Cureus* **15** e35179

IOP Publishing

Effective Science Communication (Third Edition)
A practical guide to surviving as a scientist
Sam Illingworth and Grant Allen

Chapter 8

Science and policy

Science Is Everywhere: Science Is For Everyone

—Jeanette Davis

8.1 Introduction

The flow of time is gauged and outlined by distinct and quantifiable events. Nevertheless, how change manifests in our daily lives is the outcome of guiding policy, outlined for us by policymakers, whether they be regulators, lawmakers, governments, managers, CEOs, or vice-chancellors.

Policy delineates modern civilisation, the rule of law, and the effects we have on our planet. Whether we always concur with it or not, policy characterises our world. However, 'good' policy, or rather 'optimal' policy, is that which is enlightened by knowledge, paired with the policymakers' capability to comprehend this knowledge and to employ it to make forecasts about the potential impacts that this policy may hold.

Enter science. Without informed policy, we are at the mercy of arbitrary or subjective guidance from groups or individuals that may not be experts, or who may be biased by independent or narrow viewpoints and vested interests. Science can provide the evidence base, the wisdom, and the predictive capacity for policymakers to make the best possible choices within the constraints of the political and socio-economic climate of the day; a climate which is itself a function of the science and policy that defines our expectations, aspirations, the way we think, and the way in which we live our lives. Yet the route that this important information takes into the policymakers' hands is not always as optimal as it could, and should, be.

This chapter is concerned with that pathway—the route by which science informs and influences policy. We shall explore some of the established and recognised ways that science is used in decision making in the modern world, and how you can make your scientific voice heard. Policy is often formulated by debate and by building a consensus. While other voices may have opposing views, we need to take a role in putting forward the best-informed, evidence-based facts and opinions to those that need, and want, to hear it. Expert guidance and opinion, especially from independent academics and scientists, is much valued by policymakers and trusted by the public. But that guidance is only useful if it is heard and received in a form that can be understood, while retaining accuracy and honesty.

8.2 How science informs policy

There are numerous direct and indirect pathways that science and knowledge are absorbed into the awareness of government, lawmakers, and policymakers. Indirect pathways are typically less tangible and may be subject to bias. These include opinion formed over time based on reading articles, watching TV documentaries, interacting with social media, and through interactions with organised lobby groups with a specific agenda. Such pathways clearly have an important role and can be powerful. However, communicating science through these more passive media are dealt with in other chapters in this book. Here we will concern ourselves with more direct pathways, such as submitting parliamentary evidence and guidance for best practice.

The examples we shall present are by no means exhaustive. The pathways by which science is used in policy are many and are at times indirect and often untraceable. Policies that draw on scientific evidence can apply at international, national, and local levels with impacts affecting stakeholders from multi-national industries to individuals. We shall offer some general advice and some example in-roads into influencing policy to help you think about how science is seen, heard, and used, by policymakers. And in doing so, we will be mindful of what can be done as scientists to influence decision-making more generally.

Two prime examples of modern-world policy direction and how these have been swayed by scientific evidence are those linked with the regulation of the tobacco industry and the sometimes-conflicting priorities between decelerating (or mitigating) climate change and sustainable economic growth.

In the early twentieth century, smoking was not widely acknowledged to be hazardous to human health, with some doctors, incorrectly, proclaiming its many health benefits. Consequently, the industry was not regulated in the manner that it is today. However, taking the UK as an example, the route by which the tobacco industry has been restricted by policy decisions such as limitations on advertising, restriction on smoking indoors in public places, hikes in taxation, and public health campaigns, has been relatively slow [1]. This delay is broadly observed to be due to the clash between personal freedoms, the influence of well-funded industrial lobby groups, economic arguments (with both negative and positive aspects), and the now-obvious science of a negative impact on public health

Over time, the amassed evidence of health impacts and a growing consensus by health professionals have led to the policies we observe today. Very few people on the planet are unaware of the risks; and those that opt to smoke are actively or indirectly discouraged by higher taxation, less prominent advertising, and easily accessible public health information and advice. Nonetheless, this policy success, if assessed in terms of the proportion of people smoking in both Western Europe and North America, was absolutely the result of united efforts by scientists to furnish unequivocal evidence to policymakers that there were significant public health impacts [2]. These scientists supplied policymakers with the information from which to make decisions about the optimal policies to balance health, economic, and personal freedom considerations in the face of pressure from lobby groups. However, in this new era, the emerging popularity of e-cigarettes and vaping poses fresh challenges, with health impacts and regulatory questions adding another layer of complexity to tobacco control efforts [3].

In the context of climate change policy, the discourse concerning the balanced emphasis of policy (both nationally and globally) to mitigate or lessen the impacts of the climate crisis, continues to be multi-faceted. While an almost unanimous consensus of climate scientists clearly states that anthropogenic climate change is a reality and occurring [4], a notable number of policymakers, along with a minimal proportion of scientists, assert that climate change is non-existent or not influenced by human activity; or they contend that a policy response is unjustified if it adversely affects specific industries or national economies [5]. Thankfully, most of the overt opinion among policymakers and governments is that actions must be undertaken to address this pressing issue. As such, national and international bodies and organisations such as the United Nations' International Panel of Climate Change (IPCC) are supplying and updating the evidence base and predictive capability in a form that is easily accessible and useful to policymakers [6]. Policymakers are incorporated into this process through the United Nations Framework Convention on Climate Change (UNFCCC), which facilitates international and legally binding responses to climate change—most notably through the negotiation of national greenhouse gas emissions targets.

The significant and effective organisation of science for this purpose through groups of experts such as those comprising the IPCC, which compiles and interprets the finest peer-reviewed evidence available globally, indisputably represents a gold standard and a unified (and expensive) effort. This bottom-up approach, whereby carefully selected experts examine the peer-reviewed literature for evidence, review it, and summarise and present it in an accessible form, establishes a system that does not merely heed the most vocal voice in the room (or lobby). Additionally, the IPCC reports provide a regular review that emphasises remaining sources of scientific uncertainty, which then sets a forward agenda for individual scientists to respond to, seek funding to explore, and consequently better inform on.

Such a global challenge demands a global response and the global participation of scientists. Yet, the reality persists that policy decisions need to be based on the best available evidence at hand. Without a structure such as the IPCC, policymakers would be submerged in a sea of individual research papers and individual academics, each with their own preferred climate impact and research interest, alongside vocal counter claims and agendas from lobby groups and a small number of dissenting scientists. There remains a distance to traverse to fully predict and understand this intricate field of Earth system science and its inevitable impact on humanity. Further complicating matters, in a fluctuating environment (physical, political, and economic), the evidence base may perpetually require regular updates. Nonetheless, the pathways to policy in this area have been adeptly organised; no policymaker can convincingly argue that they are not as well informed as science (and scientists) can feasibly make them.

The entanglement of inherently apolitical scientific subjects such as the climate crisis with political agendas amplifies challenges and frustrations for the scientific community [7]. The climate crisis, a global challenge rooted in empirical evidence and scientific consensus, frequently transmutes into a polarised political issue. This politicisation can sometimes obscure the factual scientific basis and undermine the urgent actions needed, as political interests and ideologies can overshadow evidence-based policymaking. For scientists, whose work is grounded in evidence and objectivity, navigating this politicised landscape can be a source of significant frustration. It underscores the need for continued, clear, and accessible dialogue between scientists and policymakers, to ensure that science-based understanding and solutions remain at the forefront of policy decisions and public discourse, unmarred by political interests and debates.

For many other fields of science, the organisation of science-policy pathways is much less formal, and individual scientists may need to be proactive in personally bringing their evidence and outputs to the attention of policymakers. In section 8.3, we shall explore some of the ways in which this can be done.

8.3 What you can do to inform policy

This section provides a few illustrative examples of how your work might influence policy. There is a multitude of ways this can transpire in practice. Specific agencies or individuals who are familiar with your expertise in a particular field might identify you. As a result, you could be approached to offer advice in the form of expert reviews of government-commissioned reports, penned by civil servants or other academics and political think tanks. Alternatively, you may be invited to bid for contracts to draft such reports yourself. To enhance your visibility in these circles, you need to maintain an exemplary academic track record whilst actively networking through science advisory groups, such as those present in many national science funding councils. Direct invitations to participate typically circulate through word of mouth within existing expert networks, or by recommendations from other academics citing your academic track record as a rationale to seek your advice and draw upon your specialist expertise.

Such 'top-down' invitations may arrive later in your academic career, after establishing your reputation as a long-standing expert and leader in your field. However, there are more proactive avenues to provide input and elevate your profile in policy circles earlier in your career. For instance, national parliaments (i.e. the legislative body of a government) habitually form specialised committees, constituted and chaired by elected representatives. These committees are charged with amassing evidence for debate on nationally pertinent policy matters before legislation and debating the impacts of introduced legislation. Regularly, these committees issue open calls for evidence, allowing anyone to contribute input.

Most democratic governments, operating at both local and national levels, employ similar mechanisms—consulting both scientists and other publics for guidance to inform debate and decision-making. An example of such a consultation will be explored the following exercise, aiding in the understanding and navigation of these significant pathways of influence and contribution in policy-making processes.

Exercise: Find opportunities to provide evidence to policymakers
Explore the webpages of your parliament's select committees to search for open or historical calls for evidence. Even if there are not any relevant open calls in your field, examining previous ones could be beneficial.

Select one of the open or historical calls and adhere strictly to the guidelines for preparing evidence, including any specific formatting instructions, such as numbering paragraphs or maintaining a certain level of formality in writing. Review past committee reports to understand how evidence has influenced the report's narrative and any subsequent debate. Contemplate how your specialism could inform that narrative and the most effective way to convey it to policymakers.

Should you opt to submit evidence to a committee, approach your writing akin to an academic narrative. Construct it with an introductory summary (like an abstract), a main body citing relevant references, and a conclusion, whilst evading technical jargon where feasible. Your submission might necessitate expanding on your knowledge to form an opinion or conclusion regarding the policy at hand. As discussed in chapter 6, delineate between your personal opinions and the evidence underpinning those opinions. Reflecting on the confidence of your conclusions and acknowledging any knowledge gaps is also advantageous, as is identifying any additional scientific inquiry needed to minimise uncertainty.

A committee within the parliament may cite your evidence in its report or during a debate, and there is even a possibility of being invited to present oral evidence. Though this might appear overwhelming, consider the significant positive influence you can wield on altering the direction of debate and policy. As discussed in chapter 3, the impact agenda is a crucial element of contemporary science funding globally. The employment of your scientific knowledge in policy and its traceability through citable policy pathways like this is a tremendously vital facet of your work. It is also beneficial for your future capabilities to secure research funding. This process highlights your skill in translating scientific knowledge into substantial impact, enlightening public and political discussions, and instigating meaningful change.

Another straightforward method to offer direct insight to policymakers, involves registering your expertise with your national parliamentary library. These libraries serve members of various legislative bodies worldwide, and their librarians' roles extend far beyond managing a book-lending service. Like civil servants in governmental departments, parliamentary librarians connect elected representatives with pertinent information in response to specific queries. These questions may originate in the legislative assembly or from the public or lobby groups. Parliamentary libraries frequently assemble research briefings for members on subjects of current debate [8].

To create these briefings, library researchers consult published literature, including peer-reviewed academic journals, and an internal database of experts for advice. You can enlist your expertise in such databases by contacting these libraries, increasing the likelihood of being approached for insight or advice in response to inquiries from elected officials. This interaction may potentially lead to direct communication with them, providing a valuable opportunity to influence policy and share your expertise on a global scale.

Parliamentary offices offer all sorts of other services to policymakers, members of parliament and civil servants. For example, the UK Parliamentary and Science Committee publish a quarterly magazine, *Science in Parliament* (see e.g. [9]), which is available to all its members. This magazine, like many of its international analogues, openly solicits ideas from academics for articles. You can suggest a topic for an article to an editor, explaining why it is relevant and topical to policymakers and you may be invited to submit an article for publication. Note that you are not likely to receive remuneration for such work; like so much in academia it is a labour of love. However, it is an excellent way to raise your profile in policy circles as a new academic with an emerging track record.

8.4 Impact from research

As explored throughout this book, the culmination of science often transcends the boundaries of a research paper. Science, as defined by both the scientific community and others, serves a plethora of constructive purposes, subsequently leading to what is coined as research impact. This impact manifests in diverse forms, encompassing economic advancement, policy amendment, environmental and public health enhancement, technological development, amplified public cognisance of science, and educational progress. Often, these various elements of impact overlap. Impact stems from effective science communication, i.e. pathways to impact (see chapter 3). These pathways could entail disseminating scientific knowledge at public forums or engaging with public, commercial, or governmental entities to instigate policy alteration or other beneficial changes.

In the context of career progression, maintaining a comprehensive and up-to-date record of your research impact and the paths leading to it is paramount, especially during public evaluations of scientific impact. Numerous countries, including the UK, periodically conduct assessment exercises such as the Research Excellence

Framework (REF) to evaluate this aspect [10]. In such evaluations, the extent and significance of scientific impact in policy, society, health, and the environment are peer-reviewed and graded, laying the foundation for calculating public funding allocations for research institutions such as universities.

The impact of science holds substantial weight not merely in its direct, palpable benefits but also in enhancing personal and institutional reputation and funding. Broadly, the quantifiable impact of science robustly supports public investment, substantiating its significance and contribution. Numerous national research funding councils scrutinise the impact of the research they sponsor, aiming to strategically allocate future funding and construct an evidence-backed argument during public expenditure assessments. This comprehensive approach ensures the sustained and enhanced role of science in various critical domains, reinforcing its indispensable contribution to global advancement.

When endeavouring to objectively quantify and contextualise the impact of research for evaluation, any claims should be fully substantiated, allowing external parties to independently trace the journey from research outputs to their ultimate impact. This evidence may materialise in various forms such as testimonials from stakeholders who have experienced benefits from your research. This could include company directors or accounts that have leveraged your findings to bolster profit, or it may appear as policy documentation citing your research or evidence grounded on such outputs.

Tracking the routes your research embarks upon towards making an impact and concurrently gathering evidence of said impact forms the foundation for future evaluations. This practice may encompass maintaining active relationships with policymakers known to be employing your research. Developing such relationships also allows for future collaboration in evidencing the impact of your research when the need arises, fortifying the quantifiable demonstration of your work's significance in real-world contexts.

8.5 Summary

This chapter lays out various pathways by which scientific evidence is used by policymakers and other interested parties, offering specific avenues for proactive contribution from scientists. We have introduced how the direct and indirect benefits of research are known as research impact, and how these can extend well beyond the policy sphere. Impact can be thought of as the practical societal justification for our scientific work, and demonstrating impact often justifies public and commercial funding of the work that we do.

Almost without exception, those tasked with decision-making and policy formulation warmly welcome input from experts, seeking robust evidence to aid in making well-informed judgements for the collective good; no one prefers making poor decisions. However, aside from global 'grand challenges' or issues of significant national importance and public interest, the integration of science into policy is typically an upward movement. It depends on the initiative of individuals or the expansion of existing expert networks. You can enhance your visibility by engaging in evidence requests and conversing with those within established networks, while concurrently building your repertoire of expertise and foundational research. Stay vigilant for opportunities, enrol for email alerts and policy publications, and nurture collaborations with policymakers who make use of your work.

8.6 Further study

The further study in this chapter is designed to help you think further about developing your science policy skills:

1. **Read a policy report.** Go to your national parliament's official website and navigate to the section for select committee publications (or equivalent). Choose and read a recent report that resonates with your field of research. These documents often provide a comprehensive summary of the topic and its policy implications. They can offer insights into the types of evidence most submitted and referred to in such reports.
2. **Join the library.** Subscribe to the email alerts from the UK Commons Library and its research service. Even if you are not based in the UK, these emails will keep you up to date with parliamentary debates, reports, and calls-for-evidence in any subject area that you wish to specify.
3. **Read a POSTnote.** The UK's Parliamentary Office of Science and Technology (POST) provides balanced and accessible overviews (see e.g. [11]) of research from across the biological, physical, and social sciences, and engineering and technology that are used to brief UK Members of Parliament. They provide excellent summaries of many different topics and are worth reading to both broaden your knowledge and look for areas that require further evidence.

8.7 Suggested reading

The *Science of Science Policy: A Handbook* [12] offers a comprehensive insight into the science of science policy, approaching it from theoretical, empirical, and practical policy perspectives. The contributors shed light from broader social science, behavioural science, and policy communities on this evolving field, providing understanding about the type of questions which drive the demand for science policy in the first place. *Using Science as Evidence in Public Policy* [13] motivates scientists to alter their perspective on how scientific evidence is used in policymaking. It examines the significance of scientific evidence in policymaking, asserting that an expansive body of research on knowledge utilisation has not led to a universally accepted understanding of the application of science in public policy. This book, accessible as a complementary online report from The National Academies Press, is particularly beneficial for scientists aspiring to see their research applied in policy making, providing advice about how to channel scientific results through intermediaries such as think tanks, lobbyists, and advocacy groups.

The article 'Co-producing the science–policy interface: towards common but differentiated responsibilities' [14] explores the persistent linear model of science–policy relations with a case study from a Dutch research institute's collaboration with a ministerial department. The research unveils the continuity of this model owing to the absence of alternative models, underlining a neglected opportunity to confront the political issues rooted in knowledge production. The article also provides insights for how to augment the effectiveness and legitimacy of knowledge production and use. Finally, *Merchants of Doubt* [15] serves as a broad interest reading and a warning narrative about the detrimental influence of substandard science on policy debate and the trajectory of policy, providing a profound exploration of the tobacco and climate change instances highlighted in section 8.2.

References

[1] Cairney P 2009 The role of ideas in policy transfer: the case of UK smoking bans since devolution *J. Eur. Public Policy* **16** 471–88

[2] Cairney P 2007 A 'multiple lenses' approach to policy change: the case of tobacco policy in the UK *Br. Politics* **2** 45–68

[3] Hawkins B and Ettelt S 2019 The strategic uses of evidence in UK e-cigarettes policy debates *Evid. Policy* **15** 579–96

[4] Lynas M, Houlton B Z and Perry S 2021 Greater than 99% consensus on human caused climate change in the peer-reviewed scientific literature *Environ. Res. Lett.* **16** 114005

[5] Kovaka K 2021 Climate change denial and beliefs about science *Synthese* **198** 2355–74

[6] Bhandari M P 2022 *Getting the Climate Science Facts Right: The Role of the IPCC* (Boca Raton, FL: CRC Press)

[7] Kunelius R and Roosvall A 2021 Media and the climate crisis *Nordic J. Media Stud.* **3** 1–19

[8] Missingham R 2011 Parliamentary library and research services in the 21st century: a Delphi study *IFLA J.* **37** 52–61

[9] Emmott S and Rison S 2008 Towards 2020 science *Sci. Parliam.* **65** 31–3

[10] Sivertsen G 2017 Unique, but still best practice? The Research Excellence Framework (REF) from an international perspective *Palgrave Commun.* **3** 1–6

[11] Allen S R and Pentland C 2011 *Carbon Footprint of Electricity Generation: POSTnote 383* (London: Parliamentary Office of Science and Technology)

[12] Fealing K 2011 *The Science of Science Policy: A Handbook* (Redwood City, CA: Stanford University Press)

[13] National Research Council 2012 *Using Science as Evidence in Public Policy* (Washington, DC: National Academies Press)

[14] Maas T Y, Pauwelussen A and Turnhout E 2022 Co-producing the science–policy interface: towards common but differentiated responsibilities *Human. Soc. Sci. Commun.* **9** 1–11

[15] Oreskes N and Conway E M 2011 *Merchants of Doubt: How a Handful of Scientists Obscured the Truth on Issues from Tobacco Smoke to Global Warming* (New York: Bloomsbury Publishing)

Chapter 9

Teaching science

The more I learn, the more I realize how much I don't know.
—**Albert Einstein**

9.1 Introduction

As readers of this book, it is likely that many of you will encounter teaching within a higher education context. Whether you are a graduate student leading a lab session, a postdoctoral researcher delivering a guest lecture, or a professor designing a new course, teaching is an integral part of your role in academia. Higher education presents its own unique set of challenges and opportunities when it comes to teaching science. The students you will be teaching are often well motivated, but they also come with a diverse range of backgrounds, learning styles, and expectations [1].

The purpose of this chapter is to focus specifically on teaching science in a higher education context. This is the area where we, as the authors, have the most experience and feel most qualified to provide advice and guidance. We aim to share our insights and strategies for effective teaching, drawn from our collective years of experience in academia. In doing do we will address various aspects of teaching, from designing engaging and inclusive sessions to assessing student progress and providing constructive feedback.

The distinction that we make in this chapter, as opposed to the other general and specific communication formats discussed thus far in this book, is that in teaching science in a university setting you are primarily targeting an audience of future scientists and graduate professionals, instilling in them the principles of scientific inquiry, problem-solving, and critical, objective and reflective thinking. While we know that many of the students that we work with at university will move outside of both science and academia [2], when working with this audience, considering them to be the scientists of the future is a useful aide-mémoire. In doing so, the rest of the advice that we have provided throughout the rest of this book still holds true, i.e. this is our audience, and we must consider both our narratives our ourselves to meet their needs and requirements as learners.

Effective teaching can foster a culture of lifelong learning, encouraging scientists to continually update their knowledge and skills in response to new discoveries and advances [3]. However, teaching science in higher education is not without its challenges. It requires a delicate balance of providing enough detail to accurately introduce and represent scientific concepts whilst ensuring that the material remains engaging and comprehensible [4].

Despite these challenges, the rewards of teaching science can be profound. There is a unique satisfaction in seeing a student's understanding of a concept click into place, or in witnessing the excitement of a student making a discovery for the first time. Teaching allows us to view our own work from a new perspective, often leading to fresh insights and ideas [5].

The landscape of teaching science within a higher education institute is continually evolving, shaped by advances in technology and pedagogical research. The rise of both online learning platforms [6] and artificial intelligence [7], for instance, has opened new possibilities for teaching and learning science. Similarly, research into how students learn has led to the development of innovative teaching methods designed to enhance student engagement and understanding [8].

Throughout the rest of this chapter, we will explore strategies and techniques that will help you to navigate this ever-evolving landscape of higher education, introducing innovative pedagogical methodologies, including flipped classrooms and problem-based learning. We will also offer practical advice on how to create inclusive learning environments, assess student learning effectively, develop materials directly related to your scientific research, and provide meaningful feedback to students. The information and strategies we share are designed to not only help you become a more effective teacher but also to enrich your experience and satisfaction in teaching science at the higher education level.

9.2 Pedagogical approaches

There are a variety of teaching strategies and methods that are employed to facilitate learning in higher education. These range from traditional lecture-based teaching to more interactive approaches such as problem-based learning, inquiry-based learning, and flipped classrooms [9]. Each of these methods has its own strengths and weaknesses, and the choice of method often depends on the specific learning objectives, the nature of the content, and the characteristics of the learners.

One of the key considerations in choosing a pedagogical approach is the level of the students. Undergraduate students, who are often new to the field, may benefit from more structured teaching methods that provide a solid foundation of knowledge. On the other hand, postgraduate students, who already have a good grasp of the basics, may benefit more from approaches that promote critical thinking and independent learning [10].

Active learning is a teaching approach that requires students to engage actively in the learning process, rather than passively receiving information. At its core, active learning is about students doing and thinking. It is not just about listening to lectures, but rather involves students in activities such as reading, writing, discussing, or problem-solving to promote higher-order thinking—the analysis, synthesis, and evaluation of ideas.

Active-learning strategies are diverse and adaptable, ranging from group discussions and problem-solving activities to hands-on laboratory work and research projects. Group discussions, for instance, can stimulate critical thinking and deepen understanding by exposing students to diverse perspectives. Problem-solving activities can help students apply theoretical knowledge in practical contexts, enhancing their analytical skills. Hands-on laboratory work and research projects provide opportunities for experiential learning, where students learn by doing and reflecting on their actions. Active learning is about transforming students from passive recipients of information into active participants in their own learning journey. It is about creating a dynamic, interactive learning environment where students are encouraged to question, explore, and create knowledge [11].

Flipped learning is a pedagogical approach that has gained significant traction in higher education. This model turns the traditional teaching structure on its head, with students first encountering new material outside of class, typically through video lectures or reading assignments, and then using class time to deepen their understanding through discussion and problem-solving activities [12]. This approach allows students to learn at their own pace and provides more opportunities for active learning during class. It also enables educators to spend more time addressing misconceptions, facilitating discussions, and providing individualised support. Flipped learning can be particularly effective in science education, where understanding often requires applying concepts to solve problems or interpret data [13].

The dialogic approach to teaching is another powerful pedagogical tool in higher education. The dialogic method emphasises dialogue and interaction as key components of the learning process. Rather than simply transmitting information, educators using a conversational approach to engage students in meaningful discussions, encouraging them to question, analyse, and reflect on the material [14]. This approach fosters critical thinking and deepens understanding, both of which are important skills for scientists. It also promotes a more inclusive learning environment, as it values and incorporates diverse perspectives and ways of knowing. In the context of science education, this approach can stimulate lively debates about scientific theories, ethical implications of research, or the interpretation of experimental results [15].

Similarly, problem-based learning (PBL) is a pedagogical approach that is well-suited to teaching science in higher education. PBL is a student-centred approach where learners work in small groups to solve complex problems, often without definitive outcomes or conclusions. This method encourages students to take responsibility for their own learning, develop research and problem-solving skills, and apply their knowledge in practical contexts [16]. In science, PBL can be used to explore a wide range of topics, from environmental issues to medical case studies. It provides a realistic context for learning, making science more relevant and engaging for students. It fosters a collaborative learning environment, mirroring the teamwork often required in scientific research [17].

However, implementing these teaching methods is not without its challenges. These methods often require more preparation time and resources compared to traditional lecture-based teaching. They also require a shift in mindset, both for teachers who are used to being the primary source of knowledge, and for students who are used to passive learning [18]. This is especially true for those who may be coming from a different educational and/or cultural background to the one that you may be teaching them within [19].

The integration of technology has had a similar significant impact on how science is now taught at universities. For instance, online learning platforms have made education more accessible, allowing students from all over the world to participate in courses that were previously geographically restricted [20]. These platforms also offer a wealth of resources, including video lectures, interactive quizzes, and discussion forums, which can enhance student learning and engagement. They provide flexibility, enabling students to learn at their own pace and in their own time [21].

Digital simulations and virtual laboratories represent another significant technological advancement in science education. These tools allow students to conduct experiments, manipulate variables, and observe outcomes in a virtual environment [22]. This can be particularly beneficial in situations where real-life experiments are not feasible due to cost, safety, or practicality constraints. Virtual labs also offer the opportunity for repeated practice and immediate feedback, which can enhance understanding and skill development. Furthermore, they can help to bridge the gap between theoretical knowledge and practical application, providing a realistic context for learning [23].

However, as the move to remote and hybrid learning brough about the COVID-19 pandemic has demonstrated, the incorporation of technology into university teaching is not without its challenges. One of the most significant is the issue of access and equity. Not all students have the necessary resources, such as a reliable internet connection or a suitable device, to fully participate in online learning or use digital tools. This can exacerbate existing educational inequalities [24]. There is also the need for both students and educators to possess the technical skills to effectively use these tools. This often requires additional training and support, which can be time-consuming and costly [25].

Another challenge is the risk of technology becoming a distraction rather than a learning tool. For instance, students may be tempted to multitask during online classes, which can hinder their focus and learning [26]. Technology should not replace traditional teaching methods, but rather complement them. The most effective learning often occurs when technology is integrated in a thoughtful and purposeful way, aligned with learning objectives and pedagogical strategies [27]. Educators need to be aware of these challenges and strive to use technology in ways that enhance learning, promote equity, and prepare students for the digital age.

> **Exercise: Explore your teaching methods**
> This exercise is designed to provide a comprehensive reflection and evaluation of your current teaching methods. It will also prompt you to consider potential improvements and innovations for your future teaching practice.
> 1. **Teaching methods inventory.** Begin by listing all the teaching methods you currently use. This could include lectures, group discussions, problem-solving activities, laboratory work, flipped classrooms, online learning platforms. For each method, briefly describe how you implement it in your teaching.
> 2. **Rationale and effectiveness.** For each teaching method listed, reflect on why you chose this approach. What learning objectives or educational principles does it align with? How does it cater to the diverse learning styles and needs of your students? Then, evaluate its effectiveness. What feedback have you received from students? How well do students perform in assessments related to this method? What are the strengths and weaknesses of each method?
> 3. **Technology integration.** Reflect on how you incorporate technology into your teaching. What digital tools or online resources do you use? How do these enhance student learning? Are there any challenges or barriers related to technology use (e.g. access, technical skills, distraction)?
> 4. **Innovative experimentation.** Based on your reflections, identify one or two teaching methods that you would like to experiment with or improve in your future teaching. This could involve trying a new pedagogical approach, integrating a new digital tool, or modifying an existing method to better meet your students' needs. Write a brief action plan outlining what you intend to do, why you want to do this, and how you will evaluate its effectiveness.
> 5. **Peer feedback.** Share your reflections and action plan with a colleague or mentor. Seek their feedback and discuss any similar experiences or insights they might have. This collaborative reflection can provide valuable perspectives and ideas to enhance your teaching practice.

9.3 Designing engaging and inclusive environments

Inclusivity is an essential element in teaching science in a higher education environment. In an inclusive classroom, all students, regardless of their background, abilities, or learning preferences, are given equal opportunities to learn and succeed. This involves creating a safe and supportive learning environment, using inclusive language, and being aware of and addressing any potential biases or stereotypes.

Universal Design for Learning (UDL) is an educational framework based on research in the learning sciences, including cognitive neuroscience, which guides the development of flexible learning environments and learning spaces that can accommodate individual learning differences [28].

UDL recognises that each student learns in a unique way and emphasises flexibility in the teaching environment to cater to these diverse learning styles. It is built around three primary principles [29]:

1. **Multiple means of representation.** Learners differ in the ways that they perceive and comprehend information. Therefore, presenting information

and content in different ways can help all students learn. For example, a teacher might present a new concept through a combination of lectures, videos, interactive models, and readings.
2. **Multiple means of action and expression.** Learners differ in the ways they can navigate a learning environment and express what they know. Providing students with various ways to interact with material and show what they have learned can increase engagement and understanding. For instance, students might demonstrate their understanding of a topic through a written essay, an oral presentation, a group project, or a digital animation.
3. **Multiple means of engagement.** Learners differ markedly in the ways in which they can be engaged or motivated to learn. Providing different ways to motivate students can help ensure that all students are engaged. For example, teachers might incorporate elements of student choice, relate lessons to students' personal interests, or use published research to make the material more relevant and engaging.

By incorporating these principles into your teaching, UDL ensures that each student has an equal opportunity to learn. It recognises the diversity of learners and provides a flexible framework for accommodating this diversity in the classroom [30].

Another advantage of inclusive design, as advocated by UDL, is the 'curb-cut effect'. This term originates from the practice of cutting curbs to create ramps, initially intended to aid those with mobility impairments. However, such changes have proven beneficial to a wide range of individuals, including cyclists, parents with strollers, delivery workers, and many others [31].

Applying this effect to education, we find that designing learning environments with inclusivity at their core results in benefits for a broad spectrum of learners, not just those with specific needs or different learning styles. By using principles like multiple means of representation, action and expression, and engagement, we effectively cut the curb of education, making it more accessible and beneficial for everyone.

For example, a lesson plan designed with UDL principles in mind might include visual aids, verbal instruction, and hands-on activities to cater to different learning styles. While initially intended to benefit those with specific learning needs, these methods can enhance everyone's learning experience by providing diverse perspectives and approaches to the material. Building on this, it becomes critical to tether the concepts we teach to the world outside the classroom.

This is where the strategic integration of recent scientific research into your teaching comes in to play, significantly enhancing students' engagement and comprehension. By anchoring abstract or complex concepts to tangible instances, students can appreciate the relevance of their learning beyond the academic confines. This approach underscores the practical utility of the knowledge, fostering a deeper understanding of its impact and value.

For instance, in a biology lesson, one could introduce the concept of adaptation by discussing various animal species and how they have evolved to survive in their specific environments. In a math lesson on proportions, the instructor could refer to architectural designs, cooking recipes, or even financial scenarios to illustrate the concept's applicability. By relating theoretical knowledge to everyday phenomena, educators can spark students' curiosity and motivation, leading to enhanced interest and learning retention.

Furthermore, the use of diverse case studies plays a crucial role in this context. Case studies present detailed scenarios that students can explore, analyse, and discuss, offering them the opportunity to apply their knowledge in a contextualised setting. This is especially important in higher education, where students are preparing for professional roles that will require the practical application of their academic knowledge.

Diverse case studies also contribute to inclusivity in education [32]. By drawing from a wide array of geographical, cultural, socioeconomic, and professional contexts, educators can make learning more relatable to a broader range of students. Case studies that reflect students' backgrounds and experiences can make the learning more relevant, while those from different contexts can broaden their perspectives and understanding of the global implications of their field of study.

For instance, geology students could be asked to study the geological attributes leading to the presence of natural resources, like the oil reserves in the Middle East or the mineral wealth in Africa. Such case studies provide insights into the practical implications of geosciences in societal and economic contexts. This diverse approach to case studies bridges the gap between theoretical knowledge and practical application, fostering a comprehensive understanding of the subject and the wider discipline.

The lack of diversity in higher education science curricula presents a multitude of issues. It often reflects and perpetuates limited, Western perspectives, causing the neglect of other valuable knowledge systems, and potentially alienating non-Western students [33]. Furthermore, the relevance of the curriculum could be limited for students from diverse backgrounds if it does not include varied contexts and applications [34]. This deficiency in diversity can stifle innovation and limit problem-solving capacities, as homogeneous viewpoints are less likely to generate diverse solutions [35]. It may also result in inequitable learning opportunities by not catering to varied learning styles. Lastly, without diverse viewpoints, science curricula may fail to address crucial social justice issues, such as environmental racism and health disparities. Therefore, enhancing diversity in science curricula is imperative for providing an inclusive, comprehensive, and quality education.

Strategies for doing so include advocating for systemic institutional change, incorporating varied perspectives in curricula, delivering the historical and socio-political contexts of a scientific subject, tying scientific principles to a broader range of geographical locations, adopting diverse communication styles in teaching to accommodate different learning styles, and promoting learner transformation and agency [32]. These approaches, when executed, have the potential to build a more inclusive and diversified curricula, allowing all students to see themselves represented and to flourish as students and individuals.

Just as UDL fosters an inclusive learning environment by tailoring the instructional design to a range of learning styles, diversifying curricula also brings about widespread benefits that extend to all students. The adoption of a more varied curriculum expands the educational horizon and provides students with a richer and more holistic understanding of the subject matter. It encourages critical thinking, adaptability, and empathy as students are exposed to various perspectives, historical contexts, and practical applications. In addition, the act of tying scientific principles to geographically diverse locations enhances global awareness and further highlights the practicality of the subject matter. By diversifying communication and teaching styles, we can reach students with differing learning preferences more effectively, thereby optimising their potential for learning. Diversifying curricula does not just cater to the needs of the marginalised or underrepresented groups—it enhances the learning environment and experience for everyone involved, fostering a more robust, comprehensive, and inclusive education.

Exercise: Diversify you reading lists

This exercise, inspired by the work of Bird and Pitman [36], will help you diversify your reading lists to encompass a broader range of perspectives, enhancing the inclusivity and comprehensiveness of their teaching.

1. **Review your current reading list.** Begin by examining the reading list for a module that you teach (if you do not currently teach any modules then consider the reading list for another module in your university department). Take note of the authors and the perspectives they represent. Are the authors primarily from Western countries? Are they mostly male? Are there any authors from underrepresented groups?
2. **Identify gaps.** Based on your initial review, identify any notable gaps in perspectives. Are there certain cultures, genders, or socioeconomic backgrounds that are not represented? Does your reading list cover the global context of your scientific discipline or is it focused on Western science?
3. **Conduct research.** Search for scientific literature that fills the gaps you identified. Look for studies and texts authored by scientists from diverse backgrounds. This might include research conducted in different parts of the world or research done by scientists from underrepresented groups. If you are unsure where to start, ask your subject librarians for assistance.
4. **Integrate diverse perspectives**. Gradually incorporate these diverse sources into your course reading list. It is not about replacing all existing material, but rather complementing it to provide a more rounded perspective.
5. **Contextualise the material.** When introducing these texts to your students, be sure to provide context. Explain why you have chosen these pieces and what unique perspectives they bring. This will help your students understand the value of these diverse perspectives.
6. **Encourage reflection.** Ask your students to reflect on the diverse perspectives they are exposed to. This might be in the form of a reflective essay, a class discussion, or even a social media post.
7. **Seek feedback.** Solicit feedback from your students about the revised reading list. Was it helpful to have diverse perspectives? Did they feel that certain voices were still missing? Use this feedback to continually adapt and improve your reading list.

By diversifying your reading lists, you are not only teaching your students about the subject at hand but also about the importance of considering and respecting diverse perspectives in science and in life.

9.4 Assessment and feedback

Assessment in higher education extends far beyond traditional examinations and essays. It encompasses a broad spectrum of methods—each with its own strengths and nuances. Such methods include multiple-choice quizzes, short answer questions, essays, presentations, projects, practical demonstrations, and peer assessments. Each of these techniques allows the measurement of different types of skills and knowledge. For instance, while multiple-choice quizzes may measure recall and comprehension, project-based assessments may gauge students' abilities in problem-solving, creativity, and collaboration. The choice of assessment method should be closely aligned with the course objectives and desired learning outcomes [37].

Regular formative assessment plays an integral role in the educational process. It helps to gauge students' understanding and progress and provides a mechanism for students and instructors alike to track performance. Assessment is not merely a snapshot of a student's knowledge at a single point in time but rather, it is a continuous and dynamic process that should reflect the ongoing learning journey. By incorporating frequent, low-stakes or non-assessed (formative) assessments throughout a module, instructors can monitor progress, identify areas of difficulty, and intervene to provide necessary support. For students, regular formative assessments provide an opportunity to self-assess their understanding, reinforcing what has been taught while promoting self-regulated learning strategies [38].

Assessments in higher education can be broadly categorised into formative and summative assessments, each serving a different purpose [39]. Formative assessments are designed to provide ongoing feedback and are instrumental in shaping the learning process. They enable educators to adjust teaching strategies according to students' needs and help students identify their strengths and areas for improvement. Examples of formative assessments include quizzes, drafts of assignments, and class discussions.

Summative assessments, on the other hand, evaluate students' proficiency in the course content at the end of an instructional period, such as a module. They are often high-stakes and include exams, final projects, and essays. While formative assessments guide the learning process, summative assessments provide an opportunity for students to demonstrate their comprehension and synthesis of the scientific principles that have been taught. It is in this junction of learning and evaluation that constructive alignment plays a vital role.

Constructive alignment is a principle that advocates for the harmony between learning outcomes, teaching methods, and assessment tasks [40]. In other words, what we want students to learn, how we teach it, and how we assess it should all align seamlessly. This principle, acting as the bridge between formative and summative assessments, ensures the integrity and efficacy of both. In a constructively aligned course, the assessments are designed to directly measure the learning outcomes. For instance, if a learning outcome is for students to be able to analyse geological data, the assessment should require students to demonstrate this skill. This principle ensures that students are taught and assessed on what they are expected to learn, promoting fairness and clarity in the educational process.

Building on the theme of constructive alignment, is a pedagogical approach known as 'authentic assessment'. Authentic assessment, intrinsically aligned with professional contexts and applications, is a pivotal part of a well-rounded evaluation strategy [41]. This approach requires students to employ their learned skills and knowledge to tackle challenges that mirror those they may encounter in their future professional or personal endeavours. Rather than simply regurgitating learnt information, students are tasked with integrating and applying their knowledge in a dynamic context. Take, for instance, a student studying climate science: they could be asked to dissect actual climate data (which might have been generated by the instructor or a collaborator) and deliver a report detailing their findings and recommendations for climate change mitigation. This assessment strategy not only provides a platform for students to exhibit their learning in a consequential context, but also nurtures indispensable skills such as critical thinking, problem-solving, and communication—skills that hold value beyond the academic sphere (see chapter 10).

Embracing the principles of constructive alignment and authentic assessment, we shift our focus to another cornerstone of effective learning: feedback. Acting as a conduit between teaching and comprehension, feedback offers a reflection of students' performance, thereby illuminating their strengths and underlining areas that need enhancement. Much more than a one-way directive, good feedback establishes a dialogue between educator and learner, crafting an environment conducive to active learning. This encourages students to monitor their progression and assume ownership of their academic journey. Feedback thus serves as a compass, guiding learners towards their educational goals and instilling a sense of purpose.

Providing timely and meaningful feedback can be quite a task, especially given the demands of teaching large classes. However, strategies such as easy-to-understand marking rubrics, making use of peer feedback, and leveraging technological tools can ease this process. Rubrics, when shared with students beforehand, provide a clear expectation and a guideline, making the assessment transparent and understandable. Peer feedback encourages a collaborative learning environment and provides multiple perspectives. Technological tools, such as online grading and feedback systems, can streamline the feedback process, allowing educators to provide more timely feedback. Feedback should be constructive, specific, and actionable, highlighting not only areas for improvement but also acknowledging areas of strength.

Assessments significantly impact student motivation and engagement. Well-designed assessments can inspire curiosity, drive learning, and nurture a deep understanding of the subject matter. By providing a clear goal and a sense of direction, assessments can catalyse students' intrinsic motivations, encouraging them to engage more fully with the material. However, poorly designed or excessively stressful assessments can lead to student disengagement or foster a surface approach to learning. Make sure that assessments are fair, transparent, and closely aligned with learning outcomes to promote positive learning experiences.

As educators, we need to strike a delicate balance between fostering a trusting learning environment and ensuring academic integrity. This requires a comprehensive approach that includes clear communication of academic expectations, promoting a culture of integrity, and implementing fair and effective policies to address academic misconduct. For instance, codes of conduct, tutorials on plagiarism, and discussions about ethical scholarship can help cultivate a culture of integrity [42]. Simultaneously, the use of plagiarism detection software and well-articulated policies can help manage instances of academic misconduct.

In this digital age, artificial intelligence (AI), including platforms such as ChatGPT, has the potential to revolutionise education, including assessment practices. While AI can offer personalised feedback and innovative teaching tools, traditional forms of assessment, such as essays, remain relevant. They foster critical thinking and articulate expression of thought, which AI tools can assist but not replace. However, the rise of AI also introduces fresh challenges concerning ethics and equity [43]. Thus, developing an AI policy for assessment becomes paramount to navigate these challenges [44]. Any such policy should address issues such as data privacy, algorithmic fairness, transparency, and accountability. It should ensure that AI is used in a way that is ethical, equitable, and aligned with the values of the institution and the educational goals of the module and/or programme. Educators, students, and other partners should be involved in the development of this policy to enable a diversity of perspectives and collective ownership.

> **Exercise. Developing an AI fair use policy**
> The aim of this exercise is to guide you in formulating a comprehensive AI fair use policy tailored to your unique educational setting. As you work through this task, consider how AI can be used responsibly to augment learning and assessment without compromising ethical principles and fairness.
> 1. **Research.** Begin by exploring how AI is currently used in educational settings, both within and outside of your institution. What are the benefits and potential challenges associated with each application? Consider the ethical implications of AI in terms of data privacy, equity, and transparency.
> 2. **Define purpose.** Outline the purpose and scope of your AI fair use policy. What aspects of AI usage in education will it cover? This could include AI applications in teaching, assessment, student support, and administrative tasks.
> 3. **Consult partners.** Identify all the partners who might be affected by the AI policy (i.e. students, teaching staff, administrative staff, IT teams). Consider how you might involve them in the policy development process for a diversity of perspectives.
> 4. **Outline principles.** Draft a list of key principles that your policy will uphold. These might include transparency (clarity about how and why AI is being used), fairness (ensuring AI does not disadvantage certain groups of students), privacy (protection of personal data), and accountability (outlining who is responsible if something goes wrong).
> 5. **Develop guidelines.** Based on the principles you have outlined, develop specific guidelines on AI usage in different aspects. For instance, if you are using AI for assessment, how will you ensure it is fair and transparent? How will you protect student data? How will you ensure students understand how AI is being used in their education?
> 6. **Implement and review.** Consider how you will implement this policy and educate stakeholders about it. Additionally, outline a process for regular review and update of the policy to ensure it stays relevant as AI technology and its usage evolve.

As we explore the nuances of assessment and feedback, it becomes evident that they are not merely administrative or evaluative tasks, but rather integral components of a holistic and learner-centred approach to education. Nurturing a culture of continual learning, they provide signposts for students, guiding them on their academic journey. They encourage engagement, foster resilience, and stimulate intellectual curiosity. At their heart, assessments should be fair, aligned with learning objectives, and provide scientific context. Likewise, feedback needs to be timely, constructive, and meaningful. Embracing a varied and effective assessment and feedback system in higher education is not just about quantifying learning or meeting curriculum standards; it is about building an academic culture that champions learner growth, inclusivity, and the pursuit of knowledge.

9.5 Turning frontier research into a module

First, it is important to clarify the terminology used in academic programming. In higher education, terms such as 'programmes', 'modules', and 'courses' often overlap but carry subtle differences. A programme refers to an entire degree or study plan. Modules, often synonymous with courses in some educational contexts, are components of the programme, focused on specific subject areas. In this section, and throughout this chapter we will use module as it offers a level of granularity suitable for the transformation of specific research topics into teachable units.

Integrating up-to-date research into higher education teaching provides multifaceted benefits, not only enriching the academic journey of students but also nurturing a dynamic learning environment that echoes the progressive nature of scientific exploration [45]. It offers students an opportunity to be at the forefront of scientific discovery and innovation, ensuring their learning remains relevant and attuned to current advancements. Being privy to the latest research findings can also deepen their understanding of the subject matter. Furthermore, it equips them with the most recent scientific tools and techniques, thereby preparing them for future professional roles in a constantly evolving scientific landscape.

In addition to enriching students' learning experience, the integration of current research can have significant implications on the pedagogical practices of educators [46]. For educators, the incorporation of up-to-date research into their teaching repertoire allows them to continually refresh their knowledge base, keeping their expertise sharp and relevant. It enhances their teaching methods, permitting them to create dynamic connections that make complex scientific concepts more accessible and engaging for students. This fusion of research and teaching thus cultivates a mutually beneficial symbiosis where scientific progress and the pursuit of knowledge coalesce into an engaging educational experience.

Creating a teaching module based on your own scientific research is an exciting opportunity to bring research relevance into your classroom. The first step is to identify the core concepts from your research that are essential for students to grasp. Break down these concepts into manageable learning outcomes—these are the key ideas or skills that students should acquire after completing the module. Remember to consider the overall coherence of the module—all learning outcomes should be interconnected, creating a comprehensive and cohesive learning experience.

Building on from this, our next step is to leverage constructive alignment, a principle we have touched upon earlier in this chapter. By bridging learning outcomes with the teaching strategies and assessments, we can ensure a harmonious learning journey for students. Think about the teaching methods that will best deliver your learning outcomes. This could range from lectures and seminar discussions to laboratory work and group projects. Simultaneously, design your assessments to directly measure these learning outcomes. This should include a mix of formative and summative assessments that offer many opportunities for students to demonstrate their grasp of the subject matter.

Next, consider how to make use of authentic assessment. Remember, authentic assessment tasks mirror societal challenges, allowing students to apply their learned knowledge and skills in a practical context. Consider assessments that mimic the tasks they might face in their future careers. For instance, students could be asked to analyse data, develop research proposals, or design and conduct experiments. Not only does this make learning more engaging, but it also cultivates critical transferrable skills.

Incorporating UDL principles in your module design will also foster an inclusive and accessible learning environment (see section 9.3). The core of UDL is flexibility—it champions multiple means of representation, action and expression, and engagement. In terms of representation, think about how you can present your research topics in diverse ways to cater to different learning styles. For action and expression, consider providing different avenues for students to interact with the material and express their understanding. Finally, for engagement, think about how to motivate and engage students using different strategies, through inquiry-based tasks or collaborative projects.

For example, imagine that you are designing a new module that explores space science. When considering representation, think about how you can present your research topics on cosmic phenomena in diverse ways to cater to different learning styles. You could employ visual aids such as 3D models of celestial bodies or interactive star maps, use auditory tools like podcasts from renowned astronomers, and provide textual references such as scientific papers or articles for those who prefer to read. For action and expression, you might assign a project where students can construct a scale model of the Solar System or use a software to simulate gravitational interactions between celestial bodies. Alternatively, you might facilitate a debate on the ethics of space exploration or ask students to write a proposal for a hypothetical space mission. Finally, for engagement, appropriate tasks might include tracking the International Space Station, analysing actual NASA data, or researching the impact of space weather on Earth's technologies. Likewise, inquiry-based tasks, such as simulating sounds made by black holes or exploring the possibility of life on other planets, would likely stimulate curiosity. Collaborative projects, like designing a Mars colony or planning a space mission, could be used to foster cooperation and shared learning experiences.

Exercise. Develop a research-based teaching module

In this exercise, you will go through the step-by-step process of developing a teaching module based on your current research. Each step will prompt you to consider different aspects of module design and delivery, allowing you to create an engaging and effective teaching experience for your students.

1. **Identify the core concepts**. Start by dissecting your research to identify the core concepts or principles that would form the foundation of your module. These concepts should also be engaging for your target student audience.
2. **Assess constraints.** Now that you have your topic, consider the constraints that might shape your module. What are your students' current knowledge levels and skills? How much time do you have for teaching this module—is it a year-long course, or a shorter, more intensive module? What resources are available to you—are there lab facilities, software, fieldwork possibilities, or guest speakers that you can incorporate into your teaching? What is the student-to-staff ratio, and how does this impact your ability to provide individualised guidance or organise group activities? What kind of spaces are available for your classes? Acknowledging these constraints can guide you in making the module more practicable and fitting to your teaching context.
3. **Define learning outcomes.** Based on the identified core concepts, outline the learning outcomes for your module. These outcomes represent the knowledge, skills, and abilities you expect your students to gain by the end of the module. Be as specific and measurable as possible.
4. **Design teaching strategies**. Next, consider the teaching strategies you will employ to deliver your learning outcomes. Think about a mix of lectures, group discussions, lab work, or project-based learning. Keep in mind the diverse learning styles your students might have.
5. **Implement constructive alignment.** Think about how your learning outcomes, teaching strategies, and assessments align. All these three components should be in harmony, each reinforcing and complementing the others.
6. **Apply UDL principles**. Consider how you can make your module more inclusive and accessible using UDL principles. Think about different ways you can represent your content, engage your students, and allow your students to express what they have learned.

7. **Create your lesson plans.** With the larger framework in place, it is time to create detailed lesson plans for each session of your module. Each lesson plan should align with your learning outcomes, include a mix of teaching strategies, and provide opportunities for formative assessment.
8. **Review and refine.** Finally, seek feedback from colleagues or a mentor. Let them review your module design and offer insights or suggestions. Be open to revising and refining your module based on this feedback.
9. **Prepare for delivery.** Make sure all the necessary resources are prepared and ready before the start of the module. This could be anything from lecture slides and reading materials, to setting up online platforms for student collaboration.
10. **Reflect after delivery.** After delivering your module, take the time to reflect. What worked well? What could be improved? What feedback did you receive from your students? Use these reflections to further refine and improve your module for future iterations.

Translating current research into science teaching can yield numerous benefits. It can enhance student engagement by connecting theoretical concepts with recent scientific research. It also exposes students to the forefront of scientific discoveries, nurturing their curiosity and critical thinking. Additionally, it can offer students a glimpse into what it means to be a scientific researcher, equipping them with relevant knowledge and skills.

Nevertheless, transforming complex research concepts into teachable content come with its own challenges. It can be tricky to simplify intricate concepts without losing their essence or depth. Furthermore, keeping the teaching content updated with the latest research can be demanding given the rapid pace of scientific discoveries. Strategies to tackle these issues include gradually introducing complex concepts, using metaphors and analogies, incorporating multimedia resources, and engaging in continuous professional development. The creation and refinement of a research-based module is an ongoing journey of reflection and adaptation. Skills that we will now look to develop in section 9.6.

9.6 Reflecting

Reflection is a fundamental aspect of teaching, often serving as the bridge between experience and learning. It allows us to look back on our teaching practices, evaluate their effectiveness, and make necessary adjustments for future improvement [47]. Reflection is not just about identifying what went well or what did not; it is about understanding how and why these outcomes occurred, using this understanding to inform our future actions.

Reflective practice is not a new concept in education. Several models have been developed to guide educators through a structured process of reflection. One such model is Gibbs' reflective cycle [48]. Gibbs' cycle (see figure 9.1) encourages educators to consider their experiences from multiple angles, focusing not just on what happened but also on their thoughts, feelings, and reactions to the situation,

Figure 9.1. Gibbs' reflective cycle. This cycle features a series of questions that help to guide the user through a process of meaningful reflection.

before concluding with an action plan for future situations. This model promotes a deep and holistic analysis of one's teaching practice, moving beyond surface-level observations to uncover underlying beliefs, attitudes, and assumptions.

However, reflection, particularly when it involves our emotions, can be challenging for scientists. We are often trained to be objective and to leave our emotions out of our scientific work. But teaching is not just a cognitive activity; it is also an emotional one. Our emotions can provide valuable insights into our teaching practices and influence our interactions with students. Recognising and acknowledging our emotions can be a powerful step towards more effective reflection and improved teaching.

Let us consider a hypothetical teaching scenario—an educator delivering a complex astronomy concept in a lecture who notices their students' apparent lack of understanding. Let us walk through each step of Gibbs' reflective cycle based on this experience, from the point-of-view of the educator.

1. **Description**. During a lecture on the Hertzsprung–Russell diagram, I noticed many students appearing confused and unengaged. There were fewer

questions than usual, and several students had a hard time during the interactive portion of the class, where they were supposed to plot star data onto the diagram.
2. **Feelings.** I felt frustrated and discouraged. I had spent a significant amount of time preparing the lesson and was excited to share this fundamental concept in astrophysics. However, I also felt concerned about the students' learning and understood the importance of addressing this issue promptly.
3. **Evaluation.** The challenging aspect was the clear disconnect between my teaching and the students' understanding. My method of explaining the Hertzsprung–Russell diagram did not resonate well with them. On the positive side, I identified this issue early in the course, providing an opportunity for modification in my approach.
4. **Analysis**: Reflecting on the situation, I believe that the complexity of the Hertzsprung–Russell diagram might have been daunting for the students. I assumed too much prior knowledge or rushed through the foundational concepts. The students' confusion signals that I need to revisit my teaching approach for this concept.
5. **Conclusion.** In retrospect, I could have broken down the concept into smaller, more manageable parts and paced my teaching more slowly. Incorporating some small formative assessments throughout the lesson could have provided early indications of student understanding (or lack thereof).
6. **Action plan.** Moving forward, I plan to revisit the Hertzsprung–Russell diagram in the next class. I will start with a brief review of the foundational concepts, use more visual aids, and incorporate interactive elements to keep the students engaged. Also, I will make sure to check for understanding throughout the lesson. Long-term, I will be more mindful about gauging student comprehension, especially when dealing with complex concepts.

The goal of reflection is not to focus on what went wrong, but to identify strategies for improvement and to continue refining your teaching practice. As can be seen from this worked example, the lessons that you learn from these reflections are applicable beyond a single taught topic.

Exercise: Reflecting using Gibbs' reflective cycle
Choose a recent teaching experience—a lesson, a student interaction, a moment of realisation—anything that stands out to you as significant. Now, go through each stage of Gibbs' reflective cycle.
  1. **Description.** What happened?
  2. **Feelings.** What were your thoughts and feelings?
  3. **Evaluation.** What was good and bad about the experience?
  4. **Analysis.** What sense can you make of the situation?
  5. **Conclusion.** What else could you have done?
  6. **Action plan.** If it arose again, what would you do?

Reflecting on your experiences using this structured approach can provide you with valuable insights into your teaching practice and pave the way for meaningful improvement.

There are many other models of reflection available, each with its own strengths and limitations. Schön's model [49], for example, distinguishes between reflection-on-action (reflecting after the event) and reflection-in-action (reflecting during the event), emphasising the value of immediate, in-the-moment reflection. Kolb's experiential learning model [50] on the other hand incorporates reflection as part of a broader cycle of learning. The choice of model depends on your needs, preferences, and the specific context.

Regardless of the model you choose, the key is to make reflection a regular part of your teaching practice. Experiment with different models, adapt them as needed, and find the approach that works best for you (and your students). Reflection is a personal journey. There is no one-size-fits-all approach. So, go forth and reflect—your teaching practice will be all the better for it.

9.7 Support and development

As demonstrated throughout this chapter, there is a wealth of considerations involved in effective higher education teaching. We have explored several of these strategies and concepts—from Universal Design for Learning and constructive alignment to authentic assessment and reflective practice. Yet, this is but the tip of the iceberg. Additional components of the teaching role, such as PhD supervision, tutoring, and pastoral care, among others, also demand our attention. With this vast array of responsibilities and considerations, the question arises: where can educators seek support and further their skills?

The good news is that there are ample avenues for educators to secure support and bolster their teaching acumen. A popular path involves acquiring specific educational qualifications, such as a Postgraduate Certificate in Education (PGCert). This certification (which is often a compulsory requirement for most teaching academics in the UK) offers a comprehensive understanding of teaching methodologies, assessment techniques, and curriculum design, tailored specifically for the higher education context. It provides an excellent foundation for those new to teaching and can also serve as a valuable refresher for more experienced educators.

Mentoring is another powerful tool for professional development in higher education. It provides a platform for sharing experiences, insights, and best practices among educators. Mentoring will be discussed further in chapter 10, but these relationships can be particularly beneficial for early-career academics, offering guidance and support as they navigate the complexities of teaching in a higher education setting. Many institutions have formal mentoring programs in place, but informal mentoring relationships can be equally valuable.

In addition to these resources, there are several organisations dedicated to supporting educators in higher education. For instance, Advance HE, based in the UK, offers a range of services including professional development courses, teaching resources, and accreditation programs. The Quality Assurance Agency for Higher Education (QAA) also provides valuable support, setting and monitoring standards for UK higher education. Outside the UK, there are similar bodies such as the American Association for Higher Education (AAHE) in the United States, and the European Association for Quality Assurance in Higher Education (ENQA) in Europe. These organisations offer a wealth of resources and support to help educators continually improve their teaching practice and ensure the highest quality of education for their students.

Teaching in higher education is a rewarding but challenging endeavour. However, with the right support and resources, educators can continually enhance their skills and make a significant impact on their students' learning experiences. Whether through qualifications such as a PGCert, mentoring programs, or the support of organisations like Advance HE and QAA, there are numerous avenues for professional development in higher education teaching. Also, do not overlook one of the most immediate and accessible sources of support: your professional network. Colleagues and peers within your institution and the wider field can offer insights, share experiences, provide feedback, and collaboratively tackle teaching challenges. By reaching out and cultivating these relationships, you can gain a wealth of knowledge and support that complements formal developmental pathways, thereby enhancing your teaching practice in a comprehensive and contextually rich manner.

9.8 Summary

Throughout this chapter, we have discussed a wide array of critical considerations for teaching science in higher education. We began by underlining the significance of educational theories and pedagogical strategies that anchor successful teaching. Here, we highlighted Universal Design for Learning (UDL) and curriculum development, emphasising the necessity of inclusive practices, and the vast advantages of a diverse curriculum.

Assessment and feedback were discussed in detail, encompassing a broad spectrum of strategies and approaches. The crucial principles of constructive alignment and authentic assessment were discussed, as well as the role of timely and meaningful feedback. We also outlined how you might turn innovative research into teaching opportunities, and highlighted the role that reflection can (and should) play in your learning and teaching journeys.

In the evolving landscape of higher education, the emergence of AI has introduced both challenges and opportunities. On one hand, AI could potentially revolutionise the classroom experience, offering personalised learning pathways, instant feedback, and a wealth of resources tailored to individual student needs [51]. It can also assist educators in identifying learning gaps, predicting student performance, and optimising curriculum delivery [52]. On the other hand, the integration of AI in higher education brings forth ethical concerns related to data privacy, potential biases in AI algorithms, and the risk of over-reliance on technology at the expense of human interaction and critical thinking [53]. As educators, it is crucial to strike a balance, leveraging the benefits of AI while remaining vigilant to its limitations and potential pitfalls.

The process of teaching in higher education is one of continuous learning, adapting, and growing. By embracing these principles, and understanding the underpinnings of effective teaching practices, you will be better equipped to navigate this rewarding journey and contribute meaningfully to the transformative educational experiences of your students.

9.9 Further study

The further study in this chapter is designed to help you enhance your teaching practice and understanding of contemporary pedagogical principles:

1. **Review a module**. Choose a module you have taught previously or one you are currently teaching. Revisit the teaching methods, learning outcomes, and assessments and see how you can apply the principles of UDL and constructive alignment. Identify areas for improvement and redesign the module accordingly.
2. **Authentic assessment design**. Create an authentic assessment task for one of your modules. This should reflect actual societal and/or scientific scenarios and require students to apply their learned knowledge and skills. Get feedback from colleagues or students, if possible, and refine the task accordingly.
3. **Continuing professional development**. Investigate professional development opportunities available to you, such as a Postgraduate Certificate in Education, or courses offered by organisations like Advance HE or QAA. Choose one opportunity that aligns with your identified areas for improvement and commit to pursuing it.
4. **Peer support**. Reach out to your networks for feedback on your teaching practices. This could involve peer observation, mentoring, or collaborative discussions around pedagogical challenges and solutions. Reflect on the feedback and insights you gain from these interactions and incorporate them into your teaching practice.

9.10 Suggested reading

When it comes to exploring the modern dimensions of teaching in higher education, including the role of technology, reflection, and innovative research, many useful resources already exist. Each of these recommended books and articles offers unique insights, aiding you in your endeavour to hone your teaching skills and practices.

Begin your exploration with *Teaching for Quality Learning at University* [54] by John Biggs and Catherine Tang. This book serves as a comprehensive guide to understanding and implementing constructive alignment in higher education. It presents both theoretical underpinnings and practical guidelines for designing and delivering courses effectively, making it a valuable resource for educators at all levels.

For an in-depth discussion of effective assessment practices *Assessment and Feedback in Higher Education: A Guide for Teachers* [55] by Teresa McConlogue presents an excellent primer on the topic. This book encourages teachers to critically examine their practices, proposes small-scale educational investigations involving various partners, explores academic standards, and suggests methods for collaboratively establishing shared standards within teaching teams and students through calibration activities.

Understanding and applying Universal Design for Learning (UDL) principles is crucial for inclusive teaching. *Reach Everyone, Teach Everyone: Universal Design for Learning in Higher Education* [56] by Thomas J Tobin and Kirsten T Behling is an authoritative source on this subject. Targeting academics, student-service staff, disability support providers, campus leaders, and graduate students, this book offers resources to enhance the engagement and performance of all college students, providing case studies, active-learning techniques, UDL coaching skills, guidance on UDL adoption, and immediate-use resources for those keen to become UDL experts and advocates.

'Roles and research trends of artificial intelligence in higher education: a systematic review of the top 50 most-cited articles' [57] summarises key applications for AI in higher education such as predicting student outcomes, intelligent tutoring, and adaptive learning. While highlighting prevalent research, it also notes the need for more studies on AI's impact on collaboration, communication, and self-efficacy. By spotlighting influential studies, it provides educators, researchers, and policymakers with an invaluable overview of AI's capabilities and limitations in enhancing teaching and learning, while also identifying areas for future research and why this would be impactful.

Finally, when it comes to reflective practice, *Reflection in Learning and Professional Development: Theory and Practice* [58] by Jennifer A Moon offers an excellent starting point. This volume provides both practitioners and students with guidance that transcends specific theoretical frameworks, empowering them to use reflection as a tool to enhance practical learning.

References

[1] Waldrop M M 2015 The science of teaching science *Nature* **523** 272
[2] Smith E and Gorard S 2011 Is there a shortage of scientists? A re-analysis of supply for the UK *Br. J. Educ. Stud.* **59** 159–77
[3] Hodson D 2003 Time for action: science education for an alternative future *Int. J. Sci. Educ.* **25** 645–70
[4] Winberg C, Adendorff H, Bozalek V, Conana H, Pallitt N, Wolff K, Olsson T and Roxå T 2019 Learning to teach STEM disciplines in higher education: a critical review of the literature *Teach. High. Educ.* **24** 930–47
[5] Gregg-Jolly L A, Kington R, Lopatto D and Swartz J E 2011 Benefits of intertwining teaching and research *Science* **331** 532–2
[6] Beastall L and Walker R 2007 Effecting institutional change through e-learning: an implementation model for VLE deployment at the University of York *J. Organ. Transform. Soc. Chang.* **3** 285–99
[7] Rudolph J, Tan S and Tan S 2023 ChatGPT: bullshit spewer or the end of traditional assessments in higher education? *J. Appl. Learn. Teach.* **6** 342–62

[8] Bowden J L H, Tickle L and Naumann K 2021 The four pillars of tertiary student engagement and success: a holistic measurement approach *Stud. High. Educ.* **46** 1207–24

[9] Abulhul Z 2021 Teaching strategies for enhancing students' learning *J. Pract. Stud. Educ.* **2** 1–4

[10] Hadi N U and Muhammad B 2019 Factors influencing postgraduate students' performance: a high order top down structural equation modelling approach *Educ. Sci.: Theory Pract.* **19** 58–73

[11] Baepler P, Walker J D, Brooks D C, Saichaie K and Petersen C 2023 *A Guide to Teaching in the Active Learning Classroom: History, Research, and Practice* (Abingdon: Taylor and Francis)

[12] Seery M K 2015 Flipped learning in higher education chemistry: emerging trends and potential directions *Chem. Educ. Res. Pract.* **16** 758–68

[13] Howell R A 2021 Engaging students in education for sustainable development: the benefits of active learning, reflective practices and flipped classroom pedagogies *J. Clean. Prod.* **325** 129318

[14] Reznitskaya A, Kuo L J, Clark A M, Miller B, Jadallah M, Anderson R C and Nguyen-Jahiel K 2009 Collaborative reasoning: a dialogic approach to group discussions *Camb. J. Educ.* **39** 29–48

[15] Hetherington L, Hardman M, Noakes J and Wegerif R 2018 Making the case for a material-dialogic approach to science education *Stud. Sci. Educ.* **54** 141–76

[16] Almulla M A 2020 The effectiveness of the project-based learning (PBL) approach as a way to engage students in learning *Sage Open* **10** 2158244020938702

[17] Alves A C, Mesquita D, Moreira F and Fernandes S 2012 Teamwork in project-based learning: engineering students' perceptions of strengths and weaknesses *Proc. of the Fourth Int. Symp. on Project Approaches in Engineering Education (PAEE'2012) (Sao Paulo)* pp 23–32

[18] Bean J C and Melzer D 2021 *Engaging Ideas: The Professor's Guide to Integrating Writing, Critical Thinking, and Active Learning in the Classroom* (New York: Wiley)

[19] Dewsbury B and Brame C J 2019 Inclusive teaching *CBE—Life Sci. Educ.* **18** fe2

[20] Ferri F, Grifoni P and Guzzo T 2020 Online learning and emergency remote teaching: opportunities and challenges in emergency situations *Societies* **10** 86

[21] Stone C, Freeman E, Dyment J E, Muir T and Milthorpe N 2019 Equal or equitable? The role of flexibility within online education *Aust. Int. J. Rural Educ.* **29** 26–40

[22] Potkonjak V, Gardner M, Callaghan V, Mattila P, Guetl C, Petrović V M and Jovanović K 2016 Virtual laboratories for education in science, technology, and engineering: a review *Comput. Educ.* **95** 309–27

[23] Lynch T and Ghergulescu I 2017 Review of virtual labs as the emerging technologies for teaching STEM subjects *11th Int. Technology, Education and Development Conf. (Valencia)* 6082–91

[24] Laufer M, Leiser A, Deacon B, Perrin de Brichambaut P, Fecher B, Kobsda C and Hesse F 2021 Digital higher education: a divider or bridge builder? Leadership perspectives on edtech in a COVID-19 reality *Int. J. Educ. Technol. Higher Educ.* **18** 1–17

Azionya C M and Nhedzi A 2021 The digital divide and higher education challenge with emergency online learning: analysis of tweets in the wake of the COVID-19 lockdown *Turk. Online J. Distance Educ.* **22** 164–82

[25] Selwyn N and Aagaard J 2021 Banning mobile phones from classrooms—an opportunity to advance understandings of technology addiction, distraction and cyberbullying *Br. J. Educ. Technol.* **52** 8–19

[26] Dontre A J 2021 The influence of technology on academic distraction: a review *Human Behav. Emerg. Technol.* **3** 379–90

[27] Laurillard D 2013 *Rethinking University Teaching: A Conversational Framework for the Effective Use of Learning Technologies* (Abingdon: Routledge)

[28] Rose D H and Meyer A 2006 *A Practical Reader in Universal Design for Learning* (Cambridge, MA: Harvard Education Press)

[29] 2019 *Transforming Higher Education Through Universal Design for Learning: An International Perspective* ed S Bracken and K Novak (Abingdon: Routledge)

[30] Gargiulo R M and Metcalf D 2022 *Teaching in Today's Inclusive Classrooms: A Universal Design for Learning Approach* (Boston, MA: Cengage Learning)

[31] Blackwell A G 2017 The curb-cut effect *Stanf. Soc. Innov. Rev.* **15** 28–33

[32] Hall C A, Illingworth S, Mohadjer S, Roxy M K, Poku C, Otu-Larbi F and Morales J 2022 GC insights: diversifying the geosciences in higher education: a manifesto for change *Geosci. Commun.* **5** 275–80

[33] Charles E 2019 Decolonizing the curriculum *Insights* **32** 24

[34] Milem J F, Chang M J and Antonio A L 2005 *Making Diversity Work on Campus: A Research-Based Perspective* (Washington, DC: Association American Colleges and Universities) pp 1–39

[35] Hong L and Page S E 2004 Groups of diverse problem solvers can outperform groups of high-ability problem solvers *Proc. Natl Acad. Sci.* **101** 16385–9

[36] Schucan Bird K and Pitman L 2020 How diverse is your reading list? Exploring issues of representation and decolonisation in the UK *Higher Educ.* **79** 903–20

[37] Martin F, Ritzhaupt A, Kumar S and Budhrani K 2019 Award-winning faculty online teaching practices: course design, assessment and evaluation, and facilitation *Internet High. Educ.* **42** 34–43

[38] Andrade H and Brookhart S M 2016 The role of classroom assessment in supporting self-regulated learning *Assessment for Learning: Meeting the Challenge of Implementation* (Cham: Springer) pp 293–309

[39] Yüksel H S and Gündüz N 2017 Formative and summative assessment in higher education: opinions and practices of instructors *Eur. J. Educ. Stud.* **3** 336–56

[40] Ali L 2018 The design of curriculum, assessment and evaluation in higher education with constructive alignment *J. Educ. e-Learn. Res.* **5** 72–8

[41] Villarroel V, Bloxham S, Bruna D, Bruna C and Herrera-Seda C 2018 Authentic assessment: creating a blueprint for course design *Assess. Eval. High. Educ.* **43** 840–54

[42] Park C 2003 In other (people's) words: plagiarism by university students—literature and lessons *Assess. Eval. High. Educ.* **28** 471–88

[43] Holmes W, Porayska-Pomsta K, Holstein K, Sutherland E, Baker T, Shum S B and Koedinger K R 2021 Ethics of AI in education: towards a community-wide framework *Int. J. Artif. Intel. Educ.* **32** 504–26

[44] Chan C K Y 2023 A comprehensive AI policy education framework for university teaching and learning *Int. J. Educ. Technol. Higher Educ.* **20** 1–25

[45] Healey M 2005 Linking research and teaching to benefit student learning *J. Geogr. High. Educ.* **29** 183–201

[46] Yadav A, Lundeberg M, DeSchryver M, Dirkin K, Schiller N A, Maier K and Herreid C F 2007 Teaching science with case studies: a national survey of faculty perceptions of the benefits and challenges of using cases *J. Coll. Sci. Teach.* **37** 34
[47] Ashwin P, Boud D, Calkins S, Coate K, Hallett F, Light G and Tooher M 2020 *Reflective Teaching in Higher Education* (London: Bloomsbury Academic)
[48] Gibbs G 1988 *Learning by Doing: A Guide to Teaching and Learning Methods* (Oxford: Further Education Unit, Oxford Polytechnic)
[49] Schön D A 1984 *The Reflective Practitioner: How Professionals Think in Action* **vol 5126** (New York: Basic Books)
[50] Kolb D A 2014 *Experiential Learning: Experience as the Source of Learning and Development* (Upper Saddle River, NJ: FT Press)
[51] Tapalova O and Zhiyenbayeva N 2022 Artificial intelligence in education: aied for personalised learning pathways *Electron. J. e-Learn.* **20** 639–53
[52] Ouyang F, Zheng L and Jiao P 2022 Artificial intelligence in online higher education: a systematic review of empirical research from 2011 to 2020 *Educ. Inform. Technol.* **27** 7893–925
[53] Bates T, Cobo C, Mariño O and Wheeler S 2020 Can artificial intelligence transform higher education? *Int. J. Educ. Technol. High. Educ.* **17** 1–12
[54] Biggs J, Tang C and Kennedy G 2022 *Ebook: Teaching for Quality Learning at University 5e* (London: McGraw-Hill Education)
[55] McConlogue T 2020 *Assessment and Feedback in Higher Education: A Guide for Teachers* (London: UCL Press)
[56] Behling K T and Tobin T J 2018 *Reach Everyone, Teach Everyone: Universal Design for Learning in Higher Education* (Morgantown, WV: West Virginia University Press)
[57] Chu H C, Hwang G H, Tu Y F and Yang K H 2022 Roles and research trends of artificial intelligence in higher education: a systematic review of the top 50 most-cited articles *Australas. J. Educ. Technol.* **38** 22–42
[58] Moon J A 2013 *Reflection in Learning and Professional Development: Theory and Practice* (Abingdon: Routledge)

IOP Publishing

Effective Science Communication (Third Edition)
A practical guide to surviving as a scientist
Sam Illingworth and Grant Allen

Chapter 10

Other essential skills

People from different backgrounds approach a subject in different ways and ask different questions.

—**Jocelyn Bell Burnell**

10.1 Introduction

Science is a vast and complex tapestry, woven with threads of discovery, innovation, and knowledge. Being a scientist, therefore, extends beyond the confines of writing grant proposals, conducting experiments, and presenting findings. It involves the cultivation of a diverse set of skills, some of which are nurtured implicitly through undergraduate and postgraduate (and basic human) experiences, while others are refined throughout a lifetime of practice and occasional formal training. These skills, though often unseen, are the pillars that support a successful scientific career. They encompass time management, networking, academic integrity, best practice, self-reflection, and personal growth.

In the dynamic landscape of modern science, the career path of a scientist often demands multitasking and adaptive responses to fluctuating workloads. This can often be a source of stress and anxiety at all career stages, and navigating these personal and professional challenges is a deeply personal journey. In this chapter, we offer insights and strategies to manage your professional life and work–life balance, drawing from our personal experiences and those of our peers. While this chapter does not provide an exhaustive list, and certainly does not constitute or substitute professional medical advice, it highlights key skills and strategies, and discusses their importance in your current and future career trajectory.

Most individuals who embark on a PhD journey will eventually find their professional calling outside the academic sphere [1]. This necessitates the development of skills that are transferable and valuable in diverse environments. Choosing a career outside academia is not a sign of 'failure' or a 'betrayal of science'. On the contrary, numerous careers outside academia remain deeply intertwined with science and may offer better remuneration or more suitable working conditions that align with your professional lifestyle preferences.

In our experience, it is common for postgraduates and early career researchers to overlook the opportunities that exist beyond academia. They may become so engrossed in their specific research field that they lose sight of the broader picture. The skills and qualifications acquired in their career are still highly valued by alternative employers and industries. Such training opens more doors than it closes.

As scientists, we possess a suite of transferable skills that make us valuable assets in the workforce, whether as potential employees or self-employed practitioners. However, we need to recognise, cultivate, and effectively highlight these skills. This might involve keeping a record of events, activities, and training programs in which you have participated. These experiences can serve as powerful examples when updating your CV, conducting personal development reviews, or advocating for a promotion. We must also strive to be ethical scientists, upholding high standards of academic rigour and integrity. We are part of a rich scientific lineage and have a responsibility to honour our heritage, acknowledge and rectify our mistakes, and foster an inclusive environment for others. This chapter also provides guidance on how to achieve these goals.

Lastly, maintaining a healthy work–life balance is a critical component of a successful and sustainable career in science. Balancing professional responsibilities with personal needs and interests can help prevent burnout, promote mental health, and enhance productivity and creativity. Sadly, we have known far too many academics that have pushed themselves too hard in their professional life, to the point that both their career and personal life (and physical and mental health) may suffer. Put simply, scientists are human beings primarily. Investing in yourself as a human being is a direct investment in yourself as a scientist. If you remember nothing else from this chapter, remember that your career is a direct result of your health and happiness as a human being. In section 10.9, we discuss the importance of work–life balance and provide some practical strategies to achieve it, as well as how to recognise when you may need help.

10.2 Time management

Procrastination and prioritisation often pose significant challenges in our scientific journey, whether it is the immediate allure of social media or the subtle distractions of over-investing in a project with limited long-term value. However, there are several straightforward strategies you can employ to optimise your time:

1. **Know *when* you work best.** Each of us has a unique work rhythm, with research indicating that people have different peak productivity times and concentration spans [2]. Identify your most productive hours and reserve them for your most critical tasks. For instance, if you are most efficient right after arriving at work, resist the urge to check emails and focus on finishing that journal article with an impending deadline. Also, remember that taking effective breaks can rejuvenate your concentration, leading to a more productive day. Quality, not quantity, of time spent working often determines productivity.
2. **Know *where* you work best.** Choose an environment that suits the task at hand. A bustling shared office might be perfect for brainstorming a future research project, maintaining friendships, and cathartically venting about problems at work. But a quieter space like a library or your home office might be better for reading journal articles or when you simply need space from other people.
3. **Avoid unnecessary meetings.** The modern workplace can be demanding. Ensure any meetings you organise are essential, well-planned and well-timed. Invite only necessary participants and structure meetings to allow partial attendance. If a meeting clashes with other commitments, try to get the agenda in advance and complete the discussed tasks beforehand. This can

help you justify your absence and prioritise effectively. Stick to the agenda and do not allow meetings to overrun if you can help it. Allowing meetings to overrun is rarely an efficient use of time (everyone has a finite concentration span) and constitutes a lack respect for other people's time and plans. Strict adherence to time and agenda can focus minds and help to avoid meandering discussions, which can be all too often hijacked by someone else's personal agenda without good chairing. Follow-up meetings can always be arranged if needed when people are more refreshed.
4. **Take control of your calendar.** Incorporate daily tasks and deadlines into your calendar, including follow-up and evaluation dates. Reserving specific days for research or development activities can prevent them from being overrun by meetings. The sense of control and serenity that can come from a well-kept diary can go a long way to managing a healthy work–life balance.
5. **Manage your email.** Despite many alternative technologies for management and collaboration, emails remain a widely used default method of communication in professional workplaces to convey important (and far less important) information. Many people become anxious about achieving 'inbox zero' and struggle to switch off until they have read and responded to every message someone else has chosen to foist upon them. Instead, consider checking emails for a fixed period at specific times of the day, such as the start, middle, and end. While the flexibility of emailing outside working hours can be beneficial, balance this with its impact on your wellbeing. Do you really need to check your email just before you go to bed? Also, consider the efficiency of your emails and whether it is the best medium for your message. Sometimes, a brief phone or video call can resolve a complex discussion far more efficiently.
6. **Embrace technology.** There are numerous apps and tools designed to help manage tasks and time effectively. Experiment with different ones to find what works best for you (see chapter 7 for some suggestions). Whether it is a simple to-do list app or a more complex project management tool, technology can be a great ally in boosting productivity and promoting a sense of calm.

The STING acronym (figure 10.1) serves as a handy guide for effective time management. Start by choosing a suitable task and estimating the time required for

Select a task

Time yourself

Ignore everything else

No breaks

Give yourself a reward

Figure 10.1. The STING acronym for time management. This provides one useful methodology for managing your work effectively.

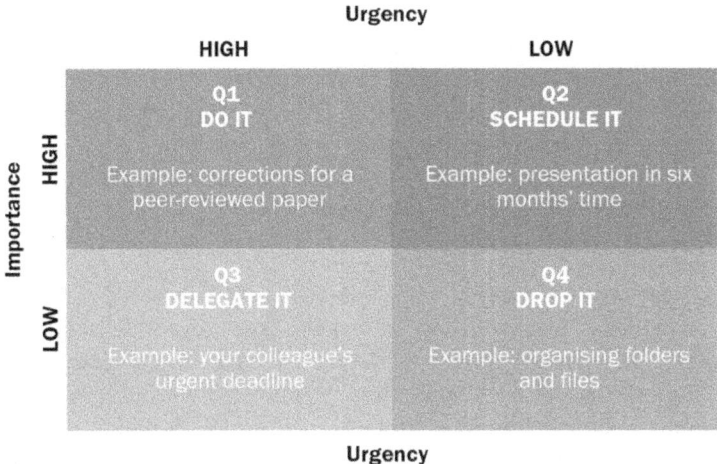

Figure 10.2. The importance–urgency matrix. This can be used to help prioritise which tasks need doing quickly, which can be postponed or delegated, and which can be dropped altogether.

its completion. For instance, 'I will write 500 words of this journal article's introduction in the next two hours'. During this period, focus solely on the task at hand, ignoring all distractions (silence your phone and disable your email if necessary), and only take breaks for comfort. Upon completion, reward yourself with something enjoyable, be it a slice of cake or a quick email check. The key is to select a task that is significant but achievable within a reasonable period. Breaking down complex tasks into shorter achievable tasks can activate our emotional reward system and maintain a constant sense of calm progress.

Another time management strategy is the Pomodoro Technique. This method divides the workday into 25 min segments, each followed by a 5 min break. These segments are known as 'Pomodoros', and after four of them, a longer break of 15–20 min is taken. This technique fosters a sense of urgency, with enforced breaks helping to prevent burnout and incorporate rewards [3]. If you wish to, you can track these intervals using a stopwatch or a dedicated app on your computer or smartphone—just be careful not to be too hard on yourself and allow for flexibility.

Lastly, an importance–urgency matrix, as depicted in figure 10.2, can be a valuable time management tool. If you have multiple important tasks, determine their position on this matrix. Tasks in Q1 require immediate attention, followed by those in Q2. Tasks in Q3 could be delegated or postponed, while those in Q4 can be dropped or ignored. Sometimes things in Q4 will migrate to Q1 over time and it is important to keep track of such changing priorities. But you may be surprised at how many things in Q4 may magically disappear or resolve themselves if left to their own devices.

10.3 Networking

Networking can be a daunting task for many of us. Few would claim to be expert networkers, and some may never feel completely at ease, opting instead to hone alternative strategies for professional engagement. However, like presenting and writing, effective networking can be nurtured with time and practice. As a scientific researcher, you will often find ample networking opportunities, whether during informal coffee breaks at conferences or at more formal events like organised dinners or dedicated networking sessions. The initial apprehension of approaching a stranger and initiating a conversation is usually the most significant hurdle. The following tips will help you to overcome these nerves and boost your confidence when networking opportunities arise:

1. **Embrace courage.** Many early career researchers hesitate to engage with senior scientists, fearing they are too 'important' to converse with. Remember, all eminent scientists were once early career researchers themselves, and most will welcome interactions with enthusiastic researchers. Most senior scientists recognise that science is a level playing field and that everyone has ideas and insights to offer to each other.
2. **Check your inner imposter.** Imposter syndrome is a recognised and near-ubiquitous challenge to scientists. Put simply, it is a false belief that we are out of our depth and have nothing useful to offer. Depending on who you are and the situation, it can manifest outwardly as anxiety and nervousness, defensiveness and over-confidence, panic, or some combination of all these traits. The authors of this book sure suffer with it. It is everywhere in academia and even the most successful scientists often question their authenticity. But knowing what imposter syndrome is, and recognising that you may be susceptible to it, is a large part of the battle in getting over it or living comfortably and effectively alongside it. Maintain your integrity and take pride in your unique expertise in your field(s). More experienced scientists may be present, but this does not diminish the value of your research or opinions. Imposter syndrome can be overcome by being true to your authentic self, valuing what you have to offer, and knowing that others really do value you too. Talking therapies, practice, and (if necessary) professional medical advice, may help if you feel that imposter syndrome or anxiety are a major barrier to completing day-to-day work.
3. **Balance the conversation.** In busy social environments such as conferences, well-known scientists may have a line of people waiting to talk to them. If you find yourself in such a situation, consider engaging with someone else and returning later. If others seem eager to talk to you, try to include them in the conversation to keep it flowing naturally.
4. **Tact over bluntness.** Networking sessions can be a great platform for early career scientists seeking potential employment. However, a tactful approach —demonstrating your skills and expertise before casually mentioning your upcoming contract renewal—can be more effective than directly asking for employment before proper introductions.
5. **Carry business cards.** Having business cards on hand allows you to continue conversations later and ensures your details can be passed on to other colleagues. Business cards with QR codes linking to your LinkedIn profile,

CV, or publication record, can be a great way to give people access to you as a professional.

6. **Follow up.** After meeting someone new, follow up with a brief message or email, especially if there is the potential for collaboration. This can help solidify the connection and open the door for future interactions. Networking is about building and maintaining relationships, not just exchanging business cards.

If networking events seem daunting, consider seeking an introduction. For instance, if you are joining a new team or working group, or wish to converse with a specific individual, you could ask a colleague or supervisor to introduce you. This can alleviate some of the initial nervousness associated with networking. Likewise, if you recognise that two individuals' work and interests align well, take the initiative to introduce them.

For those who find large social settings intimidating, consider starting with small-group or informal networking events. Attending gatherings where you are likely to encounter like-minded individuals (say, a meet-up of cat-loving particle physicists) can make the experience less overwhelming. Going to events with familiar colleagues can also provide a comfort zone. However, if you attend a networking event with friends or colleagues, avoid spending the entire time conversing only with them, as this defeats the purpose of networking.

In today's digital age, online networking has become increasingly important. As discussed in chapter 7, platforms like LinkedIn and ResearchGate offer opportunities to connect with professionals in your field worldwide. Participating in online webinars, virtual conferences, and discussion forums can also help to broaden your network. When doing so, maintain a professional online presence, engage in meaningful discussions, and respect digital etiquette. Just like in-person networking, online networking is about building relationships, so take the time to nurture these connections.

10.4 Teamwork

Teamwork, whether within a large international consortium or a small local group, is often integral to a scientific researcher's daily activities. Effective teamwork necessitates a variety of roles filled by different team members, each deserving of unbiased and non-prejudiced respect. While numerous behavioural and personality tests claim to identify your ideal role, the most effective way to discover your strengths and preferences is through experience. You might find that you excel at organising but struggle with generating innovative ideas. Conversely, you might have a knack for seeing the big picture but find it challenging to articulate those ideas in a clear, informative manner necessary for grant applications. Your preferred or most effective role may also vary depending on the project or team; do not shy away from exploring new roles in different situations, or to let people know what you feel your strengths and weaknesses are within a team objective.

Regardless of your role in various teams, it is typically impossible to do everything single-handedly, maintain high standards, and balance work and life effectively. Thankfully, the era when review panels favoured solo-authored publications and lone grant applications is behind us. Today, internationalisation and collaboration are seen as the keys to successful scientific research.

The secret to successful teamwork lies in appreciating everyone's uniqueness. Most team disagreements stem from the assumption or expectation that everyone will behave the same way. Each team member brings a unique set of strengths and weaknesses to different contexts, and what works for one person might not work for another. For instance, if you are a last-minute worker who always meets deadlines, be mindful that others may prepare their contributions well in advance and find deadlines stressful. Conversely, if you prefer to complete tasks as soon as possible, understand that others might not share your approach, so avoid pressuring them to conform to your timeline. To manage these differences in complex projects, incorporate effective planning, regular reviews, and flexibility into project management from the start. Leadership and delegation are more important to achieving a team objective than simply being seen to take on all the work that is available. Teamwork, like any relationship, requires compromise and respect. Maintaining professionalism, commitment, and politeness can make teamwork a more enjoyable and rewarding experience.

A crucial component of effective teamwork is diversity. However, diversity is not merely a box to be ticked. Numerous studies have shown that increased diversity leads to enhanced productivity, innovation, and impact [4–8]. Ensuring teams comprise diverse individuals with different approaches and backgrounds fosters a variety of opinions, needs, experiences, and solutions. If your current or future collaboration lacks diversity, question why and address it. If you are unable to enact change, find someone who can and raise the issue with them. As ethical scientists, we have a responsibility to ensure science is inclusive. A vital step towards this goal is redefining who a scientist is and what they look like.

10.5 Mentoring

Having a good mentor can be hugely beneficial, offering you invaluable advice from someone more seasoned, enhancing your skills and knowledge, and expanding your professional network. Many research institutions provide formal mentoring programs, particularly for early career researchers and new staff members. These programs can also offer a deeper understanding of your organisation and its various intricacies. However, with formal mentoring programs, there is a chance you might be paired with a mentor who does not align with your interests or future career path. To mitigate this, or in cases where no formal mentoring scheme is available, you should cultivate your own network of informal mentors.

When selecting your mentors, choose individuals you admire, whose experience and networks can aid your growth as a scientist. This network does not have to be limited to colleagues from your immediate research group or workplace. It could also include people you can meet sporadically, in a setting where you feel at ease sharing knowledge and advice. Your chosen mentor(s) should be individuals you connect with, who respect and understand you. They do not necessarily need to be in a higher position than you, but they should have expertise in an area where you feel you need improvement. For instance, if you struggle with presenting to a non-scientific audience, who do you know who excels at this? If you are new to grant writing, do you know someone who recently had a successful application? Building this informal network of mentors will also boost your self-awareness and confidence and could potentially open doors to future collaborations.

In addition to being a mentee, look for opportunities to serve as a mentor. This can be done formally or informally, and by sharing knowledge with other scientists, you will reinforce your own understanding, build networks, and gain fresh perspectives and ideas. Plus, as an ethical scientist, you will be assisting others in navigating their own scientific journeys.

10.6 Career planning

As highlighted in this chapter's introduction, many individuals who pursue a PhD will eventually find their career path leading them outside academia. Given the limited availability of public funding and the increasing number of research students viewing a PhD as a steppingstone to higher-level employment, this trend is likely to continue. In fact, it is probably more accurate to consider academia as the alternative career path. We have seen many PhD graduates and early career postdoctoral research associates battle with their own deeply held identity as a scientist when considering what to do next, sometimes to the detriment of their own happiness. A career outside academia can be a fulfilling and rewarding journey that still speaks to that inner identity and thirst for knowledge.

If the thrill of scientific research still captivates you, there is a plethora of careers you can explore outside academia. For instance, you could join a large non-university research institute or a government agency like the UK's Environment Agency or Germany's Max Planck Society. You might also be drawn to work for a global tech giant or a scientific instrument developer or manufacturer. Many of these roles will allow you to conduct scientific research, publish journal articles, and attend conferences, all while enjoying the stability of a full-time contract, a luxury often absent from many non-tenured early career positions within academia.

If at any point you find your interest in scientific research waning, rest assured, there are plenty of fulfilling and alternative paths to explore, and for which your training as a scientists provides valuable experience. For example, writing a thesis demonstrates your exceptional written communication and time management skills, while setting up experiments and analysing data highlights your ability to problem solve. Presenting your research at a conference highlights your excellent oral communication skills, and supervising undergraduates reveals your aptitude for teamwork and leadership. Recognising these experiences as evidence of the skills others may be seeking is key to crafting an engaging and effective CV.

There are many jobs outside of scientific research that would benefit from your transferable skills. The challenge lies in finding them and not allowing yourself to be too narrowly focused on the specifics of your past work. For example, in the UK (and many other parts of the world), there is a significant shortage of qualified science teachers, particularly in physics, maths, chemistry, and computing. To address this shortage, schemes like the one set up by the UK Government's Department for Education offer bursaries and financial support for teacher training.

If you choose to pursue a career in academia as a research-focused academic, you need to be realistic. The number of PhD students is growing at a rate that outpaces the increase in government research funding, as well as the rate at which undergraduate numbers may grow demand for higher education teaching. This means there simply are not enough permanent academic positions for every PhD graduate, forcing many excellent researchers to find employment through a series of fixed-term contracts that may offer less job security and might involve relocating over long distances. To maximise your chances of achieving tenure, you need a CV and expertise that demonstrate leadership and independence. Peer reviewed papers are the currency of academia and open the way to apply for fellowships, such as those discussed in chapter 3, which can often serve as a springboard into academic tenure. You may also need to be flexible (e.g. moving abroad), resilient, and reflective in your approach. Securing a tenured position in academia is not impossible, but it is certainly more challenging than ever before. And if it does not work out for you, you should not view this as a failure, but rather a reflection that sheer statistics are against it, and that may other exciting (and equally, if not more rewarding) career paths exist, at any career stage.

When contemplating your next career move, leaving academia does not permanently shut the door on a potential return. If an opportunity outside academia arises, do not dismiss it without careful consideration; many successful academics have spent time away from academia, and their careers have significantly benefited from this experience.

> **Exercise: Write a five year plan**
> Having a five year plan will help you to focus your future career objectives. Taking the time now to plan out what you want to achieve over the next five years will also help to ensure that you maximise your opportunities and will reveal which skills you need to develop further and where best to focus your time and energy. Think about what grants or fellowships you wish to apply for, how many publications you aim to produce, and any awards or accolades that you would like to receive.

> After writing your five year plan, ask one of your mentors to review your initial thoughts, and to see if you are being realistic. After another iteration, start to break down your plan into milestones and achievable tasks, and then use this as a guide to help focus your work into achieving your aims. Reflect on the five year plan during regular intervals (e.g. every six months), updating it with every major achievement, accomplishment, and setback, and what you have learnt from these experiences.

10.7 Integrity and malpractice

Without integrity, there is no meaningful research, and thus, no science. Despite the safeguards of peer-review systems, ethics boards, and academic scrutiny, the crux of our research hinges on conducting science in a fair, honest, and transparent manner.

At this juncture, we should distinguish what we mean between 'integrity' and 'malpractice'.

Integrity embodies both the ethics and the quality of academic rigour and best practice in the execution and presentation of science. This includes best practice in conducting experiments and experimental techniques, as well as the appropriate use of statistical analytical approaches, thorough transparency of methods, and data availability. The checks and balances of science work diligently to constructively elevate these standards when applied well. A lack of integrity can include instances of less serious plagiarism such as improper citation when discussing other people's work. Poor standards of integrity represent sloppy practice and less useful scientific outputs, but not necessarily wilful neglect.

Malpractice, on the other hand, represents unethical and potentially illegal approaches to science. While instances of malpractice remain extremely rare, they can be extremely detrimental to the reputation of the scientific community and society at large, especially if research based on malpractice is used to formulate policy or provide access to a new medicine, for example. Contemporary examples of fields in which malpractice must be carefully guarded against for public good include (but are not limited to): gene editing, drug development, and the application of artificial intelligence. These examples represent just a few current ethical challenges in scientific research, but other examples of malpractice include the fabrication of data and wilful plagiarism. The temptations for fabricating or copying the perfect results may be great, but the potential damage that this can cause to both reputations and knowledge mean that the negatives vastly outweigh any wrongly perceived positives. As ethical scientists, we have a responsibility to be vigilant of ourselves and others, and to ensure that we always remain beyond reproach.

Any research that you undertake should adhere to the ethical and integrity guidelines laid out by your research institute, especially if it involves the possible invasion of other parties' privacies. Most research institutions have such a policy, which sits within a hierarchy of legal and regulatory approaches to mitigate and respond to instances of malpractice. However, such ethical procedures are no longer the sole preserve of medical researchers and anthropologists and must be taken extremely seriously whenever your research might have a direct influence on the lives of others; for example, by flying a drone near to people or a built-up area, or when using satellite imagery to record high-resolution imagery of privately owned land.

As ethical scientists, we must also act with integrity towards our fellow researchers. Avoiding plagiarism, explicitly seeking permission, and dispensing appropriate acknowledgement are all ingredients for building a fertile research environment. If you are ever in doubt, then consider how you would feel if your own work had been abused in such a similarly anonymous manner. We owe it to each other, as scientists, to ensure that everyone is given recognition that is proportional to what they have legitimately earned.

With this in mind, we have a duty to challenge and report instances of poor standards or academic integrity and malpractice. To ensure integrity as co-authors, we should challenge our own research teams if poor standards are identified, and work constructively to reach solutions. As peer reviewers, we have the same duty, and as members of the academic community, we should seek to publish a rebuttal of inaccurate work. However, true malpractice may require a more formal and serious intervention. This can include reporting concerns such as plagiarism and fabrication to journals (which may lead to retractions for example), or reporting these same concerns to an institution, funding body, public or regulatory body, or in extremely rare circumstances, the police or other appropriate authority. When doing so, it may be useful to first discuss your approach to reporting malpractice with a trusted colleague or supervisor, but this should not prevent you from acting on your instincts if you have an objective reason to seriously question a potential case of malpractice.

In the digital age, the importance of integrity in science has only grown. The ease of sharing information and the speed at which it can spread means that the potential damage from malpractice is greater than ever. At the same time, digital tools also provide new ways to detect and prevent malpractice, from plagiarism detection software to open data repositories that allow for the verification of results.

Integrity is the cornerstone of scientific research and human progress. It is not just about avoiding malpractice, but about striving for excellence in all aspects of our work. By upholding the highest standards of integrity, we can ensure that science continues to be a force for knowledge, progress, and good in the world.

10.8 Promoting diversity

Section 10.4 discussed the merits of cultivating a diverse team, underscoring that diversity is not just a box to be ticked, but a potent and effective approach to conducting scientific research. However, one of the most formidable hurdles to achieving this diversity is in overcoming our own biases.

It might be an uncomfortable truth to confront, but the reality is that very few of us are entirely without bias, and research has demonstrated that most individuals harbour an implicit and unconscious bias against members of disadvantaged groups [9].

Once you have acknowledged your own biases, you can actively begin to address them, and one of the ways to do this is by proactively promoting and fostering diversity. There are several steps that individual researchers can take to do this, many of which will hinge on your personal circumstances, and often the extent to which you are 'privileged' within (and by) the scientific system. For instance, as a male researcher, you could decline any invitations to join a 'manel' (i.e. male-only panel) and instead recommend several non-male colleagues to take your place. Strategies also include seeking and providing professional development to empower and equip members of your team to address their own unconscious biases [10].

If you are organising talks, seminars, and conferences, ensure that there is diverse representation. However, make sure that you are inviting these individuals to discuss their work and research, not just to provide an opinion on what it means to be a non-white-cis-heterosexual-male scientist. Providing a platform for a diverse array of scientists to discuss their research is a powerful way to help re-normalise science, i.e. to make diversity the norm rather than the exception.

It is also important to consider diversity in online spaces. This could mean inviting speakers from different parts of the world for virtual seminars or ensuring that online discussions and forums are inclusive and welcoming to all.

Consider mentoring or sponsoring researchers from underrepresented groups. This can help them navigate the challenges of the scientific community and provide them with opportunities they might not otherwise have.

Lastly, remember that promoting diversity is an ongoing process. It requires continuous learning, reflection, and action. By committing to this process, we can help create a scientific community that is truly inclusive and representative of the diverse world in which we live.

10.9 Recognising and managing stress

In the pursuit of scientific discovery, it is easy to lose sight of the importance of maintaining a healthy work–life balance. The pressure to produce results, publish papers, and secure funding can often lead to long hours and a blurring of the boundaries between professional and personal life. However, a balanced life is not only healthier but also more conducive to long-term productivity and success in your scientific career.

Modern academic careers are stressful. They were stressful for many in the past. But in the authors' personal experiences, many of our later-career academic colleagues report that current stresses and strains in academic life are unprecedented in their view. Many recent studies agree [11, 12]. Other high-profile studies [13] highlight the impact of the COVID-19 pandemic in crystallising burnout among academic staff globally. The causes of this trend do not start and end at the door to the office, but the nature of modern academic work has a large part to play. Confounding aspects include the growing metricisation of higher education and research, the pace of work enabled by easy technological access to others, and the uncertainty and change that confronts many dynamic and ever-more business-led higher education and research institutions.

Ironically, many of the previous chapters discuss how to excel in meeting those very metrics and how to engage with those very practices. They must be recognised as a double-edged sword. Those metrics are a convenient way to demonstrate our careers in numbers, but you should not let those metrics become an end in themselves or define your career goals. Good metrics will flow from good work that you enjoy doing. Doing work solely in pursuit of some metric is rarely rewarding.

At its best, an academic career can be rewarding—academics will often describe it as vocation that goes to the heart of their very identity. But at its worst, it can consume people, destroy careers, relationships, and physical and mental wellbeing. Academic life (and a great many other careers) can make people thoroughly miserable if key warning signs are missed and no attempt is made to recognise and mitigate unhealthy attitudes to work and work–life balance. Devise and embed personalised coping strategies and mitigate problems early; and intervene and seek help if things go too far.

This section explores how negative relationships with work and work–life balance can lead to excessive stress and even burnout, which manifests so pervasively in academic life to various degrees of severity. We will offer some tips from personal experience on how to recognise it, deal with it, and recover from it. We hope to offer some personal insights and experiences that we know will resonate with many reading this section of the book (know that you are not alone). Having witnessed burnout in various stages of development among ourselves and many of our colleagues and peers, we regularly see people that are walking a hazardous path without realising the toll it may be taking on their careers, personal life, and physical and mental health. We approach this from a very personal viewpoint, drawing on experiences and a limited set of references and further reading, which we encourage you to seek out if you are affected by burnout or anything you may read here. And most importantly, what follows should most definitely not be taken as professional medical advice. If you think you may be suffering from excessive work (or other) stress or burnout, please seek professional help from a doctor or medical professional and consider raising it with your supervisor or line manager.

10.9.1 What is burnout and why does it matter?

Burnout is a state of emotional, physical, and mental exhaustion caused by excessive and prolonged stress. It can occur when you feel overwhelmed, emotionally drained, or unable to meet constant demands. Some common signs of burnout include extreme and chronic physical and mental fatigue or feeling drained most, or all, of the time. In more severe cases, it may include feelings of helplessness, feeling trapped and/or defeated and can even induce feelings of disassociation, confusion, forgetfulness, and a complete inability to concentrate. It can also include compassion fatigue (a lack of empathy for others), which can be a common symptom for those who experience burnout in the care professions, or in those caring for others in a personal capacity. Such symptoms often overlap with those of depression and anxiety disorders such that burnout can often be diagnosed (or misdiagnosed) as one or other, or both, when seeking medical help. To date, burnout is not a commonly recognised medical diagnosis, but excellent work is ongoing to raise its profile and devise more appropriate and tailored mainstream medical practises [14].

Burnout may also be known or recognised by some as a nervous breakdown, and there can be degrees of severity depending on the individual, the context, and the length of time it may have been building and gone unchecked. Likewise, recovery takes time and conscious effort, often requiring active personal and professional intervention or even suspension of work for a time. It may also require medical and/or psychological treatment. Put simply, burnout can be very serious and life changing. But the good news is that, once recognised, recovery is most often possible, no matter how bad it may seem at the start of recovery. Burnout can take many months or years to develop, often culminating in some acute episode where your mind and body may remind you that it is simply impossible to carry on as you are. But we sincerely hope that some of the experiences that follow may help you avoid getting to that point entirely.

Most people will experience stress at some time or another. Stress can be the body's way of reacting to acute pressure and preparing the body and mind for some immediate task that requires additional mental resource and energy. Stress was evolved in humans as part of our fight or flight response. But it did not evolve to deal with the constant demands that might be placed on us by our modern society. While stress can help us in some way in the very short term, it can take an extreme toll on the body and mind if it becomes chronic.

In the realm of science, where the pursuit of knowledge is implicitly relentless, burnout can be a real risk. To avoid this, set boundaries for your work and personal life and know how to recognise the pernicious creep of stress toward burnout. Recognising it is the first step to stopping things getting worse. Some important ways to prevent it from developing might mean setting specific work hours, taking regular breaks, and ensuring you have time for relaxation, hobbies, seeing friends and family, and leisure activities. It can be so easy to do less and less of those out-of-work activities as you seek to push your career. And it can be very easy to tell yourself you are tired to do them. But that tiredness and lack of interest in anything other than work can be the first sign that things have gone too far. Remember, science is a marathon, not a sprint.

10.9.2 How to recognise burnout

As discussed above, it can be difficult to distinguish between stress and burnout. It can also be difficult to distinguish between burnout and anxiety and/or depression in many cases (and each is not mutually exclusive). While again stressing the importance of seeking professional medical help if you should ever question whether you are suffering from burnout or any other mental health distress, what follows is drawn from a personal case study from one of the authors (Grant Allen) on their journey leading up to and recovering from burnout. If you find yourself resonating with what follows, we strongly encourage you to seek help.

For me, stress was relentless from the time of writing up a PhD thesis, through my years as a postdoctoral researcher and for the whole of my early and mid-career. This came from a highly self-competitive attitude, a perfectionist streak, and a strong desire to please, and be respected by, others. This combination of traits can make some people particularly susceptible to burnout and is well known in research on the topic [15]. Perfectionism is particularly indicative. Quite simply, perfection is not possible and those that strive too strongly for it can find it hard to obtain satisfaction.

Likewise, it is simply not possible to please everyone all the time. These traits go hand-in-hand with imposter syndrome, which as discussed in section 10.3 is best described as a false belief that we are out of our depth. The initial seeds for burnout can therefore be seen as far back as postgraduate studies, which for many researchers may be the first time that they find themselves among peers and not always top of the class. This can kick off a feeling that we may not be worthy or capable of performing at the level we now find ourselves at. When this feeling meets the practically infinite challenges and opportunities of academic life, the scene is set to allow you to run away with yourself if you choose to, often with very little intervention from others unless you seek it out. There is always another paper to write, there is always another proposal to design, and there is always some new duty to take on (e.g. teaching and supervision, peer review, and other service and leadership roles). Academia typically has few checks and balances on monitoring and intervening in the activities of researchers. On the contrary, academic culture encourages and praises every one of the metrics discussed earlier in this book. The peer review process and the clammer for research funding are competitive and critical by design. Everything about research teaches us to be competitive, to strive harder, and to do more and more. Quite often, we are left on our own to find the right balance and all too often we can overstretch.

Burnout is the endpoint of chronic stress. It is insidious and it can be non-linear. Because it can take many years before manifesting as a serious physical and mental issue, the gradual changes in approach to work and physical and emotional state can be missed entirely or become normalised. For me, stress felt normalised. If there were moments where I was not stressed, instead of telling myself that such moments should be the norm (and not the exception), I would instead seek out and fill that time with new projects and duties in pursuit of greater career success. Even with a very strong research track record, many funded projects and several other duties within my university, there was always the temptation to do more; not because I wanted to but because I felt almost guilty if I was not working in a permanent state of stress. Significant career success followed, but not without cost.

In retrospect, the first sign that things were not right was chronic fatigue. Weekends were spent trying to recharge batteries but not getting there. I cancelled social activities and trips out of the house, telling myself that I was too tired and needed to recharge. Social gatherings became harder and more stressful. Work travel became a chore. At one point, an international field trip that many would have been excited to take part in filled me with sheer dread. For over 10 years I suffered with insomnia to varying degrees. As time went on those symptoms worsened. In the months before breaking down, I began to suffer with very poor concentration, forgetfulness, and brain fog. I could be talking to someone, and nothing would be going in—my mind was elsewhere. I became emotional, often to the point of tears, and eventually totally numb. A ping alerting to me another email filled me with dread.

In the weeks before breaking down, I knew I needed help. I was suffering with dissociation (a feeling of detachment from reality). I had chest pains, high blood pressure, and I felt an overwhelming sense of being trapped, that some emergency was about to happen that I would not be able to mitigate, that there was no hope of a solution, and that the only way out was to finish my career in academia. I came extremely close to making that decision to leave my career. For me, the straw that broke the camel's back was a particularly challenging service and leadership role, which was poorly defined and supported. A full-time job in itself, my teaching development and research duties had become something to fit in only out of hours. On top of this, my family and I were dealing with the death of both of my in-law parents in the same year.

But then things changed. I asked for help. I told people how I was feeling. To many colleagues, it was a complete surprise. Being a highly driven and competent person, even throughout all the above, outwardly my work was seen as excellent, and I maintained a professional and productive portfolio. It is possible to be a functioning burnt-out human being for a very extended time. But not forever. When I eventually asked for help, I could barely string a coherent sentence together, had no short-term memory and felt utterly numb. Thankfully, at the time of writing, I am recovering well, but very much still learning how to be the new me. If you are reading this and can identify with even some of the above, know that there is always hope, always a way out, and that recovery is possible with help.

10.9.3 How to mitigate and recover from burnout

For me, recovery began at the time of admitting I needed help. I contacted my line managers and my university occupational health service. They were quick to intervene and offered excellent help. I was advised to take some time off work and seek medical advice. My workload was reevaluated and the leadership role that was quite literally destroying me was removed. I met with a doctor and was treated (ostensibly for anxiety). I also met with an occupation therapist provided by my university. They were able to help me reflect on the causes of burnout and the unhealthy working and mental patterns I had allowed to foster over more than a decade. I was advised to encourage myself to exercise, to meet with friends, to develop new hobbies, and to keep a journal of how I felt and any progress I was making. I was also encouraged to practice mindfulness meditation. I did all these things (slowly to begin with) and over the following weeks and months they started to work. I noticed that my memory was coming back. I was 'present'. I was not constantly anxious. I had more energy. I was able to leave the house without feeling like it was the last thing I wanted to do.

On first returning to work, I felt some residual dread on entering the office. My therapist described this to me as a form of post-traumatic stress—returning to the scene of something that had caused so much pain. Luckily, this subsided quickly, especially with the excellent support of my managers and colleagues. Six months after I first sought help, I ran a half marathon. I felt much more comfortable at work, and I found many of the activities that used to be a dreaded chore, enjoyable. I learned a new programming language. I had rediscovered all that I loved about science and my career that led me to it as a young adult. Re-reading the journal I had kept throughout these experiences clearly captured that trajectory.

At the time of writing, I still get anxious, but I have learned to recognise it and intervene, when to say no to new things that might lead me back to where I was, and how to use the coping mechanisms I had nurtured, which still include journalling, exercise, and mindfulness meditation. I know that the path to full recovery may be non-linear and that it requires constant awareness and re-evaluation. And most importantly, I know how to get help, that there is always a way back, and that so much of what I had done to burn myself out was actually because of my own perfectionism and drive. For some, there can be no greater enemy than your own potential.

Everyone's experience is different. Everyone's tolerance for stress and anxiety is different. The above is my personal journey. It may be very different to yours. But if anything you have read resonates with you, take a moment to stop and think about things, speak to friends and colleagues, talk to your manager or supervisor, and speak to a doctor or counsellor. I was lucky to have the support of excellent managers and an occupational health team. Some workplaces may be different. If you try those things and you do not get the results that I have, it may well be in your best interest to try something different. Sometimes making a career move may be the last best option, with plenty of other opportunities out there. But do not carry on as you are.

10.9.4 Practicing good mental health

Burnout is the culmination of ongoing stress, and prevention is far better than a cure. Being attuned to your mental wellbeing by recognising stress factors, understanding your personal work style, and consistently monitoring your mental health can serve as preventive measures. Just as physical health should not be neglected, mental health is equally critical, particularly in the high-stakes, high-pressure world of science. Taking note of stress, anxiety, or depression and addressing them is crucial. Actions could include regular physical exercise, mindfulness practices, or even seeking professional guidance. Remember, prioritising your wellbeing as a human first enables you to produce your best scientific work.

In the scientific community, the adage that 'no one is an island' holds true. Whether you are grappling with imposter syndrome or other challenges, it is beneficial to lean on the support of colleagues, mentors, and professional networks. Doubts and setbacks are universal experiences; do not hesitate to open up and share yours with those around you.

One of the most effective ways to maintain a good work–life balance is mastering the art of saying 'no'. Whether it is refusing an extra project, declining to review a manuscript, or opting out of a non-essential meeting, your time and energy are limited. Saying no can often feel difficult, especially when you sense that others rely on you. However, self-care must come first. The word no is not only powerful but often critical for your wellbeing. While opportunities will always be around the corner, listen to yourself and consider the commitments you are willing to make.

> **Exercise. Learning to say 'no'**
> For one week, keep a record of every time you say yes to something at work that you wanted to say no to. Reflect on why you said yes and how it made you feel. At the end of the week, review your list and consider what might have happened if you had said no. Use this reflection to guide your decisions in the future, and try saying no to more opportunities. Did anything bad happen because you said no? Did you feel better for saying no?

10.10 Summary

This chapter has introduced a range of additional skills and professional practices that are instrumental in shaping a successful and ethical scientist, including the importance of identifying and seeking help for burnout and maintaining a healthy work–life balance.

As scientists, we serve as ambassadors not only for our respective research institutes and fields of research but also for the broader realm of science. In conducting our research, we must approach all situations with unwavering standards of integrity and contemplate the broader ethical implications of our work. Furthermore, it is our responsibility to recognise signs of burnout in ourselves and others and to seek appropriate help, all while striving to maintain a healthy balance between our personal and professional lives.

In addition to these responsibilities, we also bear the onus to act as ethical scientists, to recognise and address our own conscious and unconscious biases, and to proactively champion and foster diversity in science. In the digital age, we must also consider how these practices translate to online spaces, whether that is networking digitally, promoting diversity in virtual seminars, or maintaining integrity in online publications.

Being a successful scientist is about more than just conducting research. It is about contributing to a scientific community that is ethical, diverse, and inclusive, continually striving to improve both ourselves and the world of science and being mindful of our wellbeing through vigilance against burnout and the pursuit of a balanced life.

10.11 Further study

This chapter's further study is designed to prompt you to hone the wide variety of skills that have been discussed.

1. **Seek a mentor.** Using your five year plan (see the first exercise in this chapter), pinpoint an area of expertise where you could use some guidance, be it a technical skill or a more general one (e.g. grant writing, presenting, teaching). Identify a colleague who excels in this skill, and approach them for some developmental advice.
2. **Enrol in a course.** Your research institute will offer a range of continuing professional development (CPD) opportunities, typically through its HR department. Again, use your five year plan to identify areas where you need training, and sign up for the relevant courses. Whenever possible, opt for training opportunities that offer external accreditation, as these will be most beneficial for future career prospects.
3. **Gain practical experience.** If you have decided that a career in academic research is not for you, identify opportunities to gain relevant experience elsewhere. For instance, if you are considering teaching, volunteer at a local school. Similarly, if you are contemplating a career in industry, approach a suitable company and arrange some knowledge exchange visits. Not only will this enhance your CV, but this experience will also help you determine if this is indeed the right career path for you.

4. **Cultivate work–life balance.** Set a goal to establish a healthy work–life balance. Create a routine that delineates work hours and personal time. This could involve setting strict work hours, ensuring regular breaks during the day, and dedicating time for relaxation and personal hobbies. Aim to implement this routine consistently over the next three months, adjusting as necessary for optimal balance.

10.12 Suggested reading

There are numerous resources available to help you develop your other essential research skills. For a deeper understanding of research ethics, 'On being a scientist: a guide to responsible conduct in research' [16] by the National Academy of Sciences is a must-read article.

For those looking to improve their networking skills, *Build Your Dream Network: Forging Powerful Relationships in a Hyper-Connected World* by J Kelly Hoey [17] provides insightful advice. If you are interested in understanding and addressing unconscious bias, *Blindspot: Hidden Biases of Good People* [18] by Mahzarin R Banaji and Anthony G Greenwald is a great starting point.

If you think you may be affected by chronic stress and burnout (or find yourself as a manager or colleague of someone who is), we could not recommend the following book more: *Burnout, A Guide to Identifying Burnout and Pathways to Recovery* [14]. This book is written by practising medical professionals and academics and reviews the latest research on burnout, providing useful tips and case studies on how to recognise and recover. It also offers resources for managers and helps you to objectively assess if you may be at risk.

For a more comprehensive understanding of work–life balance in academia, *The Slow Professor: Challenging the Culture of Speed in the Academy* [19] offers thoughtful reflections, while for a broader perspective on career paths in science, *Next Gen PhD: A Guide to Career Paths in Science* [20] provides a practical guide.

Finally, the journalist Angela Saini has written three very important books on addressing diversity in science (*Inferior* [21], *Superior* [22], and *The Patriarchs* [23]), all of which are highly recommended and necessary reads.

References

[1] Kruger P 2018 Why it is not a 'failure' to leave academia *Nature* **560** 133–5
[2] Goldstein D, Hahn C S, Hasher L, Wiprzycka U J and Zelazo P D 2007 Time of day, intellectual performance, and behavioral problems in morning versus evening type adolescents: is there a synchrony effect? *Pers. Individ. Differ.* **42** 431–40
[3] Wang X, Gobbo F and Lane M 2010 Turning time from enemy into an ally using the Pomodoro Technique *Agility Across Time and Space: Implementing Agile Methods in Global Software Projects* (Berlin: Springer) pp 149–66
[4] Stevens F G, Plaut V C and Sanchez-Burks J 2008 Unlocking the benefits of diversity: all-inclusive multiculturalism and positive organizational change *J. Appl. Behav. Sci.* **44** 116–33
[5] Bear S, Rahman N and Post C 2010 The impact of board diversity and gender composition on corporate social responsibility and firm reputation *J. Bus. Ethics* **97** 207–21

[6] Roberge M É and Van Dick R 2010 Recognizing the benefits of diversity: when and how does diversity increase group performance? *Hum. Resour. Manag. Rev.* **20** 295–308
[7] Díaz-García C, González-Moreno A and Sáez-Martínez F J 2013 Gender diversity within R&D teams: its impact on radicalness of innovation *Innovation* **15** 149–60
[8] Cheruvelil K S, Soranno P A, Weathers K C, Hanson P C, Goring S J, Filstrup C T and Read E K 2014 Creating and maintaining high-performing collaborative research teams: the importance of diversity and interpersonal skills *Front. Ecol. Environ.* **12** 31–8
[9] Bagenstos S R 2007 Implicit bias, science, and antidiscrimination law *Harv. L. Policy Rev.* **1** 477
[10] Gonzalez C M, Lypson M L and Sukhera J 2021 Twelve tips for teaching implicit bias recognition and management *Med. Teach.* **43** 1368–73
[11] Lee M, Coutts R, Fielden J, Hutchinson M, Lakeman R, Mathisen B, Nasrawi D and Phillips N 2022 Occupational stress in university academics in Australia and New Zealand *J. High. Educ. Policy Manag.* **44** 57–71
[12] Gushulak C A C *et al* 2023 The silent mental health and well-being crisis of early career researchers in aquatic sciences *Limno. Oceanog. Bull.* **32** 16–17
[13] Gewin V 2021 Pandemic burnout is rampant in academia *Nature* **591** 489–92
[14] Parker G, Tavella G and Eyers K 2022 *Burnout: A Guide to Identifying Burnout and Pathways to Recovery* (Crows Nest, NSW: Allen and Unwin/Routledge)
[15] Badreldin El Shikieri A 2012 *Occupational Stress in Higher Education* (London: Lap Lambert)
[16] National Academy of Sciences, National Academy of Engineering (US) and Institute of Medicine (US) Committee on Science, Engineering, and Public Policy 2009 *On Being a Scientist: A Guide to Responsible Conduct in Research* (Washington, DC: National Academies Press)
[17] Hoey J K 2018 *Build Your Dream Network: Forging Powerful Relationships in a Hyper-Connected World* (London: Penguin)
[18] Banaji M R and Greenwald A G 2016 *Blindspot: Hidden Biases of Good People* (London: Bantam)
[19] Berg M and Seeber B K 2016 *The Slow Professor: Challenging the Culture of Speed in the Academy* (Toronto: University of Toronto Press)
[20] Sinche M V 2016 *Next Gen PhD: A Guide to Career Paths in Science* (Cambridge, MA: Harvard University Press)
[21] Saini A 2017 *Inferior: How Science Got Women Wrong—and the New Research That's Rewriting the Story* (New York: HarperCollins)
[22] Saini A 2019 *Superior: The Return of Race Science* (Boston, MA: Beacon)
[23] Saini A 2023 *The Patriarchs: The Origins of Inequality* (Boston, MA: Beacon)

www.ingramcontent.com/pod-product-compliance
Lightning Source LLC
Chambersburg PA
CBHW080550230426
43663CB00015B/2780